I0134734

DEADLOCKED
A Trial Beginning

By
RM & SJ Secor

LemonWedge
Publishing

LemonWedge Publishing
Union, NJ, 07083
www.lemonwedgepublishing.com

This book is a work of fiction. People, places, events, and situations are the product of the author's imagination. Any resemblance to actual persons, living or dead, or historical events, is purely coincidental.

First published by LemonWedge Publishing 2015

ISBN-13: 978-0692562130

ISBN-10: 0692562133

Printed in the United States of America

Prologue

Imagine graduating from law school without trying very hard. *Yeah, right*, is what you're probably thinking, but it's true. Never understood how no matter what I did in life, doors just opened for me. Not many people have this happen, but I took it and ran with it.

Regarding law school, well, the only reason I chose that path is it was something I thought would be hard and just maybe for once it would be challenging and difficult to grasp. Turns out it was, but we'll get to that later. After graduating high school, I attended Sprott Shaw Community College near my house. Upon completing my Associates Degree, I decided I was going to stay focused and attend the University of British Columbia, Vancouver to get my Bachelor's Degree.

If I was to stay dedicated to finding a deeper life's challenge, I needed to push myself to do it or I would stop and forget about it. Funny thing is, deep down inside, I was actually scared not knowing what the future would hold for me. You see, when I was a little girl, I lost my mother and father to a fatal car crash. Somehow I survived and was sent to an orphanage and spent my childhood at Alexandra Neighborhood House in Vancouver, British Columbia. There is nothing worse than being in a strange place and not knowing anyone. For me, being only five when I entered the home was terrifying. In fact, I was immediately instructed that my name was now Alexandria Henson, and that was that. Being young and not knowing exactly what was going on, I just assumed this was right and never questioned it until later in life. As the years went on and I slowly started to develop into a young girl, I noticed things came easy to me, whether it was school, making friends, or just simply getting things I wanted. This talent seemed very odd to me, but I embraced it and ran with it.

I would take it upon myself to investigate how I ended up in this home from time to time from various workers there, but I just got stupid responses, or they were too busy to answer me. Quite strange how a five-year-old shows up and everything is given to her. To top it off, they always called me Alexandria when I could almost recall my mother calling me Lydia. Who knows, since those memories have faded, and when I would seek answers on my real name, they always said I was making up stories.

It wasn't long before I stopped seeking answers and just lived my life going to school, playing with others, and trying to make friends. Several years later, I came across an old, ripped box down in the basement, hidden amongst other boxes. It shocked and disturbed me. You see, the basement was off limits, and anyone caught down there would be subject to ten ruler lashes across the knuckles, no freedom for a week, and being locked in your room after school.

You're wondering what it was that shocked and disturbed me? It was an old newspaper article about a family killed in a car crash with only one survivor, a child. That's all I could read from the lit match I had struck to give off some light. It also mentioned that there was another child, yet no disclosure of it being a boy or girl or if that child had survived. A runaway bus had caused this horrific car crash. Somehow, the driver had fallen asleep, yet many think it was a hit by the Canadian Mafia. No one really knew, but from the news article, it was mentioned that the driver had a hole in his head.

How do you get a hole in your head from driving a bus? Could it have been from something that hit him when the bus collided with the car? Was it truly a bullet entering his forehead that caused the driver to die and then send the bus on its destructive course? Whatever it was, I was going to find out. Well, the unthinkable happened that day down in the basement. The warden caught me. That's what I called Miss Simons—the warden. She was a strict, tall, thin woman with nothing but meanness running through her veins. She proceeded to pick me up and shake me like a rag doll as I quickly stuffed the newspaper article down my pants. I certainly didn't want her to take it away because I wanted to read it some more.

The bad thing is that not only did I get ten lashes on my knuckles, but I also got five paddle swings on my butt for playing with matches. I was just being a kid. Apparently, that was not allowed. I studied that article repeatedly that week I was bound to my room after school. I couldn't wait to get freedom to go to the house library and see if I could dig up any information on the crash and just who the family was or even who the survivor was. I think that was my first clue to wanting to become a lawyer; I just hadn't put two and two together yet. I never could quite get any solid connections to that accident. Every time I thought I had a forward move, it always turned up a dead end.

On my eleventh birthday, I was pulled into the warden's office with some news. Miss Simons had this weird grin on her face, and that never happened. She was so delighted to tell me that I was moving out of the home because a relative of mine had sought me out and claimed me to take home. Being such a young age when I arrived, I had no recollection of any relatives, so I entertained the thought. This man who claimed to be my mother's brother offered to take me home and raise me. He sure looked like a mobster the way he dressed. He did not speak good English, having more of a French–Italian combination accent.

The man introduced himself to me as Nicholas Rozzito, the brother of my mother, Carolina. He explained how he had searched for me all these years and had finally found me. I quickly blurted out that this is where I had been, and he could have found me if he had searched harder. The look on the man's face scared me as he reached his arms out to me. I didn't want to move as Miss Simon pushed me toward him, feet scraping the floor.

My time at the orphanage was over, and my new life began with this newfound family member. It was quite obvious that my mother's brother was well off. I will never forget that day as I left the orphanage and climbed into a dark-glassed, stretched-out car. The car spun off, and so did my life. Not in a bad way, for sure.

Soon, I had everything I had ever wanted, just on a larger scale: fancy homes, expensive cars, and extravagant parties. My uncle always had men around the home. I just thought that since he was well off, they were his security, and I never questioned it.

When I graduated from high school, I thought about going to law school. My uncle always tried to persuade me not to, saying, "Someday you might find something you might not like and end up hurt or dead." I always argued with him, insisting that would never happen. He always said he would be there for me but wished I would reconsider and take on a job that didn't involve digging into people's lives and exposing them for who they really are. That's the thing that drove me to become a lawyer. It was in my blood, so to speak.

I eventually graduated at the top of my class from Seattle University School of Law across the pond. Not exactly across the pond—I live on Vancouver Island in the city of Victoria. The best way to get there was by air, which would take forty-five minutes to an hour, and if the airports were closed due to weather, I had to take a two-to-three-hour ferry ride across. Not exactly the fastest way to travel, but I preferred to take that way whenever I could. It just seemed less stressful. The ferry would leave Seattle, travel up Puget Sound, and turn left towards the Strait of Juan de Fuca before turning back right and heading north to the port of Victoria. From there, my apartment was two miles inland.

My uncle's gift to me for graduating law school was a trip to wherever I wanted to go, and I could take a friend or two on him as well. I chose to go to Paris, France, with my classmate and longtime friend, Daniele Ramos. Besides, I had picked up some basic French from my uncle and his acquaintances over the years, but just enough to say my name, where I lived, and "I love you." Every time I said "I love you" to my uncle, he would tell me his heart melted and I was forever in his heart. That was my secret weapon to get out of being in trouble sometimes as well.

After graduating law school and enjoying a wonderful trip to Paris, I returned to my home and to begin my new career working as a newbie trial lawyer for Winslow and D'entremont LLP, Washington State's top law firm. Funny how when I started applying for firms to work for, my uncle mentioned he could pull some strings as a favor to me and get me into Winslow and D'entremont. I never second-guessed his offer and took him up on it. Truth be told, I really didn't search very hard, but once I told my uncle the place I wanted to work, he somehow made it happen.

The trip to Paris was fun, exciting, and straight out of a fairy tale. Paris was full of young love and old love, and the city was vibrant with energy. It was quite sad to leave. Daniele and I had fun partying and meeting some new friends, but it was time to become a working adult and fend for myself, even though my Uncle Nicholas always stated he would help me out whenever I needed it. Daniele had landed a job at the same firm as well but silently hated how I didn't have to struggle to get in and she did. Needless to say, we hugged each other after the trip, said our short goodbyes, as we would always get together every other weekend for girl time, and parted.

The weather in Seattle was slightly cold with a hard rain, which made traveling cumbersome. Stepping out of the airport terminal, I knew I was in for a long night traveling home. The bad thing was, I had to present an opening statement on a preliminary case the next morning, and I had barely touched the material mailed to me. Since it was only five o'clock in the evening and I would be taking the ferry home, I had plenty of time to read through the material and come up with a statement. Grabbing my suitcase in one hand and my overstuffed backpack in the other, I went to throw the backpack over my shoulder, but I missed. It fell on the ground out from under the terminal shelter and into the pouring rain.

Shaking my head, I dashed for it as rain pelted my head, when suddenly I was pulled back and out of the rain as a taxicab slammed on its brakes right in front of me. I turned around, and a tall, young, handsome man had grabbed me, thinking I was going to get hit, and pulled me back to safety. He smiled at me, turned, and walked away without even saying a word. I probably scared him off since my hair was wet and partially covering my face.

The strange thing was, though, that it was as if I had seen that face before but could not recall where. It could have just been a coincidence. Nevertheless, I was quickly brought back to reality when the driver of the taxi yelled at me as he picked up my backpack. He asked if I needed a ride, all the time mumbling the words "crazy lady" to me.

I just wanted to get home where I knew it was dry, warm, and comforting. The taxicab driver asked me where I wanted to go, and I told him to take me to the ferry down at the harbor. From the airport, it was only ten minutes, but that night it seemed like forever as I entered the cab and quickly dozed off while listening to the rain hit the windows and roof. My eyelids felt heavy as I looked at the driver several times. My eyes forced themselves shut.

Suddenly, the cab stopped, and the wet brakes squealed. The driver waved for me to get out and told me it would be fifteen dollars. He popped the trunk open and didn't even get out of the car to get my bags, so I had to grab them and place them to the side of the road and come around to pay him. My purse was still in the backseat, and I told the cab driver to wait so I could get it. I walked back around to the other side of the cab, opened the door, grabbed my purse, and slammed the door as the taxi started to take off. I noticed my coat was caught in the door. I yanked at it, and it almost dragged me down before tearing off. I yelled at the driver, and his rebuttal was a horn honk. Cold, wet, and tired in the pouring rain, I turned, grabbed my stuff, and looked down towards the ferry.

Chapter One
Pier Sixty-Nine

The ferry was less than a hundred yards away down a slight slope, but it looked very dangerous, and the rain was splashing against the wooden dock extension. I had better suck it up and get down to the end of the dock. My only reservation was breaking my new black Prada high-heel dress boots that cost me three hundred dollars on sale and tumbling onto my butt. At least I knew if I hurried, I could make it to the ferry and have enough time to grab a cup of coffee from Old Merl's diner inside the terminal before the ferry arrived.

I started down the dock and noticed the rain was not letting up. The air seemed to be cooler since I could see what looked like fog rolling in from the water's edge. Nothing was more eerie then traveling across the waterway with little to no visibility, and I was not the one driving. Out of nowhere, a lightning bolt shattered the skyline and made the hair on my arms stand up. I stopped, grabbed my wits, tried to shelter my

1

head with my purse, and started to walk faster towards the terminal entrance.

My only concern now was to get out of the rain and put an end to the day's hustle and bustle. The problem was, I had rushed off and left my luggage at the spot I had stopped at and didn't realize it until I heard someone behind me shouting and whistling at me.

"Hey, you left your bag!" A whistling sound rang out. "Hey, you forgot your bag, ma'am!"

I turned around to see what the shouting and whistling was about. I looked down and noticed I had not even thought about my luggage. I am so stupid at times, it scares me.

Holding my purse up above my eyes, I managed to brush enough of my drenched hair away and out of my eyes to see a fellow walking towards me with my bag. I could not make out what he looked like, but he looked like a younger man. As he approached me, I could see he was not thrilled to be bringing me my bag, as he looked a little miffed. It could have been that he wasn't too thrilled about the pouring-down rain, either.

"Thank you so much for bringing me my bag. I am so sorry," I said.

"It's all right. I just hate the rain."

My feelings exactly, I thought as he offered me the handle of my bag. In fact, this young man was rather good looking, and I figured if I gave him a sweet smile and a thank-you, that would make up for his having to bring me my bag. "Thank you again" is what I wanted to say, but I just smiled at him, took my bag, and turned around and started to walk again.

I did not get but a few steps forward before I felt awkward for not even acknowledging my thanks again. I decided to turn around to thank him, but to my disbelief, he was gone. It was as if he had vanished and had never been there. I realized I was standing in a heavy downpour of rain and half blinded by hair in my face, but I swear, I was not imagining this. How could it be? Well, I was certainly not going to stew over it. I was cold and wet and needed coffee. Besides, my arm was killing me from holding my purse up so long. Being sore was not going to make for a productive evening looking over papers.

"OK, Alex," I mumbled out loud, turned around, and was shattered by a horn blown from a fishing boat leaving the dock to the left of me. I did not even see this boat, which is how freaking heavy the rain was coming down. Talk about being scared, I almost crapped my pants in utter fear. Not that it mattered even if I had seen the boat. I still would've been shaken by the horn blast. This night was going to get the best of me, and my nerves were shot.

I managed to get out of the rain as I entered the terminal entrance under the metal awning. The fog had become so thick, it seemed right out of an old Hollywood movie. Strange, as I had never seen it so thick on my previous trips, but that was because I had never taken the last ferry across at night. Typically, during the day, all you can hear is the sounds of boats coming and going and seagulls crying out as they dive to the dock in hopes of snatching up some morsel of food dropped by passing travelers or from the old geezers tossing scraps of unwanted leftover bait before casting their lines over the side of the dock.

The only thing I could hear now was the water running up against the dock and splashing, with a constant distant bell sound, possibly from an anchored boat swaying in the water a ways out and covered by the blanket of night and fog. Quite spooky, if you ask me, but nevertheless, I had made it, and now I could go and grab a cup of "Devil's Blood." That is how Old Merl referred to the coffee he served. To me, it was a lifesaver. The taste of the coffee was less desirable to some and could be compared to tree bark, but it was nothing a little cream and a whole lot of sugar couldn't do to tame it.

I had almost made it through the terminal door when the door slammed on my luggage bag. I was abruptly halted and twisted my foot, and my right heel snapped right off.

"Are you freaking kidding me? First my coat, then my bag, and now my heel. This has got to be some cruel joke, and I am not laughing," I said aloud. Looking around, I noticed a few folks staring at me as if I were an idiot.

"What?" I said. "Never seen someone talk out loud to themselves before?" Funny how quickly their heads turned away as if they had not been looking at me.

After realizing how ridiculous I was for snapping out loud, I bent over to pick up my heel that had broken off and hobbled towards one of the people to offer my sincere apology.

"I am so sorry for speaking to you that way. It's just that it's getting late, and I am drenched, tired, and moody. I didn't mean it. I'm just having a bad day."

The little old lady I had approached and offered my sincere apology to for my outburst looked at me with a frown and said nothing back, just stared and shook her head in disbelief.

I was about to offer up my sincere apology again when the old lady turned to me, extended her left arm, and pointed her wrinkled old index finger. She just shook it up and down for a few seconds before mumbling the words, "You young people today have no class," and walked away. Boy, was I left with such an odd feeling, and to top it off, I got a finger pointed at me. That sure reminded me of Miss Simons, and the hair on the back of my neck stood up as a cold shiver ran through my body.

Looking around, I could see this section of the terminal had no seats, and lighting looked to be kept at a minimum, probably to save on costs. It did not matter as the section that

4

did have seating was behind glass doors and at this hour was locked, so there no sitting down like a civilized human being and taking my Prada's off. Funny how I never paid attention to such little details of the terminal before; it had never dawned on me to.

I decided to walk over to a wall so I could brace myself and try to pull off my boots one at a time even though I sure didn't want to. This floor didn't look too clean, but I had no choice—it was either hobble along with one broken boot or toughen up and go barefoot. Besides, I was a lawyer; I was supposed to be tough, and who cared if I walked barefoot? The reality of it was, I cared and didn't really want to.

Bracing myself, I tried to pull the broken boot, but the stubborn thing wouldn't come off. Tug after tug just made me so frustrated, I wanted to cry. Suddenly, I felt a tap on my shoulder, which startled me. I adjusted my posture, tugged on my dress, and started to turn around to see who it was. A little quirk I had adopted over the years, which my uncle had instilled, was to always be a lady. It just came naturally now. The only person I could think it could be was the little old lady, but to my surprise it wasn't.

"Looks like you need saving now and not your bag."

A slight smirk rolled onto my lips as I said with hesitation, "Ha-ha. Sure looks that way. My day is just not ending well."

"You know, I turned around to offer my thanks to you, and you had vanished. I never got to introduce myself." I offered my hand to shake his as I mentioned my name.

"Alex? Wait, isn't that a guy's name?"

"Well, it is, but it's short for Alexandria," I replied, blushing.

"Wow. Now, that is a hot and sexy name, like Nefertari, and it fits you well."

5

"Well now, that is the first time I've heard my name compared to the great wife of Ramses the Great. Not sure if I should be scared, flattered, or throw myself on you and kiss you." Grinning with excitement, I asked, "So, what is your name?" It felt like minutes as I waited impatiently to find out the name of this young, handsome man who had come to my rescue twice.

"Well, first, give me your hand, and then I will tell you."

"Oh, OK," I said with hesitation as if I was not going to, but I knew damn well I was. Before I could raise my left hand up all the way, he had grasped it firmly, but not too tightly, as I watched him bow his head with his eyes focused on mine. He ever so softly caressed the tops of my fingers with his thumb, sending shivers up my spine. He kissed my hand and said, "Alex, my name is Beauford."

Instantly, my emotions stopped like a screeching needle running across a record. Nothing like an odd name to buzzkill the moment. I certainly did not want to show him my emotions outwardly, so I slowly withdrew my hand and pretended I was not shocked and said, "Oh, Beauford, um, such a nice name." I could think of many things to respond with as I quickly turned my head to the side and rolled my eyes, but that was not ladylike, and he was just so darn handsome.

Beauford smiled as he stood there waiting for what looked like a response from me. I did not know what to do other than to make a move to sit, but I couldn't.

"Here, let me help you. Take off your other boot."

I had no idea what he was up to but played along and tried to balance myself and pull off the other boot. I knew this wasn't going to be easy and felt I was going to end up embarrassing myself if I fell over. Suddenly, after trying to pull my good boot off, I lost my balance and started to fall right towards him.

6

Luckily for him, I fell right into his arms. His face lit up like a Christmas tree, but I, on the other hand, felt like a total idiot. What is it with men? You accidentally fall towards them and they get all googley-eyed as if you had planned it.

"Whoa, easy now," Beauford quickly responded to my dumbest act of the night. Well, not exactly, as I could have fired off a few others that would take the cake.

Even though it was an accident, both my arms landed on his shoulders as he slowly lifted me up to safety. My lips and his were so close, I could feel the breath rapidly escaping from his nose. I knew he was excited by the way his eyes were focused on mine and my lips. His heart was racing. I needed to back off, or it would explode. The truth is, I was excited too and had started to feel a little lightheaded. Sweat was building on my forehead. That always happens when I get nervous or excited.

"Oh, I am so sorry. I thought I had my balance."

"I don't mind at all. Seems tonight you have a knight in shining armor to save you. Well, minus the knight's armor and being shiny and all."

OK, now I know he was excited about me since he was talking so awkwardly. Knight's armor missing and not shiny. For a moment, he felt like my knight in shining armor, right up to the point he started talking like a geek and back stepping his confidence.

"Alex, tell you what. Sit down on the floor and let me help you remove your boot. We surely wouldn't want you to fall totally on top of me next," Beauford blurted out while looking around the terminal as if to brag, yet there were not many folks around.

This man was truly a geek or had been instantly love-struck. *Caution, Alex,* was all I could think of at that second. Well, looking down at the floor, I knew I didn't want to sit on it,

7

germs and all. So I glanced down at my wrist as if to check the time and stall, yet I don't wear a watch. If that wasn't an outward cry to stall, I don't know what the heck would've been.

I could see in his eyes that he knew I was stalling and motioned me with his hands to sit on the ungodly dirty, unsanitized floor. "Fine," was the only word I could think of and blurted it out. This way, he would at least know I was going to do it but wouldn't like it, just like a teenage girl refusing to hang up the phone when told to while talking to a boy she liked—same thing here; I just didn't want to do it.

"Come on, now. Nothing is going to happen by sitting on the floor."

So I dropped my purse to the ground and unstrapped my backpack as Beauford offered his hand to help me down onto the floor.

"I'm good. I've got it. I can sit on my own."

"Oh, relax. Take my hand and let me help you. I've got you. I promise, nothing will happen, and you'll sit down safely."

I grabbed his hand and slowly descended to the floor, taking my focus off him and looking down at the ground. This was going to get my dress dirty, and I was not at all amused.

Suddenly, out of nowhere, he blurted out a yelp and jolted my arm. "Look out!"

I panicked as if there were something there. As I looked up, I saw his eyes were closed, and he was shaking his head and laughing softly. This almost made me pee a little, and now my heart was beating fast. Touché, I would presume if a score were being kept.

"Ha-ha-ha. Not funny. You almost made me pee, and you scared the crap out of me. Now if that happened, how would you respond to that?" I quickly responded as my heart rate slowly withdrew from the edge of possible death.

Letting go of his hands, I managed to sit down the rest of the way. That was so stupid, thinking that there might've been something on the ground to frighten me.

"OK, I am down on the ground. Now what?"

"Give me your other leg, and I will show you."

Beauford reached for my leg at that moment and began slowly raising my dress up over my knee area. His eyes were not focused on mine now but on my leg. All I could do was watch this unfolding as he managed to unzip my boot and begin to remove it.

"You're going to have to bend your knee more so I can get a good grip and pull it off."

"More? Wait, why? Can't you just pull it off?" I said, muttering several other questions as if to argue with him.

Bending my knee more upward made it easier now for him to unzip the boot and pull it off. However, I noticed his eyes light up as he stopped pulling the boot off and gazed at my now slightly exposed inner thigh, revealing a little too much for him to concentrate.

"Hey, focus on my eyes, not my thigh," I blurted out as I tucked my dress to cover my exposed thigh.

I was starting to think this was all an act so he could get a glimpse under my dress, but for some reason, in a quirky way, it didn't bother me. Yet I was not going to let him think he could just do that and get away with it. He had just seen parts of me you don't get to see unless I want you to.

"Wow, so what's that tattoo all about?"

"Never mind what you just got to see, and hurry up and finish with my boot."

Beauford, with a gleaming shine to his face and body language, removed the boot from my foot. What is with guys? They accidentally get to see a part of a woman's body, and they

9

go nuts with no self-control, as if they were animals with perverted tendencies.

Beauford took my boot and began to observe it like it was a piece of evidence at a crime scene. I just looked at him. One second he was handsome, charming, and easy talking; then another, he was something different, more like a young teenage boy with a high sexual drive wrapped with the outer shell of a geek.

I had no idea what he was going to do with my boot but was really was hoping he would speed up the examination, as I was dying for a cup of coffee and to get off the godforsaken terminal floor. I snapped my fingers in hopes of gaining his attention. Beauford raised my boot; then I watched him slam it down to the floor. My eyes lit up like an explosion, and my jaw dropped, trying to utter a few single words to save my three-hundred-dollar boot.

There was nothing I could do or say as I was frozen to my spot. I was suddenly speechless, my mouth feeling as if it were stuffed with cotton balls. The word *STOP* was unnecessary since Beauford spoke from his look. I had never been speechless, and this was a first. *Oh my God, he's destroying my Prada boots! Does the man have no conscience over what this boot is worth?*

The sound of a quick snap rang throughout the immediate terminal area as I leaned back. I slowly closed my mouth and just blinked in astonishment. My breathing once again was forced beyond natural human limits. My heart pounded against my chest as Beauford brought the boot closer for me to witness the destruction.

"You see? All better."

All better? I wanted to lunge over, grab my decimated boot, whack him across the face, and beat him to a pulp, but I quickly realized that was a split-second out-of-body experience, and I looked at the boot in front of me. The heel was snapped right off as I glared my eyes up towards him.

"I'm speechless. I...I...I...do you know?...wow," is all I could get out as he motioned me to lean back and raise my leg again so he could place my boot back on my foot and leg. This time, he would not be getting a glimpse of me. I tucked my dress in and completely wrapped it around my leg, revealing not even the slightest hair on my leg if there was one. My boot was now safe and sound back on me.

This whole charade on my behalf was really silly and stupid, as it was just a boot. But it was a boot that I wanted for a long time, had window-shopped for, had desired, and was finally bought from Saks Fifth Avenue as a gift for graduating college. They were Prada boots, and nothing speaks with louder volume then a woman wearing Prada.

Beauford stood above me and reached down to help me get back to my feet. As he pulled me up this time, I distanced myself so I would not be so close. Besides, I was angry for what had just happened.

"There. Now you can walk the rest of the night without hobbling."

Slowly moving my foot from side to side, I realized he was right. It wasn't the best option of the night for me, but it would do. I knew I just didn't want to have to go the rest of the trip barefoot.

"So tell me, Alex, now what?"

"Well, for starters, how about you buy me a cup of coffee from Merl's, and we'll start there?"

Chapter Two
Stranger amongst Us

Walking in Old Merl's diner as the little bells above the door jingled, I was greeted by that smell of deep coffee that Merl always had brewing. The smell to me was intoxicating. Beauford was a gentleman as he held the door for me. I could see a familiar face behind the counter peeking through the kitchen to the front. Old Merl smiled and waved me in as he stopped what he was doing to come and greet me.

"Ah, my little Bella. *Ciao, venire qui.*"

That is what Old Merl said to me every time he saw me, speaking old school in his native tongue. It meant, "My little beautiful. Hello, come here." I reminded him of his granddaughter, whom he said didn't come around anymore much. That was a shame, if you ask me, but I did not mind bringing a little happiness to him when I got the chance to visit. Old Merl was an immigrant from Sicily, Italy, right off the boat many years ago. He fell in love with Seattle and never left.

Owning a little diner next to an ocean inlet reminded him so much of the time when he was a little boy, when his father would bring him to an old diner once a month when he visited. His father did not live with his mother and him, so it was a treat for them to spend time together.

"*Ciao,* Merl."

"Ah, Bella, so good to see you. Here sit...sit." Merl motioned Beauford and me to sit down.

Merl was always so inviting and quick to have anyone and everyone who came into the diner sit down as soon as they walked through his door. It was his pleasure to have them there, and he wanted to please everyone.

"So, let me guess...a hot cup of Devil's Blood for you."

"Oh, I would love you to death if you brought me that goodness."

Beauford had no idea what Devil's Blood referred to, but seeing how he felt like a fifth wheel since I hadn't introduced him to Old Merl, he leaned in and asked for the same. "Ah, sounds good. I will have a cup as well," he said, smiling at me and sitting back in the booth.

Well, I guess it was OK to interrupt, as I realized I had not introduced him to Merl since we were seated so quickly, but it still was a little rude, if you ask me. Old Merl just looked at him for a few seconds with no expression, just a straight face. Looking up at Merl, I rolled my eyes with a smirk on my face to break his stare. It worked.

Old Merl looked back at Beauford, then back at me, and smiled and said, "Two cups coming right up." Old Merl's diner was also famous to me as he always had fresh cannoli filled with white cream and chocolate chips. I was a bit hungry, so I quickly made sure to add that to my cup of coffee.

"Merl, can you bring me one of your famous cannoli as well?"

13

"Of course, my Bella."

As I glanced over at Beauford across the table booth, he looked back at me. I could see he was thinking the same thing and called to Merl a second time, "Make that two!"

"So, tell me, Alex, what is Devil's Blood? This some sort of concoction that I'm going to like?" Beauford asked me in a lowered tone voice.

Laughing slightly as I looked at him, all I could do was sit there and smile. I could see he wasn't too sure about what he had ordered to drink and was feeling a little uncomfortable—kind of how I felt when I was sitting on the ground as he gazed at my inner thigh revealing my tattoo.

Ah, the mystery of not knowing, such a potent drug for the mind. Men always go in half-cocked and don't even know why. What would the world be without us? This place would fall apart, and to think, over a simple cup of coffee ordered without asking its contents. Several thoughts came to my mind for me to play with his mind and let him believe it was some sort of concoction, but I decided to just keep it simple.

"Oh, don't worry. You will like it. Trust me." I smirked at him to keep the mystery going for a bit longer. The look on his face was priceless. Asking a guy whom I'd just met not more than an hour ago to trust me without even knowing who he was—for all I knew, he could have been some sort of stalker, rapist, or kidnapper, and I was his new target. Maybe he was a hit man and had been sent to kill me. Or here's one that is even more stupid—maybe he was hired by my new law firm to watch out for me and to protect me because this case that I had not even had a chance to look at involved some sort of Mafia ties, and they knew who I was and were coming for me.

Laughing under my breath with my eyes closed, for a split second I actually pondered that as true. I needed to know who this person was sitting with me. The sound of silence filled my ears for a second, and I could briefly hear the ringing of a bell outside as a nearby boat jostled in the water. Old Merl had a few windows left open all the time to let out the aroma of the diner to attract people to come in. The sound of the bell eased my concerns, and I opened my eyes to see Beauford still sitting there with a smile.

"You OK?" Beauford asked me as I reopened my eyes.

"Yes, I'm fine."

"You sure? Because you seemed to have blanked out for a bit."

"No, I'm fine," I said, insisting to Beauford that nothing was wrong even though I was letting my mind take the best of my thoughts for a second.

Just then, I could see Old Merl walking our way with the coffee and cannoli. They could not have come at a better time, as I really didn't want to show Beauford I was in a vulnerable state.

"Here you go, Bella and friend. Two cups of Devil's Blood and two delicioso cannoli. Enjoy while you have time; the ferry doesn't arrive for another twenty minutes. *Tu mangi*."

"Thanks Merl," I responded to Merl as I lifted my cup of coffee to my nose, taking in a huge hit of aroma.

"Ah yes, there is nothing like a good ol' cup of coffee to wake you up!"

"Wait, so Devil's Blood is just a cup of coffee?" Beauford uttered with a strange look on his face.

"No. *Non solo una tazza di caffe'. E' una splendida tazzi di caffe'!*" Old Merl reiterated in his native tongue— referring to not just a cup of coffee but a fantastic cup of coffee—before walking back towards the kitchen, waving his hands in the air and shaking his head. Well, I thought that was what he meant; I had picked up some Italian living with my uncle.

15

"Wow, what's up with him?"

"Oh, that's just Merl. He's quite fond of his Devil's Blood—I mean coffee," I said with a smirk, "and he's proud to serve it to the locals. Just a family recipe. To some it is just coffee, but to him it is everything. That's how his family survived when he was growing up in Italy."

"I guess I'd better go and tell him I did not mean any disrespect."

"Oh, don't worry about. I'll talk to Merl before we leave the diner and smooth things over. Besides, it sounds to me like you're not from around here, are you?"

"Not exactly."

"Well, Beauford, where are you from?

"From the great state of Texas. Corsicana, Texas, to be precise."

"Texas? What brings you to Seattle?"

"Cow pies."

"Excuse me, did you just say cow pies?" I said, responding quickly as that certainly took me off guard. "So, are you some sort of baker?"

The image I had for this handsome man was quickly getting contorted as I tried to imagine him wearing a baker's white hat.

"I guess you could say I am sort of a baker."

I didn't really hear his last statement as I was imagining him as a baker, shirt off, showing his chest and firm abs with flour stuck to them, white hat on and looking at me with lust, trying to seduce me, and boy, was it working.

"Hello?" Beauford interrupted my dreaming gaze at him.

"So, a baker. I would've never guessed that. I would've thought possibly a model or a geek or…I don't know."

Beauford really didn't like my response. He picked up his cup of coffee to sip it to avoid responding, this time not looking at me. I decided it was time to ask him about his name, hoping not to offend him, but it didn't quite come out the way I had envisioned it.

"Oh, you wouldn't mind if I just called you Beau for the rest of the night? Something about your name is turning me off, and I can't get past that."

"Oh, sorry, don't want to offend you with my name, too. Listen, maybe this isn't such a great idea after all. I should go. You seem fine now." Beauford quickly moved sideways to get out of the booth and stood up.

"No, please, sit down. I didn't mean to offend you. Sometimes I say things before I think. I'm sorry. Please sit back down, drink your coffee, and eat your cannoli." I looked up at him, showing with my eyes that I hadn't meant it.

Boy, I was feeling like a total jerk for saying what I just did—not one of my grandest moments, making this guy feel uncomfortable after he had helped me out. Beauford sat back down and took a bite of his cannoli.

"So, tell me more about being a baker."

"I think you got it all wrong, Alex. I am not a baker as in cakes and pastries. I work with manure."

Well, that was certainly not what I had expected to hear. He worked with manure and was some sort of a baker. I was not following that and was not sure I really wanted to know more, but I did.

"Well, gosh, Beauford, that must be a crappy job," I said, making a joking comment in hopes to see a smile on his handsome face. I wasn't sure if it had worked as he paused for a second or two without speaking. Then it happened. He cracked a smirk.

"I get it…crappy job...working with manure...I can see the connection. I like you. You have a way with words, don't you?"

"Yes, I think so," I said, smirking back and sipping my coffee. "So, I am not quite sure what it is exactly that you do."

"I am an agricultural scientist who specializes in fertilizer anatomy and structure to enhance the growth of plants and crops."

Listening to his definition of what he was and did seemed to lure me in, as he said it with such poise and confidence. He seemed pretty proud of his work, and I yearned to know more.

"So, this work of yours brought you to Seattle?"

"Well, not exactly. My research and experiments that I did back home got me here. As a boy, I grew up on my granddaddy's farm in southern Texas and witnessed the struggles he and his workers went through to grow crops in the hundred-degree heat and drought."

"Wow, that must have been rough."

"It was, and sad, too. Anyway, I wanted to help him succeed, but I didn't know how. He was related to a public figure, and the thought of failure would've devastated him, not to mention the media harassment."

"So, your grandfather was related to a public figure? Who, if I may ask?" I was enthralled with his story and didn't even think about my coffee as it slowly became engulfed in coldness.

"You sure this isn't boring you? Other women I talk to don't seem interested, and, well, I never hear back from them."

Looking up and to Beauford's side, I tried to glance at Old Merl's lighthouse tower clock to see what time it was, but the clock was not working. Merl had said the previous month he was going to get it fixed, but obviously he hadn't. It seemed to me that thirty minutes had already passed, and there was no sign of the ferry coming into port. Usually you would hear the horn blow. I certainly did not want to miss my ride home.

"Is something the matter?" asked Beauford.

"Oh no, sorry. I was just looking for the time. Do you know what time it is? I'm not wearing a watch."

Beauford looked down at his wrist to see what time it was but realized he wasn't wearing one, either.

"I don't know. I must have forgotten to wear my watch. Could've sworn I had it on earlier."

Beauford looked around him on the booth seat, on the floor, even stretching over to see the booth behind him, but no luck. I needed to know what time it was, but I figured if I looked outside the window, I might be able tell if folks were starting to walk towards where the ferry would have docked. Who knows? I could have not heard the horn blast while I was enchanted by his story. As I looked out the window, all I could see was darkness encompassed by heavy fog, but I leaned further in, pressing my cheek into the window. I was startled by a glimpse of a man's face protruding through the fog and threw myself back into my seat.

"Oh my God, did you see that man looking in the window?" I cried out, surely with fear in my voice.

I could see Beauford had not seen it as he was ducking his head under the table to look for his watch. He replied, "What window?"

"This window. I swear, at first I was looking out through a dark, foggy window, and out of the fog a man's face appeared and scared the crap out of me. Funny thing, though."

"What's funny?"

"Can you please stop looking underneath the table for a second and listen to me?"

19

Beauford quickly raised his head, banging it on the bottom of the table, causing my coffee to splash out of the cup. It landed on the table and on my dress right above my chest. The table made a shaking sound, and Old Merl came running out of the back of the kitchen to see what had just happened.

"What happened?"

"Merl, you've got to go outside and check it out. I swear I saw someone looking in the window at me. I swear I have seen his face before, but I cannot for the life of me think of where."

"OK, Bella, I will go and look. How did you get coffee on your dress? Did he do that? That dress is going to be ruined now."

"Calm down, Merl. It's OK."

Merl looked down at Beauford, who was holding his head where he bumped it, and then back at me. "Are you OK, Bella?"

"Yes, I'm fine, but I'm not too sure about him." Looking at Beauford rubbing his head, I felt bad for asking him to stop talking and listen to me. And I thought Merl thought this guy had made a pass at me and I got coffee all over my dress fending him off.

"Merl, he did nothing to me other than accidentally bump his head on the bottom of the table looking for his watch. I had asked him for the time." I paused for a second to change the subject. "Anyway, that doesn't matter. I swear, I think someone outside was watching me."

"I'll go and see." Beauford made his way out of the booth and went out into the terminal. He made his way to an exit, quickly walking towards the window. He stopped to look around and then darted off out of sight, looking for a stranger who might be lurking around and looking suspicious.

"Do you know what time it is, Merl?"

"Yes, it's about that time the ferry should be pulling in." And just at that moment, the ferry's horn blast went off.

"Hey, how did you know that?"

"It's a gift," Merl said, shrugging his shoulders up and down and squinting his eyes.

"I guess I'd better get going. Don't want to miss my ride home."

Reaching over to my purse in the booth, I said, "How much do I owe you, Merl, for the coffee and treats?" I pulled out my pocketbook.

"Ah, it is on the house. Go now before you miss your ride."

"You are such a sweet man. Love you." I kissed Merl on his check, grabbed my belongings, and started to exit the diner and head out the terminal towards the ferry.

Merl always loved it when I kissed him. Made him feel warm and fuzzy inside. As I pulled on the diner door, the bells jingled. Merl raised his voice to get my attention. Turning around, I saw him motioning me to wait as he ran behind the counter, wrapped up some cannoli, and headed back towards me.

"Here, take these and enjoy them. And come back soon and make an old man smile, my Bella."

"Oh, thank you, Merl. I will."

Heading out the door with both my hands full, I could hardly hold onto my stuff let alone the cannoli, but there was no way in hell I was dropping those. So, grasping the cannoli in my mouth and smiling back at Merl, I exited the diner and quickly darted down the terminal to the exit with my luggage bag wheels bouncing from side to side, up and down. I almost lost my grip on the handle several time as I held onto my backpack on my shoulder for dear life.

21

Pushing open the terminal door to the outside, the taste of aluminum foil literally filled my mouth. Saliva was running down the side of my mouth, but I was not dropping the cannoli. I didn't give a rat's ass what I looked like; I was not missing my way home. Besides, I had to go find Beauford, too, and see if he had found the man who I felt for sure was spying on me through the window.

As eerie as it felt, I hadn't even noticed that the fog was not as dense. The rain had let up as well, to a mere light drizzle. Outside the front entrance to the terminal, standing on the dock, I could see the ferry lights getting brighter through the fog as the boat was pulling into the dock. I made my way over to where I needed to be, hoping to spot Beauford.

The ferry was now pulling up, waves crashing into the side of the dock. Seagulls flew away into the dark so as not to be hit by the big boat. Standing there, all I could do was watch this massive ferry move in with such majestic rhythm. Big black letters, one by one passed in front of my eyes: V-I-C-T-O-R-I-A C-O-V-E.

I had never seen the *Victoria Cove* pull into the dock. In fact, I had never really paid attention to it in the past. It could be that before, there were too many people around to distract me, but wow, this ferry was massive and such a beauty, I say that even though it was dark out. I just climbed aboard and took her for granted. I guess I was always wrapped up in my schoolwork and never took the time to actually pay attention to it.

Many lights illuminated her outer shell and decks, dressing her with poise and character as she came to a stop. What a magnificent sight to see. One last horn blast to alert everyone she had arrived caught me off guard. I dropped the cannoli out of my mouth and watched them almost hit the ground, but a hand came out of nowhere and caught them. It was my missing man, Beauford.

"Easy now. Seems like I came back in the nick of time."

Looking stupid and relieved at the same time, all I could do was look at him and smile. Beauford noticed that the cannoli's aluminum-foil package was profusely drenched in some sort of slobbery liquid. He paused for a second before handing it back to me. Little did he know it was my saliva. Gross, huh?

"Sorry. I rushed outside to see what happened to you and to get over here for the ferry, but Old Merl stopped me and gave me a few cannoli for the road. It was the only way I could think of to carry them since my hands were full."

"Oh, that's all right. Kind of reminded me of my childhood dog Dingo's chew toy. But nevertheless, here you go."

OK, I deserved that. I'd been taking shots at a total stranger for the last hour, and it was about time I got some of that handed back into my lap.

"Did you happen to see anyone who looked suspicious out here?" I asked.

"Well, seeing how dark and quiet it is out here, I didn't see anyone out of the ordinary, but..." Beauford hesitated for a second before I jumped back at him with my plea for more information.

"But what?"

"It was nothing."

"Nothing? It has to be something or you would not have said it. You said you didn't see anyone out of the ordinary, followed by a 'but,' and your voice changed pitch. To me, that means you did see someone or something. What were you going to say after the 'but'?" I was anxiously cross-examining his statement, looking for a response, and I didn't want to wait any longer to see if someone was truly spying on me.

"Easy now. Relax. Give me a second to respond. Geez, you would think you were some sort of lawyer by the way you hammered me there."

"Well, kind of, sort of, I am a lawyer."

"Lawyer? Hmm, you know, that doesn't surprise me, the way you've been responding to me."

Feeling rather foolish for my outburst, I could see in his face that he wasn't surprised. It's not like I had been putting him on the stand questioning his responses and motives that night, or had I been? I couldn't even think straight right then. My feet were killing me from these damn broken boots, my back was tight from dragging my luggage around like a maniac to get out there, my mouth tasted like aluminum foil, and now my pride had gotten the best of me. *I hope he still likes me* was all I could think of at the moment, looking into his eyes as water ran down my face.

To make matters worse, the rain changed from drizzle to a downpour again. If it weren't for rain, what would Seattle be known for? It was my destiny tonight to be wet, cold, and humiliated by my own words and actions.

"Here, let me cover you with this umbrella."

I didn't recall his having an umbrella the whole time we had been together. Strange, if you ask me. It was as if he had pulled it out of his sleeve as a magic trick. I didn't care, as I was delighted to at least have my head covered for just a moment out of the pouring rain, although I was curious as to how he had obtained it.

Beauford managed to come under the umbrella as well, moving in close to me, within an inch or two. This closeness jump-started my heartbeat once again as I could see and feel his breath on my face. The warmth of his breath felt good and still smelled of coffee, and the heat his body was letting off thawed my chilled body. I glanced at him scooting closer, touching my body against his. I could tell from his reaction he didn't mind. I wanted to lean over and kiss him. That was how attracted I was to him at that moment, but I dared not.

"Now, isn't that better?"

"Much better, thank you."

"What a beautiful sight," Beauford whispered to me in a lower tone, looking at me.

"Yes, she certainly is a beautiful boat."

"No, I mean you."

Chills shot up my spine and goose bumps ran the length of my arms as my cheeks tightened with an overwhelming desire to jump into this man's arms. I wanted to wrap my arms and legs around his body, to grind mine against his in hopes of arousing him. I was so attracted to this quirky, geeky, clumsy, yet come-to-my-rescue handsome man whom I had just barley met.

I do not usually fall for a guy that fast. Something was definitely odd about him, or maybe Old Merl had spiked my drink. Laughing from within, I did not want to let on that I was so easily taken by him, so I did nothing and stood there for what felt like an eternity before he spoke to me again. The rain was tapping the top of the umbrella like the sounds of a snare drum marching into battle as I could see people lining up to board the ferry off to the side.

So, without responding to his comment on my being beautiful, I figured I would dodge that bullet by getting back to finding out if he had seen anyone suspicious when he had left the diner to look for me.

"So, did you find anyone, and how did you come up with this umbrella?"

"Well, not exactly. By the time I got out here, if there was someone truly spying on you through the window, he was gone. However, I did run into a guy around the corner who was selling umbrellas and asked him, but he said he hadn't seen much of anyone around here other than a few folks walking about and the two of us about forty-five minutes ago walking into the terminal."

Very odd, if you would have asked me, as I hadn't seen anyone hanging around the corner as I walked into the ferry's terminal. But that didn't mean there hadn't been as it was foggy and raining, and I wasn't particularly looking for that sort of thing. Yet my childhood upbringing would have led me to spot that person even if it was under those conditions. I credit my time at the orphanage and my uncle's house for that.

I had to know for myself even though Beauford had mentioned there wasn't anyone around. The sky began to cry more as the rain intensified. I knew it would be difficult to see, but I had to know.

"Give me a minute. I need to see for myself." I quickly left the comforts of Beauford's warm body and umbrella and darted off towards the edge of the building to see what or whom was around the corner.

"Alex, come back here. It's raining hard, and besides, I wouldn't imagine him to still be there," Beauford shouted to me. He was about to drop the umbrella to chase me but decided not to.

I really didn't care at that moment about the rain. I had been soaked for hours by then, so what was the difference between standing in the rain and running in it? I needed to know if I was being followed. My inner Spidey sense was going off, and I had to find out.

Well, I rounded the corner of the building to the far east of the dock, and Beauford was right. I could not see anyone through the blurring rain. I decided to walk a few feet more and stopped. This was stupid. Why would anyone be following me in the first place? I had nothing on anyone, no enemies that I knew about. Besides, I was a brand-new trial lawyer with no cases under my belt. I hadn't even begun to make enemies.

As fearful as I felt from letting my mind get the best of me, I stood there as the rain came down even harder, soaking my hair and face. It was Mother Nature's shower, and with just the simple thought of that, I closed my eyes, opened my mouth, and twirled right there as I did as a child. I must have been crazy, and to think I had made all this up in my head. I was starting to think I was my own worst enemy.

Just then, I could hear my name being called from behind me. Beauford had come after me, calling my name as he approached me. He had all my belongings with him, too.

"Alex...Alex...ah, there you are. I was starting to worry about you."

"You were right."

"Right about what? Here, come on, tell me as we walk back to the ferry. It's about to leave. Come here. Get closer. You're shivering."

Beauford seemed to be my knight in shining armor that night after all as he placed the umbrella once again over my head and his. He wrapped one arm around me, and I was once again embraced by his warm body. Strapping my backpack over my left shoulder, Beauford motioned me to take the umbrella as he grabbed my luggage in his other hand, all the while dazzling me with his beautiful smile.

"OK, let's get you back to the ferry. Oh, I hope you don't mind, but I stuffed your purse in your backpack. I didn't want to run off looking for you and leave your belongings behind."

I wasn't the least upset that he had done that. Besides, I had run off, leaving it all behind, not thinking about someone running off with it or even that someone being Beauford. I still had hardly any background on him, yet I had subconsciously let him guard it.

"Oh, and I also stuffed your cannoli in there as well, but I might've kind of squished them. Sorry."

"It's OK. Thank you for being so caring. Sometimes I run off and don't think twice, and well, you see what happens. Again, not one of my finest moments." I smiled up at him, and I could see he knew I must be one crazy girl.

As we walked back, rounding the corner, I could see it was time to board the *Victoria Cove*. A few folks were walking up the connecting stairs to enter the vessel. This was a good sight since I knew I could rest a spell before getting home.

"So maybe we could get back to our conversation over another cup of coffee on the ferry?" I suggested. "I would really like to know more about the man who has rescued me time after time tonight."

"I would love to, but I'm not going your way."

I was puzzled because I had thought he was going to the same place as I was. It had never dawned on me to even ask him why he was at the ferry terminal. Wow, I felt stupid.

"What do you mean? So why are you down here tonight, if I may ask?"

"Well, funny thing. I was supposed to pick up my grandmother, who was traveling back to Seattle this evening, but when I didn't see her, I decided to walk down to the terminal."

"And that is where you ran into me and my luggage that I so stupidly left behind. Oh my God, I am so sorry. Your grandmother, she must be worried about you. I feel like an idiot distracting you from her," I said, pleading to Beauford because I felt so bad for my actions.

"Relax, Alex. It's OK."

"OK? How can it be OK? Your grandmother must be worried to death that you haven't found her."

"No...no. She's fine. I had the days mixed up. In fact, I'm a day too early."

"How do you know that?"

"Well, after I went outside to check on your mysterious man, I didn't see anyone other than the guy selling the umbrellas, so I bought one, walked back up to the dock entrance, and used the pay phone to call my family where she's staying. It turns out she answered the phone, and, well, I felt foolish that I had come a day early. But if I hadn't, I would not have met you."

I felt bad for him because he could have found out earlier about his grandmother, but he was glad he ran into me. As selfish as it sounds, I was glad Grandmamma was not there, or I would not have had the pleasure as well to meet him.

"So now what?" I asked him as if to get some sort of commitment from him to follow up with me. "I would really like to know more about you and your manure business."

Beauford smiled as he replied, "As well as I. I want to know more about you, Alex the lawyer. And it isn't a manure business; it's science."

Whatever he wanted to call it, to me, I could not get the image of him playing with crap, but I felt compelled to lean in and kiss him. What was a girl to do? It was at least one thing I could do to repay him for his kindness that night. Besides, who would refuse a kiss from a beautiful stranger like me? We both leaned in and were about to touch each other's lips when the horn blast from the *Victoria Cove* signaled it was about to depart.

"Well, I must go. I don't want to miss my last chance at getting home. I have a very long day tomorrow, and I haven't even read over the case." I pulled away from him and walked aboard the ferry, looking back at him.

"Wait...how can we meet again?"

"Call me. I'm in the phone book under Henson. Alexandria Henson."

I boarded the ferry, turned around, and waved at him as he stood there in the pouring rain waving back, watching me fade away as the ferry pushed forward away from the dock, engulfed once again in the Seattle fog.

Chapter Three
Victoria Cove

Several more horn blasts rang through the night air to clear the way as the *Victoria Cove* came about to the left. I could feel that she was gaining momentum and figured it was best to move away from the edge where I had boarded the vessel as Deckhand Bailey secured the area.

"Good evening, Miss Henson. Been a month already?"

"Hi, Josh. How are you tonight?" I responded, as I hadn't really noticed it had been a month since I last had ridden the ferry.

"Oh, a little tired. Been a long day."

"Oh, I can relate. Been quite a day and night for me, too. Looking forward to getting home. How are the waves tonight?

"Captain says it should be smooth sailing for a bit, but it might be a tad bumpy once we near the strait. But other than that, should be a pleasant ride. Here, let me take your luggage and stow it away behind my stand."

"You sure? I don't mind lugging it around."

"Not at all. Looks like to me like you could stand to not have to bring it with you." Josh smiled at me while looking down at my boots.

"Don't ask. Too long of a story."

"Well, I'm surprised to see you on such a late ride. Usually you're on an earlier ride."

"Again, long story. Maybe sometime I'll share the story with you, but for now, let's just not speak of it."

"You got it, Miss Henson. Look forward to it. Hey, just to let you know since you are on the last ride, the main restaurant near the aft is closed, but the bar on the top deck near the front is open. If you're hungry, they have a few snacks and some ice-cold submarines."

"Oh, OK. Thanks, Josh. Not feeling hungry, but I could use a stiff drink right about now."

"Well, you are in luck as drinks from the bar are free for riders at this hour."

"Maybe I should ride the ferry more often at this hour. Free drinks and a handsome deckhand to take my luggage…a girl can't go wrong." I said, making Josh blush a tad. I felt I would head towards the bar.

"Have a pleasant ride, and when we dock, your bag will be right here with me."

"Thank you, Josh. See you on the flip side. Time for a drink, and I have got to read over some important papers or I am going to be in big trouble."

"Oh, that's right. Last time we talked, you were about to graduate law school and head off to London, right? So I take it you must have landed a job as well, too?"

Turning to walk away from him, I stopped to answer since he hadn't finished conversing. I was under the impression he had, but nonetheless, I responded, "Yes, and if I intend to keep my very first job as a trial lawyer, I'd better get reading. And no, no Big Ben, just the city of love, Paris."

"Ah yes, well, welcome back, and tell Bernard at the bar to hook you up with the special. Trust me, you will love it. Glad to see you again."

You see, Josh was an eighteen-year-old boy fresh out of high school working on the ferry, and I think he had a crush on me. And well, he would tend to distract me as long as he could to avoid doing his duties. I'd been told I was rather a distraction for him in the past by his cousin, the ship's navigator.

The ferry was pretty much run by his family. Seems he once told me that he was either going to have to work on the ferry, learn respect, and gain a valuable skill, or he would be sent off to a juvenile institution since he was a teenager who seemed to run with the wrong crowd and would get into trouble.

I believe he had also mentioned that his dad was or had been a detective for the Vancouver Police Department, and this was his last straw with his son. From what I could recall, his father had sweet-talked the judge into letting his son "do time," so to speak, here on the ferry. If you asked me, it seemed Josh would rather work here to avoid going to Juvie. I didn't mind at all. I kind of liked the attention he gave me when I was aboard the ferry…made me feel safer knowing I was riding with protection.

"Well, I'd best be getting back to my duties. So good to see you again, Miss Henson."

"You can call me Alex. When I hear 'Miss Henson,' it kind of makes me feel like an old woman for some reason."

"OK, Alex, you got it." Josh was still red in the face as he smiled. I turned and walked into the entrance from the aft of the ferry.

I realized that Josh was just being polite and that I was going to be hearing "Miss Henson" a lot being a lawyer, but coming from a guy just a few years younger than me made me feel really old. It's not that I looked old; I was only twenty-two. I work out regularly and try to keep my slim, girlish figure and feel like I am sexy. Well, not right then, as I must have looked rather scary with my brunette hair covering part of my face and my clothes soaked to the bone. But other than that, I feel good about myself.

Ha, these days, it seems men don't really care. If you smile at them, they think it's a free ticket to romance or even more. Not in my book. If I don't like you back, you don't stand a chance. Makes me think Beauford, as geeky as he seemed, might've been a good catch for me, although I might've come across a little harsh at first and a tad easy before we departed. There was just something about him that drove me crazy.

It probably wouldn't matter since I might not ever hear from him, but it was nice that we had bumped into each other. It isn't every day a girl gets to experience such chivalry.

Walking around inside the *Victoria Cove,* I never realized how nice and elegant it was laid out. How could I have overlooked this on my past voyages? It could have been because I had never entered this way before. I usually followed the crowd and just went with the flow and usually ended up in the front of the boat, sitting in the chairs that faced forward. I had never really given much thought to getting up and exploring around other than using the ladies' room.

Of course, walking through the hall up to the center of the ferry wasn't elegant, but I noticed the pictures of old vessels hanging on the wall and some maritime artifacts as well. I just never gave it much thought and really only thought of it as a means of getting across the sound to home. Besides, I usually fell asleep, woke upon arriving, and just exited the boat. There was so much more to this vessel and would have loved to see it while there was hardly anyone aboard, but I knew that if I did, I would not settle down and open my case and review it. It seemed to me my first case was either going to be a hit or break me, but I did have a three-hour ride ahead of me, and would another thirty minutes kill me?

Walking into the open middle section, I could actually see a bright full moon silhouetted by the night sky from the glass-covered ceiling. It just lit up the area and was a sight to see. The center of the boat was the passengers' heartbeat, as I could see shops along the edge of both sides of the ferry surrounding hardwood floors, small tables, and chairs placed about. Elegant light fixtures lit up the area and up and down the halls, leading to other places on the boat. Lounge chairs neatly facing one another on opposite sides of the area could potentially spark conversation between passing riders. An inner top deck wrapped around the entire area with a shiny brass handrail and glass below to keep little ones from falling through.

It was not what I would have imagined. To some, it was just a boat, as I had thought, but for others, it was not just a means of getting from point A to point B, but rather a social mingling center that made their lives thrive. I could envision many people going their way, passing one another, talking, drinking, and even going outside to sightsee, to breathe in the ocean breeze, and to just have a good time.

"I do the same thing." Josh had walked up behind me unannounced, startling me.

"Oh my God, you scared me."

"Sorry, Miss Henson…I mean Alex."

"It's OK. My heart will stop racing in a few minutes."

I wanted to turn around and punch him in the arm but didn't. I did that once in school to the boy whom I was in love, just for horseplay. Besides, Josh meant no harm and I was just edgy, so I brushed it off as my pulse settled back down.

"You do what the same? Not following."

"I come here on my breaks around this time, and if it's nice out, I usually grab one of the chairs and sit it in the middle of this open area and look upwards, staring into the night sky."

"Wow, Josh, that seems not so teenage of you."

"What is that supposed to mean?" Josh looked at me, bewildered, as if I was making a bad comment directed at him.

"No, I wasn't meaning anything bad. I was actually referring to you in a good way. What I mean is, it sounded like you were an adult rather than a teenager, and if your dad had heard you just now, he would see that in you as well."

"Well, he really doesn't call me very often."

"That's too bad. He should." Just then, I realized I had not called my Uncle Nicholas since landing hours ago, and now I was going to be in trouble.

"Oh shit. Sorry, excuse my language. Do you know what time it is, Josh?" I said, reading into my purse. I pulled out my BlackBerry and realized it was dead. No wonder I hadn't gotten a call from my uncle.

"It's ten-forty-seven."

"I'd better go find a place to charge my phone."

"Wait. You can do that up in the bar area, but first try sitting down here. Let me grab a chair."

"No need to do that."

"Please, I insist. You'll feel much better after you've experienced it."

"What the hell, OK." Looking at Josh, I figured a few more minutes would not hurt. Besides, he was admitting about getting me to do this, so I agreed.

"OK, sit down here and look up," Josh said.

I dropped my backpack and purse on the wood floor next to the chair and looked up.

"No, relax and lean your head back," Josh said. "Look up at the sky and see the stars and moon. Visualize that for a few minutes, and then close your eyes and take in a few deep breaths and let them out."

"This seems silly, Josh."

"Trust me, just try it."

I could not believe I was going along with this little charade, sitting down in the middle of the floor, looking up at the night sky and listening to him. There had to be a catch to this, and I wasn't sure what it was. But sitting there looking up at the sky was relaxing. It was peaceful, and I noticed that the rain had stopped, and it was just a clear night.

"Now lean back, close your eyes, and breathe in and out."

Josh managed to guide my head back against the top of the chair with his hands, and I let him. I didn't think anything was out of the ordinary as it was the first time that night I had actually relaxed. Little did I know that this young man had other intentions? Josh was speaking to me softly while my eyes were still shut. I could not make out what he was saying but went along with it as he moved up closer behind my head. I had not noticed he was about to do something he would regret, but I was relaxed for the next few seconds.

Josh leaned over and was able to see Alex's chest poking through the top of her dress. His eyes lit up as he kissed her left ear while sniffing her wet hair. Sensing his close proximity, I quickly leaned forward, opened my eyes and give him a piece of my mind.

"What the hell are you doing?"

"Um, I'm sorry. I meant no harm."

"You meant no harm? What do you call kissing my ear and sniffing my hair?"

Josh stood there with a giddy look on his face, grinning. "Alex, please let me explain."

37

"Call me Miss Henson, Josh. I can't believe I fell for that teenage move. I have to give it to you, Josh; that was quite smooth."

Again, Josh felt quite proud of his move and agreed by nodding his head.

"No, stop it, Josh. Even though this might've been a romantic gesture in your mind, it was creepy. You took an innocent moment and twisted it."

Standing up, I noticed what might have sparked all of this as my top few buttons on my dress were unbuttoned, revealing more than I would have liked to have shown. Knowing that, I felt stupid and foolish for yelling at him. Besides, being a young man, this might have been a pinnacle moment for him, and I had just killed it. Nevertheless, I played it as if he was the one who was wrong.

"Listen, Josh, I apologize if I gave you the wrong impression, but next time, try not to be so eager. Let it happen naturally."

"So you're not mad at me?"

"No. Just don't try that again, mister," I said, smirking back at him since it was a little funny as well.

"I promise I won't. I'm not sure what came over me. Must be that you are so hot."

So much for feeling angry towards him. This young man had just called me hot. If he had been just a few years older...I had to stop and refocus just then.

"Thank you, Josh. I appreciate the compliment."

"No, really, you are smoking hot."

"OK, I get it, thank you, but stop saying that. You're going to make a girl blush and get all hot and bothered by that." I figured that was the wrong response to an already heightened sexual drive in a young man, so I quickly made a rebuttal. "What I mean is, thank you."

"Please don't say anything to anyone. I meant no harm. I do apologize for my actions."

I could see in his eyes he was sincere in his apology, and I was not going to alert his boss anyway. But I felt I needed to play it to him as if I might.

"I won't, but you have to make me a promise that you won't try that again with me or any other woman unless they let you. You got it?"

Boy, I sure sounded like an adult there, almost like my uncle scolding me when I would do something stupid as a teenager.

"Yes, I've got it. But you did say there might be a next time, so..."

"Hey, don't count your chickens before they hatch." I paused for a few seconds. "I guess I did just say that, but what I meant was, the next time you find yourself in this situation, you think twice, that's all. Don't go all cocked in."

Josh giggled like a schoolboy as I said that. I just gave him the look, nodding my head. I could see in his eyes that the fire was slowly dwindling, and his posture was not so correct anymore. It was like the big letdown of being turned down by a pretty girl after asking her to go steady. I felt compelled to redeem him somewhat by giving him hope, even if I really didn't intend act on it.

"Listen, tell you what. If in a couple of years we both find ourselves still single, who knows? I might take you up on it. I mean, for a casual date, not sex. So, for now, when we see each other, let's just be friends. Deal?"

I knew in the back of my mind that if this eighteen-year-old good-looking man was single in a few years and looking as good as he did then, I would entertain the thought. Who knows? He might even get lucky then if he played his cards right. In fact, I might even let him join the Mile High Club, but from a maritime standpoint on this vessel. What am I saying? My mind is drifting and it seems my hormones are heighten from this little incident.

I waited for Josh to respond glaring at his eyes. He hesitated for a moment but responded like a good boy.

"Deal!"

"Good. Now, tell me how to get to that bar. I need a stiff, cold drink."

"If you go straight across to your left, right next to the coffee shop, and hang a left, you will see a spiral staircase. Take that to the level right up above us. Then just walk towards the left side of the boat and hang a right, passing Le café, and take the next set of stairs you see. Once you reach the top deck, the bar will be towards the front."

"Well, that seems pretty easy. See you in a while, Josh."

It didn't really seem easy, but I got the drift of it. Basically, find my way to the top deck and locate the bar. Couldn't be that difficult. I was actually mostly relieved to say that that awkward moment was over. Twice in one night being hit on may be a booster for some, but under my circumstances, I was a little frazzled. Men have no self-control, and it usually gets them in trouble.

Josh left as quickly as he came, and to me, that was no shock. His feathers were ruffled, but at least now he knew not to try that again. Looking up at the level above to the left, I could see that I needed to get over to the hallway and head to the bar. I just needed to visually stamp the path in my mind. Still, I could not get over the beauty this vessel possessed and many probably would never know unless they saw it the way I was seeing it.

I had no idea exactly where we were at the moment on the seas, but the boat barely bounced against the water's skin, and it hardly even felt like we were moving. Making my way to the stairs and up to the next level, I could see out the windows, and it was majestic. The glow from the moon reflected on the water as the ferry glided across the water.

I saw the hallway entrance as well as I walked past an older gentleman who happened to be seated in a lounge chair, smoking a cigar. I would have imagined smoking on a vessel like this would have been prohibited and enforced, but who was around to do that? Funny how a clearly visible sign was across from him to my right— "NO SMOKING" in bright red with white letters. A fire extinguisher was right beside it as well.

The thought crossed my mind to tell him to put the cigar out because a fire caused by his ashes falling on the carpeted floor due to his neglect would be horrific on this boat. I also thought about pulling the fire extinguisher off the wall and dousing him to put it out. But those were just thoughts, and the less I interfered with what I could not control, the better off I would be.

Still, I could see he wasn't aware of the ashes that had fallen on the carpet, yet there were no burn marks that I could tell. He just looked at me with a smile as I passed him. I offered him a simple greeting without showing a smile.

"Hello."

"Marvelous evening, wouldn't you say?"

"If you had the day I've had, you would respond differently."

"Hmm, I guess by what I just saw down below, I can agree. Young Josh seems to have taken a liking to you."

"Sorry, I did not realize anyone was around to see that. Not what I expected from him."

"Well, can you blame him?"

Great. Another man on the verge of referring to the way I look. It must have been the getup I was wearing: broken Prada boots, drenched clothes, coffee-stained dress with buttons that seemed to not want to stay buttoned. "Listen," I said, "all I want to do is to go upstairs, get a freaking cold one, and sit my butt down in a chair and relax. Not looking for a romance."

"Easy, little lady. I was just referring to your—"

I quickly interrupted him as I knew what he was going to say next. "I know, my beauty. Yeah, yeah, been hearing that all night. What is with you men? Can't a girl be just a girl without all the hubbub?"

"I see. You seem to know what we men are always thinking. Well, now, if you'll excuse me, I'll be going now."

Feeling rather stupid then for my actions, I offered my apology. I could see from his wrinkles on his cheek and chin that he had to be in his mid-sixties, but I could not see his eyes as the fedora he was wearing covered them.

"Hey, mister, I am sorry. I didn't mean anything by my words. It's just been a crazy day, and I guess I took it out on you, and you had nothing to do with it."

"Call me Pierre—Pierre Gustave, to be exact—and don't think twice about it. I accept your apology." Pierre removed his hat and bowed in front of me gracefully. You don't see that level of response anymore.

"Wait, *the* Pierre Gustave? Pierre Gustave, the famous yacht racer? The Pierre Gustave who crashed into rocks near Puget Sound during the nineteen-eighty-eight Canadian Sailboat Racing Olympics? No way. I grew up reading about you and your races. You and your team were unbeaten."

"In the flesh." Pierre bowed again while stretching his arm out with his hat.

"Shut up!"

Just then, I could see the awkward response from Pierre. I meant it in no derogatory sense, but he was baffled and speechless. He was just standing there. I think I had just insulted him again. It seems my mouth was my biggest problem that night.

"No...no, I don't mean that in a bad way. I wasn't telling you to shut up. I was just reacting in a heightened moment."

"Ah, yes. I seem to have that effect on women," Pierre said, making a joke.

"Oh, where are my manners? I forgot to introduce myself. Hi, Pierre, my name is Alexandria Henson," I said, reaching out to shake his hand. I was greeted with a kiss on top of it instead.

"Well, nice to meet you, Alexandria. And allow me to offer my apologies as well."

"For what? You didn't do anything wrong."

"Well, that is where you are wrong, little lady. I am keeping you from your cold drink. If I may ask, can I escort you to the bar and buy you that drink?"

I liked the sound of that, and besides, when a man offers to pay for a drink, I am not going to turn it down, especially from one of Canada's famous sons.

"I would be honored, Mr. Gustave."

"Please, child, call me Pierre. It makes me feel much younger," he said, smiling as he turned to put out his cigar, which was still smoldering between his fingers.

"You know, smoking isn't really allowed in here, and those ashes on the carpet could've caused a fire."

"Really? I hadn't noticed." Pierre cracked a smile. He knew but didn't seem to care.

"Well, I won't tell the owner if you won't," I said, looking at him with a firm face.

"Good. I won't, either. I don't think I would like it so much that I was smoking inside the vessel."

"So, you are the owner of this vessel?"

"Indeed I am. I like to ride the ferry every now and then late at night because it's peaceful. And I was actually trying out a new prototype fireproof carpet when you came upon me."

"Oh, and to think I thought you were just being inconsiderate and dangerous."

"No, not inconsiderate, but dangerous as a mouse." Pierre was being funny again—quite the joker if you ask me. "This new carpet I was trying out will aid in keeping vessels like mine safe from passengers carelessly dropping their smoking products on the floor and causing a maritime disaster."

"That is a great idea."

"Enough talk about carpets and disasters. Shall we?" Pierre straightened his posture and offered up his arm while standing like a gentleman as I accepted. He pointed the way towards the hallway with his other hand. We both walked out the exit and walked up to the top level towards the bar.

As we approached the bar, I noticed a huge sign calling it the Gnarly Gar. That definitely was fitting. Pierre, still being a gentleman, pulled out a barstool for me. I dropped my backpack on the ground in front of the stool and sat down.

"What will it be, mateys?" the bartender asked in a horrible attempt at a pirate's voice.

"Well, that sure sounded like a sick pirate," I said, addressing the bartender with a smirk on my face.

Clearing his throat after that failed attempt, Bernard the bartender replied with, "Sorry. Guess I don't have to keep doing that silly voice this late at night. The owner of the vessel sent out a letter requesting we dress and act like our names for where we work. If you ask me, I think it's silly, and so do the customers, but I guess he doesn't care. I've asked my boss to ask him if we could stop, and, well, I am here still doing it."

"Have you ever met the owner?" I asked Bernard while looking at Pierre.

He shook his head slightly side to side. "No, I just started here a few months back. I've heard he never comes around. Besides, I also heard that he sort of was linked to some sort of scandal in the past and was paid off, and, well, the rest is history, as you can see from this vessel being in service."

I could see from the dim lights that his facial reactions were not pleasant. I sat there hoping he was going to keep calm. I was about to reply to Bernard that he was standing right in front of the man who owned this vessel when Pierre reached over with his right arm and motioned me to quietly back off, so I leaned back and sat there with a grin on my face.

"Bernard is it?"

"Yes."

"If the owner were standing right in front of you, face to face, would you tell him again as you just told us about the silly little gig he has you doing?"

"I might. He doesn't scare me. I would tell him exactly what I just said."

"OK, then. How about right now?" Pierre looked at him with conviction in his eyes and voice.

"What? Now? Is he here?" Bernard was not so sure of himself. He started to shake a little while rinsing a glass.

"You are looking at him in the flesh."

The look on Bernard's face was priceless. Not only did he freeze right before us, but I think he peed a little, too, but I wasn't sure. I would have after making a remark like that in front of the owner and not knowing it. I could see Pierre wasn't mad at all. He felt redeemed as he saw Bernard tremble.

"I...I am..."

Pierre held his hand up, gesturing to Bernard to not say anything. He replied, cutting Bernard off, "Relax, young man. It is quite fine. Point taken, and I agree—you don't need to do that anymore. I will make it official in a few days with a letter to the staff. It takes courage to speak the way you feel, especially doing so without even knowing I was right in front of you." Pierre giggled lightly. "I admire your confidence. However, just remember to always be confident no matter what the situation is."

Spoken like a true mentor. Pierre's words even inspired me as I sat there listening and watching him. How could this man ever be accused of being caught up in a scandal? He seemed too honest and professional.

"Enough of this. I promised this little lady a cold drink, and by golly, I intend to make sure she gets it. What's your pleasure, Alexandria?"

"Well, Josh mentioned to me to tell Bernard to ask for the special, and I would like it. So how about that?"

"The special? Hmm, what is the special, Bernard?"

"It's my own creation. Pineapple chunks mixed with the house rum, a touch of vodka, lots of ice, and some lime, blended."

"Wow, that sounds like a potent drink. But hasn't that been discovered already?" I asked Bernard even though my mouth was beginning to want that drink anyway.

"No. Some have tried to make similar drinks, but it all depends on the type of rum and the added vodka, and I also put a splash of chocolate sauce on top with whipped cream."

"Not sure if this is a mixed drink or a dessert, but I like the idea. Make one for me as well," Pierre said, giving Bernard a thumbs-up on his drink creation. We sat there for a few minutes watching Bernard make the drink before he handed them to us.

"Here you go."

"Now we just have to see if it lives up to its taste. What exactly do you call it?" Pierre responded while holding the glass at eye level.

"Um, well, don't get mad, but I kind of chose your last name and added the word crush to it—Gustave Crush."

Pierre and I sipped our drinks, and I was amazed how well all the ingredients tasted. I was blown away. I could see Pierre was licking his lips as well and taking another huge sip.

"I like it! This is an excellent alcoholic beverage, and the name is a smart move, too! Tell you what…why don't you add that drink permanently to the menu, and I will give you rights and credit for the drink? In fact, I will also pay you something for it as well. Mighty fine drink."

"Thanks, Mr. Gustave. I really appreciate it."

"You are welcome. That will be all for now." Pierre told Bernard that he could relax now and go about his duties.

"So, Alexandria, tell me, what it is that you do?"

"I just landed a job as a trial lawyer in Seattle. My first day is tomorrow, but I graduated law school a few weeks back and went on a celebration trip to Paris."

"Lawyer? Now, that seems quite the challenging job."

"If it is anything like my life, then it will be a piece of cake since I already have the necessary skills to do it."

"Sounds like you had a hard upbringing."

"You can say that, but I don't really want to bore you with that."

"No worries. Maybe another time, perhaps? I like hearing stories like that."

"OK, sure, if our paths cross again."

"Well, how about this Saturday?"

"Wow, OK. I think I can make it."

"I am having a get-together for all my friends on my private yacht, *Wanderer*, docked in Sooke just a half hour from Victoria near my home. I welcome you to attend as well. Bring a friend if you like. Food, drinks, mingling, and overall good times."

"That is quite the invite. I will be there. What time?"

"Any time after two in the afternoon is good. My pleasure to have met you, Alexandria. Please excuse me, and enjoy your drink." Pierre picked up my hand once again and kissed it. He excused himself and walked away towards the outside of the ferry. I could see he was going outside this time to smoke his cigar.

What a night so far. I hadn't even realized that two hours had gone by since stepping on board the *Victoria Cove*. Time flies, I guess, when you are having fun, sort of in a weird way. All I knew was that I had to look at those papers, and I needed to plug in my phone to charge it. I could almost bet I was going to get a call the next day from Uncle Nicholas, and it wasn't going to be pleasant because I hadn't let him know I had landed hours ago.

"Hey, Bernard?"

"Yes, ma'am?"

"Is there a place where I can sit that has enough light that I can read some papers and charge my cell phone?"

"Yeah. The table behind you against the column. It has a candle for light and a plug on the column that you can use."

Chapter Four

Feelings Mutual

I have to hand it to Bernard the bartender for his frozen alcoholic concoction. It really hit the spot. Who would've ever thought of mixing such ingredients? Wow, I felt overwhelmed, too, as I just had had the pleasure of meeting a man who was a local legend and one whom I looked up to for inspiration from reading magazine articles on him.

Strange, though—if my memory serves me well, Pierre was favored to win the nineteen-eighty-eight Canadian summer sailboat race with the odds of his losing not likely. I also remember Uncle Nicholas talking about the race as well because he had some sort of bet on it, but I'm not sure for whom to win. It was a big deal back then in his house and drew quite the audience of folks coming and going. That day of the race seem to be a big deal that many gathered around the television in his bar and throughout the house talking and drinking. Some even a little too much and recall hearing my uncle raise his voice and suddenly the place was quiet until he waved his hands. When this happened I would disappear and go off looking for a hiding spot.

At times I even thought of my uncle as being some sort of gangster the way we lived, with a lavish house—well, more like a compound if you ask me, with all the security that was in place—black limousines always driving him and his friends around, and fancy parties every other night of the week.

I chose to stay out of my uncle's way and business, but at times I wondered about it and attempted to sneak around, but I only ended up getting caught by one of his friends or security people. Uncle just told me he was wealthy from an inheritance his father had left behind, and I was lucky to be a part of this household. He was right; I had no plans to go back to the warden's torture chamber…well, that's what I called the Alexandra Neighborhood House, especially with that wicked old lady Miss Simons being there.

I never really did get along with anyone at the orphanage other than Tina. She would sit next to me at breakfast, lunch, and dinner, and sometimes I would see her sitting alone on the playground, but she never spoke to me there, only through the walls. Tina stayed in the room next to mine. She was constantly crying, yelling, and fighting with the staff, but at night she would randomly whisper to me. I never really could make out what she said other than to run and escape.

My childhood was cast with sorrow until my uncle found me. He said that all those strange men coming around were just friends or business partners. Sometimes those friends would act stupidly out of the blue or say something wrong and my uncle would smack them around, but then he would hug them. I sure didn't want to be one of his friends.

One time I was where I wasn't supposed to be in the house—the attic. The attic was off limits, and if I was ever caught in there, I would be punished severely, and I didn't want to have that ever happen. I heard my uncle yelling at someone I had never seen or recognized before down in the back courtyard. He was walking around the fellow pushing him around, and every minute or two, I would see my uncle slap him. Then some of his friends would kick him, even when he was on the ground in the fetal position, until he wouldn't move. After my uncle and his friends left, I watched the man slowly get up. Blood covered his face, as he stumbled out of sight.

I never saw that man again and never spoke of it to my uncle since I surely didn't want to end up like him. I feared my uncle because I had seen firsthand how mean he could be, yet he was so loving and gracious—to me, too—as well as well-respected by others. Still today, I love him to death even if he doesn't agree about my choice to become a lawyer. I do recall seeing a rather unusual tattoo on the man who was beaten that day. He had an eagle of some sort on his right arm, but I really couldn't make it out clearly.

Wow, that drink had to have been the most potent drink I had ever had in order to conjure a flashback like that. Chills popped up on my arms and ran down the back of my neck, stiffening the top of my head. This was one hell of a good drink, and I loved it. Something told me I was going to need another one as that one was almost gone, and that couldn't happen.

"Hey, Bernard."

"Yes, ma'am?"

"How about another one?" I called out to him while raising the empty glass and tapping it with my index finger with my other hand. "Easy on the rum this time," I said, smiling back at him.

He quickly replied to me, "Coming right up." Bernard was delighted to mix up another, and I saw the smile on his face as well.

I decided I'd better plug my BlackBerry in so I could check to see if I had any messages, especially from my uncle, and get down to business looking over the case. Leaning over to my backpack, I unzipped it and first removed the semi-smashed, aluminum-foil-wrapped cannoli and placed them on the table. Smashed or not, I was still going to devour them. As I reached for my purse for my cell, Bernard caught me off guard placing the drink on the table, startling me.

"You all right? I didn't mean to startle you."

"I'm OK. Just a little tired and frazzled from my travels today."

"Well, this should fix you up."

"That's what I'm afraid of. Too many of these and I'll need more than just someone startling me to get me up." Looking at Bernard, I could see he was as happy as a pig in shit, so to speak, as he walked back to the bar to attend to washing the glasses. In fact, I felt that if I didn't stand upright that second and walk outside for a few minutes and take in some fresh air, I was going to pass out from that drink.

"Hey, Bernard. Can you watch my cell and back for a moment? Think I need some fresh air to go along with this drink."

"Sure thing. No one is here except you and me. Don't think anyone will slip in on me and take it, so go."

"You sure?"

"Yeah, go ahead."

"I'll be just a few minutes, and then I'll be back."

"No need to worry, ma'am. Take your time. We have roughly twenty-seven minutes before we pull into harbor."

Time sure was flying by, and I thought I would have had plenty of time to relax and look over my case, but it was looking less likely as I headed out the side door to the deck outside. I figured it would be best now to read over the papers quickly when I got home instead of trying to then since I was half wasted with a strong buzz and didn't feel like doing it.

I had but a few hours left on my vacation trip, and I was going to enjoy them. What better way to end the trip than with a cold drink, the wind caressing my hair, and the light of the moon dancing across the water as the *Victoria Cove* pushed towards my home?

What a fantastic view of the distant lights to either side of me as far as my eyes could see, far-off vessels traveling about…made me wonder what they were doing and where they would end up. There were also fisherman's boats flooded with lights shining down on the water circling the boat, doing what they knew best to make ends meet as we passed in the night sky. How could I have missed this all along? Surely it wasn't a secret. I just had had no idea how majestic and peaceful it was traveling on the ferry at night.

Brave as I was, I inched my way closer to lean on the railing that kept me from falling overboard the bow of the *Victoria Cove*. Resting my forearm against the top railing with my drink in hand, I played freely with the passing wind with the other. I had loved doing that as a child, rolling down the window inside my uncle's limousine and just playing like my hand was a car going up and down on a roller-coaster ride, nothing touching it but air as we drove along.

"I see you are enjoying the night air." Pierre had come around and had seen me standing there and sparked up another conversation.

"Very peaceful and relaxing."

"Indeed. In fact, this is why I had this vessel built."

"Why is that? There are already other ferries traveling the same waters."

"Oh, besides the fact that the others are aging with signs of rust and are not very fast, I built her because it reminded me

RM & SJ Secor

how wonderful it is to be sailing at speeds that almost feel like you are walking on water, yet with all the luxuries and amenities."

"I guess I can understand. It truly does feel like we are gliding across the water." I was truly amazed that I had discovered this ferry and looked forward to the next time to enjoy more of her.

"I honestly never paid much attention in the past. I would hop aboard, find a seat, fall asleep, and leave when the ferry docked. I had no idea how much more existed to her."

"Alexandria, there are some things in life that are important to do, but there is much more worth experiencing, and that is my vision." Pierre spoke like a true visionary as he stood there next to me turning around with his hands out pointing to the ferry.

Pierre, with his back against the railing and cigar in one hand, marveled at his dream as I gazed upon the water. It was quite refreshing up until he blew his cigar smoke my way. Coughing and waving my hand to clear the awful smell, I tried to ignore it, but Pierre offered up his apologizes since he hadn't meant to do that. His cigar was still on his mouth, and one eye was looking towards me.

"Oh, forgive me. I should put this nasty habit to rest for now." Pierre turned towards the bow of the ferry and looked over the railing, pausing for a moment.

"It is OK, right, to flick my ash in the water? Nothing should happen, right?"

Was this guy for real, or was this his sorry way of trying to be funny? Shaking my head as I gave him a quirky smile, I said, "Well, that all depends on if the water is fireproof."

Pierre giggled in response and sucked down a long drag. I could see the red glow move back towards his fingers. He inhaled just enough smoke that I swear I thought it was going to come out his ears. Yet he slowly exhaled it out his nose, and the white stream of smoke drifted in the wind.

"Now, that was funny. I have to say I had that coming. Fireproof water...now that would be something to market."

I could see the wheels turning in his eyes as he pondered that for a minute. I guess maybe he thought that could be a profitable business. It was just me being silly. Besides, really, fireproof water? That would never happen.

Looking out in the distance, I could now see that we were getting close to the shoreline on the left since lights were more visible and it seemed like the *Victoria Cove* had slowed a bit; it didn't feel as smooth as before. The water had started to get a little choppy, and I grabbed onto the railing just in case it got really rough.

"Don't worry. We're slowing because we are about to change our heading, and this is where it gets a little rough; the current from the Pacific merges with the Strait of Juan De Fuca. As you can see, the lights off to the left are Port Angeles, and the lights off to the northeast are home, the city of Victoria. Won't be long now."

OK, I kind of have a good sense as to where we are at the moment. Pierre was right as I could see we are getting closer to home, finally. Just then, I heard a cell phone ring. The ringtone sounded like a Frank Sinatra song as it rang again. The theme sounded sort of like "when a moon hits your eyes like a bigga piece of pie, that's amore."

I was about to say, "I think your phone is ringing, Pierre," but I could see he was looking at the phone number on the screen. He excused himself by walking to the other side of the deck, but I could still hear him, although it sounded like he was speaking French to someone. I guess that would make sense seeing how he was originally from Quebec, if I recalled correctly. I figured I would inch my way closer, perhaps to eavesdrop on his conversation, but as soon as I started to move, he stared at me, turned around, and began to speak back into the phone.

"*Que voulez-vous dire, aucune affaire? J'ai investi des milliers dans cette épreuve. Faites-le juste arriver. Bon au revoir!*" Pierre's tone rose as he spoke, and I kind of got the impression he was angry. He hung up, muttering under his breath, "You son of a..." He stopped and didn't finish what he was about to say, just turned around and smiled at me. I guess he thought it would be impolite to swear in front of me. It didn't bother me. I think I learned every bad word in the book from my uncle just by listening to him talk to his so-called friends and business partners growing up and sometimes now.

I don't speak French, but I have picked up a few things listening to my friend Daniele, who does speak French. That saved me from botching the language when we were in Paris. The best I could make out from it was something, something, no deal...lots of money...something, something...goodbye. That's about as good as it gets when it comes to my understanding the French tongue. I giggled a little after thinking that; it reminded me of French kissing and my desire to kiss Beauford. I knew I should have kissed him before boarding, but wouldn't that have come across as too sudden?

The call didn't really pertain to me, and I could not have cared less since I didn't know Pierre from Adam, but still, we were the only two outside on the deck, and, well, it just happened. I mean, come on, unless he walked out of sight, I would have heard him anyway.

Pierre walked closer to me, and I smiled back at him. I think he felt kind of embarrassed for his actions because he offered up another apology and excused himself. "Sorry about that. I have to excuse myself and take care of some business. See you Saturday?"

I didn't respond right away to him. Saturday? What was going on Saturday? I could see he knew I had already forgotten his invite, and just then it came to me.

"This Saturday. Yes. Wouldn't think twice about not coming. Yes siree, Bob. You got it. Two o'clock," I said, nodding my head rapidly to confirm my invite. I felt so stupid for rambling on and not taking him seriously when he invited me.

"A simple yes would've sufficed, but I gotcha." Pierre smiled, went back inside the bar area, and then went down the stairs and out of my line of sight. What a strange man, yet I liked him. Meanwhile, without being detected, the stranger that had peeked into the window at Alex had been lurking around the corner listening to Pierre and Alex talk. He watched her walk back into the bar as he pulled out his cell phone and called someone.

"Hey, she was just talking to an older man who called himself Pierre Gustave. I thought this guy was dead or something."

"Impossible," replied the voice on the other end of the phone. "Pierre Gustave was killed when he died from complications resulting from a boating accident back in the late eighties, if you get my drift."

"If you say so. I don't know; he also said something about this upcoming Saturday, some sort of gathering, and she was invited. Want me to find out more?"

"No, stick to the plan, Nicholi. I need that envelope. If I don't get that envelope, it is your head that will be rolling and not mine. You got that?"

"I got you, boss. Chill. I'll get it even if I have to follow her all the way home and rough her up a bit."

"Do not touch her. Just get the damn envelope and get it to me. You were supposed to do that when you followed her to

Paris, you dumbass, and now see where you are? I repeat, do not touch her, and do not get spotted."

Nicholi, the mysterious man's name, watched me from a distance outside the bar door as I checked my BlackBerry for any missed calls and messages. Just three voice messages, which were probably from my uncle. I couldn't call him then. It was really too late. I would just have to call him in the morning before I left for Seattle and explain something to him regarding why I hadn't called him.

I had to find the ladies' room. The drinks were going through me, and I had to pee badly. I could see Bernard was still in the bar area, making his rounds to close up the place. I yelled out to him. "Hey, is there a ladies' room near here?"

"Um, yeah. If you go back down the stairs and head straight, you'll find it on the left."

"OK. Do you mind watching my things again so I don't have to drag them with me? I promise I will be right back."

"Sure, no problem. I'm just tidying up since we're almost near Victoria Harbor. Go on; I'll wait for you to come back."

"Thanks, Bernard. I'll hurry."

Leaving the bar area, I quickly walked down the stairs and down the hallway and found the ladies' room. Meanwhile, Nicholi saw that Alex had walked away and noticed her belongings left behind. This was his chance to get the envelope; the damn envelope that her case pertained to, the case Alex had no idea about and has yet to read the contents.

Bernard had his back to the door that Nicholi had walked through. Nicholi slowly crept up behind Bernard. The only way he was going to nab that envelope was to get rid of Bernard. Pulling out a handgun tucked between his back and pants, Nicholi stopped for a second and looked at the gun and then Bernard. If he fired and killed the bartender, the gunshot noise would alert others. He would be caught since the only quick way off the ferry was to dive overboard, and Nicholi wasn't about to do that; he was deathly afraid of water. Nicholi was almost drowned when he was little by none other than a hit put on him, a retaliation against his father by the Canadian Mafia, yet he was rushed to the hospital and miraculously revived. It seems the lesson didn't take because he grew up and was leading a life of crime.

Nicholi had to think of something fast. He quickly grabbed the envelope while staring at the butt of his the pistol nodding his head up and down with a devious smirk on his face and whacked Bernard on the back of the head, knocking him out cold. He dragged his unconscious body by both feet behind the bar, quickly grabbed Alex's backpack, and headed for the stairs.

No more Bernard concoctions for me. Man, they were good, but I was going to have a bad headache in the morning. Way too much rum, or was it the vodka? Looking into the mirror, I could see the coffee stain on my dress as it stood out. I could also see my cleavage showing. I just stood there laughing the night off, as it was kind of funny. Straightening my hair with my hands, I was ready to grab my stuff and get off this boat.

Pulling the door to the ladies' room open and exiting to my right, I started to walk down the hall when I saw young male coming down the stairs. He stopped. I saw that he was carrying my backpack.

"You! You are the face from earlier! I knew it! I knew someone was spying on me, and I wasn't imagining things. Hey, give me my backpack. Bernard! Bernard, help! Come quick! This man has stolen my stuff!" Yelling for Bernard to come help as I ran towards the stairs, Nicholi darted back up the stairs, past the bar, and out the door to the deck. I quickly made it up the stairs and to the bar, but there was no Bernard around.

I couldn't believe he had left after saying he wouldn't. That pissed me right off. I noticed my phone was still lying on the top of the table. I ran towards it to get it. I unplugged it from the wall and ran out the door, stumbling over my broken boots. I tumbled to the deck surface as my cell skidded away, still attached to the charging cord. I saw that if I didn't think fast, I would lose my phone over the side of the deck through an opening. I yanked on the phone, and it stopped.

In an overly panicked outburst, I got up, grabbed my smartphone, and unzipped my Prada boots as fast as I could. Struggling for a second with one of the zippers, I pulled them right off my feet and threw them over the side of the ferry. I screamed bloody murder as I darted off down the deck of the ferry barefoot. I spotted Nicholi as he looked back before taking the midship stairs down to the next level.

What the hell could I possibly have that this stranger wanted? All I had in my backpack was my purse, cannoli, and…oh my God, the case papers. I could not believe the thoughts going over in my mind as I quickly ran towards the stairs in hopes of catching this guy and fighting him for my stuff and my trial case. I was in deep shit as it was for not looking over the papers, and now I was even more so because confidential information had been stolen.

I made it to the stairs and jumped over several at a time to the next floor. I heard a loud door swinging as it hit the wall of another stairway entrance. I didn't care that I disturbed three people as I ran past them barefoot and to the door. The sign on the door read "Vehicle Garage Level." All I could think of was that this guy was trying to get down to a lower level and possibly get off the ferry before we docked.

Looking at the stairs going down and then back behind me at the folks staring at me, I said, "You could've at least helped me, you know. I know you heard me scream, and you saw this man running fast. You could've tried to stop him." I got nothing in return other than a few shoulder shrugs and glares.

"Figures" was all I could think of to say, and I bolted down the dirty set of stairs to the vehicle garage level.

Rounding the door at the bottom left of the stairs, all I saw was one car off near the stern of the ferry, every possible light on, and what looked like Josh lying on the ground next to my stolen backpack. I rushed over to him and found him conscious but dazed.

"Oh my God, Josh, are you OK?"

Josh turned his head in my direction as I helped him sit up by pushing on his back. He said, "You are an angel."

"What? Josh, snap out of it. It's me, Alex."

"Alex? Oh, did you get the license plate number on that guy?" Josh was talking gibberish. I could see he had been hit maybe a little too hard on the head.

"Did you see him? Where is he?" I said, asking for the whereabouts of Nicholi. I saw my backpack lying with the top open, the trial case envelope still in it along with my purse. A huge sigh of relief overcame me, but I wondered what he did take. I did have another envelope in there, but it just contained pictures of Paris. Well, if anything, he would get to see Paris photos.

"All I can say is, I was coming towards the door, and this guy came running through at the same time and crashed into me. We both hit the floor rolling, and I somehow grabbed one strap of that bag. All I can remember is that he rushed over and grabbed something out of it and..."

"And what?"

"I watched him run to an exit at the stern. It seemed like he was talking to himself, walking in place, and, well, he jumped into the water. What's going on?"

61

"This guy was spying on me back at the Seattle terminal."

"What? Why?"

"Obviously, he was thief and wanted my belongings, but thanks to you my backpack is still here. He must have hopped aboard and was following me and at the right time grabbed my backpack. And, well, you know the rest of the story. Here, let me help you up." I helped Josh to his feet. He brushed off his pants and straightened his shirt.

"Wow, that was not cool at all." Josh was still rambling on, dazed.

"Alex I thought I saw him take something."

"You have got to get some help so we can catch him," I said while looking at my backpack to see if anything might be missing.

Just then, the *Victoria Cove*'s horn blew as the captain signaled its entrance to the harbor.

"No need, Alex. We are entering the harbor and will dock in a few."

"Yeah, I get that, but hey, he must be caught."

"Alex, if he jumped into the water, especially at the knots we were doing, he is dead. His body will be floating, and once we get to land, I'll alert the captain and authorities, and they'll take care of it. Let's get you up above and reclaim your luggage. What happened to your boots?"

"Don't ask, but I'm sure if they find that guy floating dead in the water, I imagine my Prada's will be close behind."

Motioning Josh to go towards the stairs, I reached for the backpack and helped him up the stairs. By the time we made it up to the top, Bernard popped his head into the stairway. He was holding the back of his head and was dazed as well.

"What the hell happened to you?" Josh asked Bernard.

Bernard replied, "One minute I was blowing out the candles on the tables, and suddenly my light was blown out. I felt a bang on my neck, and that was it."

"Here, let me take a look at it," I said. I could see he was hit pretty hard. No cuts or bleeding, just a huge lump. So he hadn't run off and left me. Nicholi must have knocked him out in order to grab my backpack.

"Go put some ice on it, Bernard," said Josh, "and I'll take Miss Henson up to her luggage near the exit. I'll inform the captain of what just happened."

"Yeah, sounds like a plan to me." Bernard stumbled off towards the stairs to the bar as Josh and I made it to the exit where my luggage was stowed away.

"Here, sit down, Alex, and let me inform the captain."

Chapter Five

Home, Sweet Home

What a sight for sore eyes, literally. My eyes were being affected by the bright lights surrounding the docking area as well as the lit-up Parliament Building just above Victoria Harbor. That is the name of my town's harbor, named for the queen many years ago when she visited.

To the right of us was the Port Angeles ferry, already succumbing to retiring for the night as the waves made by the *Victoria Cove* bounced off her hull as the vessel ever so gently rocked. Amazing how peaceful it is coming in at night as this place usually is hopping with boats heading out and coming in the inlet. The dock is usually packed with vendors and food stands; the aroma is always overwhelmingly delicious. People are usually frolicking about their business, yet tonight, all I could see were lifeless boats snug against the marina when we passed by.

All I could hear were the sound of buoys and the harbor water meeting as they brushed up against and between the dock and boats anchored. Not a soul was in sight; they were long gone since the other ferry's last run would have been nine o'clock. I could see what Pierre referred to because it didn't look to be in the best shape. I had never really given it much thought as I just rode her every day from Victoria to Port Angeles across the strait and back for work.

I was starting to think Bernard the bartender had been trying to impress me, as I concluded he had put a little too much alcohol in those drinks. Either that or it was just now hitting me. The ferry stopped and the engines quieted once we were docked. I could see Josh hanging up the phone as he looked over to me.

"Hey, sorry about all that has happened to you tonight. Gosh, and to top it off, my little unjust move on you. I'm...I'm really sorry, Alex."

"Josh, stop apologizing for what happened. Besides, what happened between you and me, you had no idea that would've happened. All that matters is that it's over, and I just really want to forget about it."

"Do you have another pair of shoes you can wear? The rain is coming down again, and since the dock area is metal and wet now, you could slip and fall being barefoot."

It never did cross my mind what I was going to do between the ferry and home in regards to my feet. As ridiculous as it sounds, I would have gone back and jumped into the water and retrieved my boots I threw overboard in a fit of rage. Somehow, I doubt they would even have been there. Some fish had probably claimed them for their new home.

What an idiot I was for doing that. That was three hundred dollars down the drain. Oh well. It wasn't like I could file a report for a lost item with the local authorities. They would surely think I was crazy. But don't get me wrong; I did think about it. Come on, hello? We are talking about Prada, for God's sake. All I could do was laugh out loud.

"What's so funny?" Josh asked me as I was giggling.

"Nothing…just a girl thing."

I could tell he had no idea and didn't expect him to understand the meaning of owning and wearing Prada. Typical for a man not to dial into a woman's thought process, but again, as they say, men are from Mars and women are from Venus. I still have no idea what that means, but it sounds weird enough to just believe it. Josh prepared the manual walkway as he guided it from the side of the ferry by the cables and winch it was attached to.

"Hey, Josh. Did the captain alert the authorities while you were speaking to him?" I wanted to make sure it had been reported.

"No need to respond, Josh. I will tell her in person." The captain had shown up where I was, but who was steering the boat if he was down here?

"Aren't you supposed to be driving the boat?"

"I could, but no need. This vessel is equipped with a state-of-the-art computer system that auto steers and docks on its own with the touch of a button. Hell, sometimes I think I'm just here for nostalgia. Ah you see, she has completed her journey for the night." The captain smirked as he held out both his hands towards me as the ferry made a slight bump motion.

As the captain coupled both my hands in his, he pulled me aside, offering up his sincere apology. Josh finished guiding and lowering the walkway. What few folks there were on this ride and standing behind me exited towards the walkway. I saw the same folks from before who hadn't helped me and just stared as they passed.

All I could think of at that second was to fake-lunge my head towards them and say "boo!" Such a stupid gesture on my part, but it felt good as I saw them quickly turn their faces forward and squirm to the exit and out and down the walkway.

One of them actually bumped into the railing, making it rattle for a second, as she looked back at me. I just tilted my head to the side and said sarcastically, "Have a wonderful night." I could tell the captain was not at all amused, but Josh got a kick out of it as he held onto the side of the walkway rails to stabilize it.

"Miss Henson...Miss Henson," the captain blurted out, calling my name to refocus my attention on him. I turned around to face him.

"Sorry, just a little humor. They know I was kidding."

"I alerted the local authorities and the Coast Guard, and they are on it. I am going to need you to file a report with the police department, and I will with the maritime authorities."

"Word gets out about this foul play and a dead guy, this ship will be permanently docked, and I can't imagine how Mr. Gustave would react to that."

"How I would react to what? What are you talking about, Jean-Paul?" Pierre made his way up to the captain and me standing near the exit of the ferry.

"No need to worry, Mr. Gustave. We just had a little incident that involved Miss Henson, but we have it under control."

"Alexandria, is that true?" Pierre said, looking at me.

"Well, sort of," I said, responding to Pierre.

I could see he was looking down at my exposed feet. "For heaven's sake, my dear, what happened to your boots?"

"You see, after you left—" I was cut off again by the sound of Pierre's cell ringing. He looked at it and lifted it to his ear, turning his back on us.

"Listen, hang on a second," Pierre said into the phone. He turned back around and said, "Jean-Paul, just handle it. I have got to take this call. I don't need any bad PR right now.

Make it go away. Excuse me, Alexandria, I must go. My ride is here. See you this weekend."

Pierre left as quickly as he arrived, walking towards his limousine and chatting away with someone on his cell. It was quite obvious he was an important man and could not be bothered with bad press attention, but why? Not that anyone needs bad press, but what was he up to that he could not afford any? Was it related to his earlier conversation that he had to end and run off from?

It must have been, since I recall him switching to speaking in French as if to think I would not understand. *Something is strange about him,* I thought. *I just can't figure it out.* I couldn't worry about that. I needed to worry about getting home to the Brownstone, my condo. In all this, I hadn't even thought about calling ahead for a taxi. Stupid me; now I was going to have to wait in the rain again, but this time with no one to come to my rescue and barefoot.

"Miss Henson, don't worry about a thing. We will take care of this. Just make sure you call the police and report what happened, but also make sure you leave Mr. Gustave's name out it." The captain looked at me with firm eyes as if to emphasize his request.

"I will, but it will be later on in the day. I have a preliminary trial case hearing that I will be involved in, and then I will call the police sometime afterwards."

"Well, on that note, I bid you a good night, and thanks for riding on the *Victoria Cove*. Josh!" Captain Jean-Paul excused himself, calling on Josh.

"Yes sir."

"Square away your area, and let's go home."

"Aye aye, captain." Josh looked at me, smirking, as I grabbed my luggage and backpack and stepped into the opening to the walkway.

DEADLOCKED: A Trial Beginning

There was no doubt about it; this had to be the same rainstorm that was in Seattle earlier. *What is with all these downpours?* I thought to myself. It had never rained this hard before, and I imagined some of the roads would be flooding. As I left the ferry and stepped onto the cold, wet walkway, a huge sensation hit me, as my feet instantly felt chilled. I danced across the walkway and onto the concrete connecting dock.

I could see the rain had changed direction to more of a sideway pour as it reflected off the lights on the dock walkway. In order for me to get up to the street level, I had to carry my luggage and backpack up fifteen metal stairs where I could wait inside the see-through bus stop structure. From there, I would use my phone and call a taxi.

****

At that same time, Nicholi had survived jumping off the ferry into the semi-cold water and avoided being sucked under by the current. Against his better judgment, he had no choice but to jump and not get nabbed for what had just happened. Swimming to the shoreline just outside the harbor inlet, Nicholi, with envelope still in hand, climbed up the rocky side and darted across the Laurel Point Park terrain in the dark towards the outside of the Parliament Building on Belleville Street, where his contact would be parked in a dark blue Chevy Tahoe facing towards the harbor. Nicholi had been instructed to meet up with his contact and they would drive off with the envelope that contained Alex's trial case, but little did Nicholi know that he had, in a desperate moment, grabbed the wrong one, and what he really had was Alexandria's photos of her vacation in Paris.

I made it up the stairs to the top and slipped a few times, catching myself on the railing, but I made it. All this commotion tonight—running, chasing strangers, breaking my shoes, my dignity, and my integrity—had really put a strain on my back. I could feel it tensing up, and I was going to a wreck the next day.

If I recalled correctly, before I headed up the stairs, the stationary clock on the pole right before the stairs said it was one-thirty a.m. I really just wanted to sit down and cry, but I was stronger than that. My uncle would never let me cry as a child because he said it was a sign of weakness and I was above that.

"OK, Alex, toughen up. You are a strong woman. Don't fail me now," was all I could say out loud as I dragged my luggage and myself inside the bus stop, plopped my butt down, rested my head against the structure, and closed my eyes.

****

Meanwhile, Nicholi had managed to find Belleville Street and had moved quickly to find his contact. He approached the Parliament Building and saw the blue Tahoe. Walking up to the passenger side of the vehicle, he knocked on the window.

For a second, all Nicholi could see was a dark glass window with his reflection and that of the Parliament Building in the background. The window slowly rolled down, revealing the contact's face. It made Nicholi step back. He knew his contact was feared by many, including him.

"You got the envelope?" It was Rozzito's captain recruited from the Toronto crime family, Bobby Sidermo. Bobby was known for being the stiff arm for his family, and his trademark was cutting off both thumbs of his victims and shoving them up their nostrils before shooting them in head.

"Yeah, I got it. Why are you here?"

"Because Mr. Rozzito didn't think you would deliver, and if you didn't, well, let's not talk about not delivering the package. So, again, do you have it?"

"I already said I did. Relax."

"Good. About time. Get in." Nicholi looked at Bobby, opened the door, and climbed in with a scowl on his face.

"Jesus, you're soaking wet. What the hell happened? You run into a sprinkler on your way here?"

"No, wasn't like that all."

"*Qual e il problema con te?*" Bobby looked at him, shaking his head and uttering, "What's the matter with you?"

"What? Don't start with me. Nothing's the matter with me other than I just survived jumping off a moving ferry and barely made it to shore." Nicholi snapped back at Bobby since he was convinced he had almost died in the water. Bobby lifted his hand and motioned as if he was going to smack Nicholi but stopped.

"You know, I outta knock you upside your head. Good thing Mr. Rozzito thinks you have potential, 'cuz if not, I would take care of you myself. Personally, I don't know what he sees in you."

"Take it easy. Back off. I'm sorry. I just almost died trying to get this. How about cutting me some slack?"

"If your butt leaves a stain on my freshly installed Italian leather seats, you will pay for it, but not in cash. Here, get up. Sit down on this." Nicholi noticed Bobby had grabbed a bloodstained dry towel and placed it on the seat.

"Relax, kid. It's not mine."

"Yeah, well, I don't want to know."

"Don't worry about it. I just had to rough up some friend of Mr. Rozzito for not delivering."

Nicholi looked at Bobby, squinting his eyebrows down and with a nasty look on his face as he tossed the envelope into his contact's lap. Carefully sitting on the stained towel, he said, "You see, I did deliver. Let's get out of here. I'm tired and cold."

"Not yet. I'm supposed to confirm that you did get it."

71

****

I opened her eyes as I sat inside the bus stop, only to see that it was still raining. It felt like a lifetime since I had closed her eyes to rest for a few minutes.

I'd better call a taxi service or I'm not going to get home, and I am not walking from here to the Brownstone, I thought. My condo was on Cook Street next to the Cedar Hill Golf Course. Reaching for my BlackBerry, I discovered it was not turned on.

It was quite obvious as I held the smartphone that the back cover was off, and apparently the battery was gone, too. So much for that idea. It must have come off when I fell on the deck. Now what was I going to do? The rain was pouring, the bottom of my outfit was drenched, and my feet were cold. I wished Uncle Nicholas was there to help me. He would have probably hugged me and yelled at me at the same time, but it wouldn't have bothered me. He always took care of me. I guess I should have called him earlier.

****

Back at the Chevy Tahoe with Bobby and Nicholi, Bobby opened the envelope and discovered that what Nicholi had in fact retrieved was a bunch of photos and not the trial papers.

"This some sort of joke, Nicholi?"

"What? What do you mean, a joke? It's the papers."

"No, you idiot, it's just a bunch of photos of her."

"What? You're lying. Let me see."

Bobby angrily threw the envelope of photos back at Nicholi, hitting him right above his left brow with the sharp corner, cutting him. Bobby pulled out his cell and scrolled for Nicholas's number.

"Ouch! You didn't have to throw those at me. You cut me." Nicholi touched his forehead above his eye. He knew he had been cut because blood had started to seep out of the wound.

"Just sit there and shut up while I call Mr. Rozzito. He'll know what to do with you."

"Ah, come on, Bobby. I tried, honestly, but I must have grabbed the wrong envelope."

"Yeah, well, you sure did grab the wrong one, stupid."

Nicholi flashed back to the scene when he had bumped into Josh down in the garage area on the *Victoria Cove* and had tumbled to the ground. Seeing the envelope protruding from the top of Alex's backpack, he could see himself grabbing the envelope and noticed this time from memory that there was a slightly lighter colored envelope that was still in the backpack when he stood up and ran off.

"Wasn't my fault. I ran into someone and was knocked down. I saw the bag that had the envelope sticking out, so I grabbed it and ran towards the exit of the ferry and jumped off into the water, and I hate water."

"Stop your whining." Bobby cut off Nicholi as Nicholas answered the phone. "Hello? Yeah, Mr. Rozzito, I got Nicholi, but he doesn't have the papers. Seems the little twit grabbed the wrong one, and she must still have it with her. What do you want me to do?"

"Scare him," said Nicholas. "Tell him if he wants to be a member of this family and not just an associate, he needs to do as I say. Don't hurt him, Bobby. Just push him in the right direction."

While on the phone with Rozzito, Bobby reached down between his seat and the center console and grabbed his weapon of choice, a .38-caliber six-shot revolver made by none other Smith & Wesson. He pulled it up slowly and when Nicholi wasn't looking placed it near the temple of his head. Nicholi was distracted and did not realize that Bobby had a gun aimed at his head. He was focused on the photos of Alexandria, looking at one after another.

"So, Mr. Rozzito, about that. I am ready."

"Ready for what?" Nicholi responded to Bobby's response to Rozzito without looking up. In fact, for some reason, he was enthralled by the pictures of Alexandria. He liked what he saw, as she was truly beautiful, even in photos.

"Say, what did he mean by 'ready'?" Now Nicholi raised his head. Bobby tapped it with the end of the gun barrel and pulled back the hammer.

"Whoa...whoa. Wait, no, Bobby. Please don't," Nicholi, frightened and trembling, pleaded with Bobby and began to cry.

"You see, you little punk, this is what happens when you don't deliver to Mr. Rozzito."

"Bobby, just scare him enough so he will finish the job. Don't overdo it," said Nicholas, coaching Bobby to stay calm and just scare Nicholi. If he didn't remain calm, Bobby would snap and end up killing this kid.

Bobby placed his phone down on his left leg, still on, allowing Nicholas to hear him taunting Nicholi. Shoving Nicholi forcefully up against the passenger window with the barrel of his gun, Bobby pushed the automatic button to lower the window just enough so Nicholi's head would fall out the top of the window. Bobby raised the window back up, wedging Nicholi's head halfway in and out.

"You sick son of a bitch...let me go," said Nicholi, pleading and screaming for his life as he tried desperately to get free but to no avail. As it seeped through the open space, the rain poured against his forehead and ran down his face into his right eye, causing him to temporarily lose sight in that eye.

Bobby reached over and grabbed Nicholi's exposed right thumb and began to bend it in a direction it was not meant to be.

Nicholi's screams filled the air as he squirmed in pain and agony. His screams of pain were not heard as thunder rumbled across the night sky with intense lightning streaks.

"This is what happens when you don't do as you're told. You are nothing but a punk. You want to be part of this Mafia family, then you do as Mr. Rozzito said and finish the job, or I will snap your finger back and break it."

"Bobby, knock it off! Just scare him," Nicholas repeated several times, but Bobby could not hear him because he was so into his act against Nicholi.

It wasn't long before Nicholi managed to contort his torso enough to face Bobby. By squirming around, he freed his right leg and managed somehow to raise it and kick Bobby right under his chin. Bobby's head lunged back like a punching bag as he dropped his .38-caliber right between Nicholi's legs. Nicholi, in a desperate act to free himself, found the window button and lowered it, freeing his trapped head. Panic-stricken, he opened the door, falling out onto the wet pavement almost face-first. Without worrying if he had hurt himself, Nicholi stumbled to his feet and bolted off across the parking lot towards the Parliament Building.

Nicholas was still live on the other end of the phone, shouting for Bobby's attention. "Bobby! Bobby! What the hell is going on?" Nicholas was ranting on his phone from within his private office in his home.

Bobby slowly regained consciousness after being dazed for a moment and heard Nicholas shouting to him from his phone. Reaching down between his legs and the steering wheel to retrieve the phone, he realized Nicholi is gone.

"Sorry, boss. The little punk must have kicked me when I was trying to only scare him. Guess he thought I was really going to shoot him in the head."

"Shoot him? You stupido. I said scare him, not kill him. You'd better find him, and both of you'd better get the envelope or I will kill both of you myself, *capisci?*"

"*Capisci*," Bobby said, indicating he understood. He ended the conversation, angrily tossed his phone to the passenger side floorboard, and growled. He turned on the lights, revealing the heavy rain as the lights shined on it. He slammed the Tahoe into drive, screeched the tires for a few seconds, and drove off out the parking lot at high speed.

****

Still down at the ferry bus terminal, I heard sounds of screeching tires and stood up. I watched a Tahoe swerve in and out, cross over a median, and almost sideswipe a black limousine. The driver of the limo swerved as well to miss being hit head on.

The limousine stopped, its light beams shining in the rain as I walked out of the bus stop enclosure and into the rain to watch the car. The limo driver put the car back in drive, and I watched it make a U-turn, drive back towards the bus stop, and stop right in front of me. The smoked-glass window rolled down, and inside was Pierre.

"Well, that was close," said Pierre. "The idiot in that truck almost hit me. Luckily, Frederick, my driver, missed him"

"Mr. Gustave, what brings you back here?"

"Well, I was banking on the possibility that, seeing how it was very late, you might need a ride to your home, and I guess I was right. Poor girl, you look exhausted. Do you need a ride?

"Yes, I do. I couldn't call a taxi because my phone is broken."

"Frederick, please get Miss Henson's things and open the door for her."

"Yes sir, Mr. Gustave, right away." Frederick exited the limousine, walked up to me, and said, "My lady, allow me." He grabbed my luggage bag and backpack, popped the trunk open, and placed my stuff in. After closing the trunk, he walked around to the opposite side of the car and invited me to hop in.

There was no argument from me as I was not about to stand out there any longer, drenched, tired, and shivering. Pierre welcomed me and handed me a dry towel. Frederick closed the door and quickly got back in the driver's seat and pulled away.

"Seems to me I was right about my hunch that you might need a ride. Not to mention I hadn't gotten too far down the road when I realized how rude I had been as we left the *Victoria Cove* and wanted to offer my apology."

"How sweet, but you could've just called my home phone. I think I'm still listed in the phone book."

"Yes, I could've done that. Now, why didn't I think of that?" Pierre said, smirking across from where I was sitting in the back of his limousine.

"I guess I should be the one apologizing since you felt you had to come back here to the harbor during this torrential rainstorm."

"Nonsense. No need to apologize. Why, a lovely girl like you…this is no place for you to be, especially this time of night."

"You mean this early in the morning, sir, right?" said Frederick, chiming in since it was in fact early morning. He was looking through the rearview mirror as he lowered the interior privacy window that separated the front from the back.

I could see it took everything in Pierre's good gentlemanly character to refrain from saying something right back at him, so he just looked at me and gave a silly smirk before responding to his driver. I was truly thankful that he had come back to check on me but not really sure of his motive.

"Why, Frederick, you are quite right. I guess I seem to have lost track of the time."

"Why, yes sir. That is why you hired me—to keep you on track." Frederick was grinning through the rearview mirror, looking directly at me. I could tell he was kidding around. It seemed to me they had a love–hate work relationship going, but I still thought it was humorous.

"So, Alexandria, where can my driver drop you off?"

"I live at the Brownstone off Cook."

"Ah, yes, the Brownstone. Very nice luxury townhouses. I see being a lawyer has its perks."

I was taken totally off guard. I forgot I mentioned to him that I was a lawyer when we had met. Still, feeling slightly out of sorts thanks to those yummy drinks, I felt I needed to ask him how he knew.

"I don't recall mentioning to you tonight that I was a lawyer."

"No, you are right. That is true."

"I'm not really a lawyer yet."

"How exactly is that?" Pierre seemed confused as he looked at me with disbelief.

"No, what I mean is, yes, I am a lawyer, a trial lawyer, to be exact. It's just that I have yet to actually set foot in a courtroom."

"Ah, you are that good that you don't have to appear in court, and you get your cases settled outside?"

"No...No, not exactly. Although that sounds like a terrific gift if I could. I just graduated law school a month ago, applied for a job as a lawyer, and was recruited rather quickly by Winslow and D'Entremont LLP."

"Winslow and D'Entremont? Not too shabby, Alex. I can call you Alex, or would you prefer Alexandria?"

"Alex is quite fine, Pierre. Alexandria reminds me of when I was a little girl, and I'd rather not go there."

"I understand. You realize that that law firm holds the highest respect in Seattle and Vancouver?"

"I had no clue. It was the first one my uncle suggested and it just so happen to be the one I was hired. Of course my uncle made a few calls too that helped.. Very strange, though, seeing how they were recruiting only top A-game trial lawyers, but my uncle can be very persuasive."

"Your uncle? What's his name?"

"Nicholas...oh, I am sorry. Can you have your driver stop, please?" Alex blurted out. She noticed they had passed the one place she needed to go to on her way home.

Pierre quickly motioned for Frederick to stop. The car came to a halt suddenly, chirping the back tires, the backlights illuminating the road behind it. The limousine sat there for a few seconds as the pouring rain pelted the top.

"What is it, Alex?"

"I was planning on stopping at that little grocery store we just passed on my way home, and I just remembered."

"What the devil for?"

"Don't laugh, but I am hooked on coffee, and I need my dairy for it."

"You made us stop in a panic over creamer?" Pierre started to chuckle and then laughed rapidly.

"I just said don't laugh."

"Oh, for heaven's sake, Alex, I thought it was something urgent."

"Well, if you lived in my house, you would understand how creamer is urgent. I think coffee was singly invented to dominate our body as a controlling drug, but a good one, to be exact."

"Well, I would say coffee is indeed an excellent beverage over a morning conversation or paper to read, but I wouldn't think it needed the attention you have dedicated to it. Nevertheless, if it is that important to you, it is important to me that we get you your creamer. Frederick, do Miss Henson a favor. Back up a ways to the little grocery store we just passed on the left, and run in and get some coffee creamer, will you please? It is on me."

"Why, of course, Mr. Gustave. Anything for the little lady."

This over engaging hospitality was not normal, or at least I was not used to it. What was Pierre's angle? He had to have an angle; no one just did this. Well, not exactly true—my Uncle Nicholas saved me from my childhood, and his hospitality is overwhelming to me all the time. Guess I wasn't expecting a second stranger to do the same.

****

Over off of Government Street, Bobby was frantically looking for Nicholi through his soaked driver-side window. Nicholi couldn't have gone far, he thought to himself, but he knew Rozzito was going to be pissed as hell if he lost Nicholi as well as a chance to obtain the papers that seemed to contain information obviously with some sort of allegations that had links to Rozzito.

Bobby wasn't about to find out what the consequences of not delivering would be. He could do it himself and nab them from Alexandria, but the thought of actually laying a finger on her would expose the fact that this was being conducted by her uncle and spoil the plot. No, he needed an expendable little punk kid like Nicholi to do it, a kid who had tried to work his way into the Rozzito family. That way, if he failed, it would fall back on him.

Bobby spotted Nicholi as he was running along the sidewalk and sped up to catch him.

****

I sat for a few minutes waiting for Frederick to return from the grocery store with coffee creamer. He walked out of the store, walked over to my side of the car, and opened the door.

"Here you go, Miss Henson. I was not quite sure what type of creamer you wanted, so I got you two different kinds."

"Thank you, Frederick," said Pierre. "That was a wise move. Let's get Alex home. I am quite sure she needs her beauty sleep, and I could sure use some sleep myself. Big day tomorrow."

"You can say that again," I said. "Later on today is my preliminary trial hearing, and I have yet to read over the case. I have absolutely no idea who I am defending or cross-examining. Sounds rather bad on my part, it being my first case and all, but I did try last night." I tried to explain my actions as if it would even matter to Pierre.

"Well, just make sure you at least glance at it before you go in tomorrow. Who is the judge presiding on the case?"

"I couldn't tell you, Pierre. I feel like I am going to look like an idiot tomorrow and blow everything."

"Relax, Alex. You will do fine. Here, let me give you a bit of advice. I seem to be going to more and more meetings lately. I despise meetings, but I look at it this way. I am there to add to the meeting, and I don't give a rat's ass if I stumble over my words or not. In the end, if I sound confident, I am confident, and whatever is left, I usually offer a check and that shuts them up." Pierre tried to sound funny as he gave me these tips, but I wasn't buying it.

"I don't know, Pierre. Seems to me I should have my A game on."

"That is what I meant. When in doubt, be yourself, and you will do well. Ah, look at that, the Brownstone. We are here."

I looked out the drenched window as Frederick pulled up to the entrance to the Brownstone. He put the limousine in park, popped the trunk, and got out.

"I am so happy to be home. Thank you, Pierre, for coming to rescue me out of the rain. I'm very grateful."

"It was my pleasure. Just do me the honor of coming to my shindig, all right? I promise you will have a great time. Besides, I would like to hear how things went at your trial hearing."

Frederick pulled my luggage and backpack out of the trunk and placed them underneath the Brownstone entrance out of the rain. He then walked back and opened the door for me.

"Thanks again, Pierre. I promise I will be there." I couldn't resist. I leaned over, kissed Pierre on the cheek, gave him a smile, and exited the limousine. Pierre smiled back as Frederick closed my door, hopped back in, and drove off. Wow. I could not believe how this trip had ended. I was so relived to be home.

Chapter Six
Shakedown

Nicholi had no idea what to expect when Rozzito found out that he didn't have the envelope. If what he had just endured from Bobby was any indication, he'd rather avoid that at all costs. Thoughts of hiding out somewhere and then disappearing crossed his mind. However, that wouldn't have worked because Rozzito would have his foot soldiers tracking him until he was caught, then beaten or killed and left for the public to view.

The best thing Nicholi could do was confront Rozzito, beg for him to spare him and give him a chance to make it up, and pray that he didn't end up dead. There was really no way around it. Being part of a Mafia family left no room for retirement, let alone being able to walk away from it all. The only way out was to be taken out against his will.

Since Nicholi was still a newbie within the ranks, perhaps Rozzito would feel compassionate and allow him to redeem himself. Bobby had almost caught up to him as Nicholi rounded left on Battery Street, heading towards Beacon Hill Park. Bobby had to stop briefly at the stop sign but did a touch and go and turned left to follow Nicholi.

If he was going to get Nicholi back in the Tahoe, he was going to have to convince him without showing his ugly side, even though he was just following Nicholas's orders. Bobby had never had an in-between switch on his actions; it was all or nothing, soft or hardcore in a manner of speaking, but usually the situation was elevated rather quickly to hardcore each time. It was the way he was raised by his family back in Toronto.

The Tahoe pulled up beside Nicholi, and Bobby drove slowly to keep right beside him. Nicholi glanced up for a second, avoiding his face getting wet, then put his head back down and kept walking. He suspected it was Bobby following him. Bobby started to fall behind for a bit as Nicholi picked up his pace walking in the rain.

Bobby sped up a little. The sound of the engine made Nicholi stop and turn his head. He saw through the rain that it was Bobby and started running down the street. Trying to avoid running into anything, he darted across the street accidentally right in front of Bobby and almost got hit. Bobby slammed on the brakes, screeching the tires. He threw the Tahoe in reverse, looked over his right shoulder, and stomped on the gas as Nicholi ran as fast as he could down the street. Fearing for his life, Nicholi ran frantically and ended up turning right down a side street, which turned out to be a wrong move on his part. Not being familiar with this area, he had run into a dead end street.

Bobby, driving in reverse, passed the street and slammed on the brakes once again, the air ringing with a loud screeching noise. He threw the Tahoe in drive and turned into the street. Nicholi just stood there with his back to Bobby as he stopped the vehicle a few yards behind him. Dark as it was in the dead end road, Bobby's headlights lit up Nicholi as rain poured from the night sky.

Nicholi's first thought was to run to the left and jump the first fence he saw, but if he didn't make it, Bobby would catch him and probably use brute force on him. His second thought was to turn around and flip Bobby the finger, but that, too, would just end so wrong. Running out of options, he decided to turn around and just stare at Bobby. If this was how he was going to die, then he thought it would be better to be run over than shot or be manhandled by his pursuer.

As the lights from the Tahoe shined on Nicholi, Bobby looked at him through the rain-soaked windshield. The wipers made a thump...thump sound working their way across the viewing area. Bobby just sat there and waited to see what Nicholi was going to do. Was he going to run again, or was he going to just stand there?

"Just get it over with, you freak show, and run me over," shouted Nicholi. "That would be better than Mr. Rozzito having me chopped up into little pieces."

Bobby shook his head and smirked. He said nothing back but rolled down his window and revved the engine. The exhaust fumes billowed in two sets of white smoke coming out the dual pipes. As the anticipation grew, every second that went by made Nicholi's heart pound faster and faster. Several more times, Bobby revved the engine, each time a little longer. Nicholi finally closed his eyes, stuck out both his hands, and flipped Bobby off. This way, it would end, and he would hear the sound of the tires screeching and quickly feel the metal from the front end taking his life from him. But nothing happened. Bobby just sat there laughing his ass off as he looked at Nicholi fearing for his life.

"If you're going to kill me, just do it."

"Shut up, kid. It was just to scare you, just like before. I was just following the boss's orders," said Bobby, confessing to Nicholi. This was his way of apologizing without having to do so. "Are you done playing in the rain? We have a job to do still, and you haven't delivered the goods yet, so stop messing around and get in the damn truck."

As bad as it was, Nicholi knew it was his best option to stay alive, so he walked over to the Tahoe and climbed in. Bobby just gave him that evil smirk, placed the Tahoe in drive, made a three-point turn, drove to the opening of the dead-end street, and turned right, heading back towards Belleville Street a few blocks up.

****

I realized just how tired I was after seeing that the keys I had tossed onto the table had fallen to the ground. I couldn't have cared less, though, since I was so freaking exhausted. Wow, what a roller-coaster night of events. First, the cab ride and tearing my clothes, and second, this awful torrential rainstorm making my life much more miserable than my heels breaking. That set me back. And meeting Beauford. Who names their child Beauford? Good thing he was good looking because with a name like that, there wasn't much of anything else going to happen, if you get my drift.

To top it off, what was left of my Prada boots? Probably sunk to the bottom of the strait. Oh my lord, the very thought was making my stomach churn. After all this, what could have possibly been next?

Sudden lightning flashes filled the living room like lights of boundless energy. The hair on my forearms stood up as I waited, squinting my eyes and grinding my teeth, waiting for the thunder boom that always follows. I counted one one thousand, two one thousand, three one thousand, four one thousand, and then the rolling thunder sound rumbled in the distance.

DEADLOCKED: A Trial Beginning

The storm seemed to be off in the distance—four miles, as far as I could tell by the amount of seconds I counted. Well, I am no meteorologist. This was just something I learned as a kid in school—count the seconds before you hear thunder after a lightning strike, and somehow it would add up to the miles away. If after the next one your count was less, you knew it was getting closer.

I can't tell you enough how much I despise lightning and thunder. It was very scary to me as a child growing up in an orphanage. I can recall lying there in my room when a storm was upon us, scared as can be as the room flashed over and over again with thunderclaps echoing off the walls. The shadows of the trees that appeared from outside my window moved like animated monsters across the wall.

It sounds very stupid to be that much afraid of storms as an adult now, but that fear has been permanently etched in my memory. It is associated with bad things, and well, that night was no different. I was just very glad to be home, out of the rain, not being stalked by strangers, and not embarrassing myself by breaking my boots and tumbling to the ground, and I couldn't wait to take a hot shower.

One thing was for sure—I had to remind myself sometime that day to file that report, just as Captain Jean-Paul had asked of me. If they found a dead body in the water, I needed to make sure I was not a suspect. I was the victim, and if that stranger had jumped off and killed himself after trying to steal my stuff, then so be it—no skin off my back.

I was so convinced that whatever lay within those court case papers would have the answers to everything that had happened to me that night, but I would not look at them not until after taking a shower. I felt so dirty, like my skin was crawling, and I needed to get that feeling to go away.

I didn't bother to pick up my keys. I just left my luggage and backpack right next to the front door in the entryway and headed upstairs to my bedroom. Nothing was going to matter right then, and being in the comfort of my home was enough to ease my stressful night.

In my bedroom, I stripped my dress off and then walked inside my master bath to turn on the shower. Within seconds, the steam rose around the shower, and the warmth of the mist felt good against my naked skin. I unsnapped my bra and bent over to remove my underwear one leg at time, then flung my underwear across the floor with my left leg. It caught on the doorknob and rested there. I grinned, as that was quite amusing to me for some reason. I entered the shower.

"Oh, you sweet fountain of water. God, I have longed for you tonight."

The steady stream of hot water poured over my head and down my neck and back as I leaned in under the showerhead and let the water begin to de-stress my body.

****

It wasn't long before Bobby and Nicholi approached Alexandria's home according to the GPS coordinates from the address Rozzito gave Bobby just in case he had to go there. Pulling up to the side of the road roughly two doors down, Bobby put the Tahoe in park and turned off the headlights. He turned the key to the off position, killing the engine.

"Now what?" asked Nicholi.

"We sit for a moment and see if we see any lights and movement coming from her place," Bobby responded, cracking both front windows down a little to allow air in.

"Hey, why did you roll down my window? The rain is coming in."

"What's the matter? The rain going to make you cry like a baby?"

"Stop calling me a baby."

"When you grow a pair, and I say that loosely, then I will stop calling you a baby. We wouldn't be in this predicament if you would've just gotten ahold of those papers while she was in Paris. I warned Mr. Rozzito to not let you handle it, and I was right. You are a little punk-ass kid and lucky to be here, let alone be alive still."

"Whatever, you freak. One of these days, someone is going to do to you what you do to them, and they will have the last laugh."

Bobby was getting quite aggravated, but Nicholi maintained his bearings and just looked away. Reaching inside his coat pocket and pulling out a half-crinkled pack of Players cigarettes, Bobby shook one out enough for him to grab it with his mouth. Looking at Nicholi, he just smirked, lit the end of the cigarette, inhaled, and a few seconds later exhaled as the smoke escaped out the cracked window.

"Now, that is better than sex," said Bobby.

"Whatever. Those things are going to kill you." Nicholi rolled his eyes and looked out his window.

"You say that only because you haven't had sex."

"No, it's because smoking causes cancer. Don't you ever read or watch TV ads on what smoking does?"

"Why bother? It's all stupid. Besides, when I die, it will be when I say so."

"I'm going to get out and walk around her home to see if I can find a way in." Nicholi opened the door and got out.

"Nicholi, remember, Mr. Rozzito does not want his niece to know that we are the ones trying to get the papers. It will look really bad seeing how he is family. So don't mess up."

"I am not going to mess up."

"Good, 'cuz if you do, I won't be the one coming after you, and you're going to wish I was. Look, I have to run an errand for Mr. Rozzito and will be back in a little bit. Get the envelope and meet me down the street. I'll pick you up, and then we'll go see Mr. Rozzito." Bobby exerted his captain's role by telling Nicholi what was going to have to happen.

"Who the hell died and left you in charge?"

"I'm the f'in' captain, you little shit, so you need to listen and listen well. I was only playing around before, so you need to do as I say and cut out your stupid remarks or I won't be playing next time. *A madam a pasta fagoili!*" Bobby yelled out the words that didn't even make sense to Nicholi while he started the Tahoe and pulled out from the side of the road like a moron.

"What the hell was that? You think I'm stupid, don't you? What a freaking idiot. Lady and bean soup? What, and he's captain?" Nicholi yelled back, raising his leg as if to kick the Tahoe as Bobby sped off. None of what Bobby said as he drove off even made sense.

Seconds later, tires screeched from an oncoming car as it swerved, dodging Bobby's reckless driving. The car drove into a light pole right outside Alex's townhouse, sending a hubcap from the passenger side down the road. Nicholi watched it go by. Looking up, he saw smoke starting to billow out from the front of the car as the horn blew constantly.

Not wanting to be spotted, Nicholi took off around the side of Alex's place and squatted down between the bushes to stay out of sight. This would be a perfect time to slip inside the front door and grab the envelope if Alex came running out to see what all the noise was.

A woman inside the car lay motionless with her head drooped against the deployed air bag. Nicholi watched from the side of the building. He was not about to go and help her and risk missing a chance to get what Nicholas Rozzito ordered him to do.

DEADLOCKED: A Trial Beginning

****

My eyes opened in a horrific motion. With the water rushing past my ears and covering my face, I could swear I heard a car horn going off. I wasn't sure if it was my mind playing tricks on me or if it was for real. Could it just have been someone next door with their TV on too loud? I reached and turned the shower handle to stop the water from running. All I could hear was a horn blowing, and it wasn't my imagination.

Stumbling for my towel and robe, I dried off as quickly as I could, climbed out of the shower, and opened my bathroom window facing the street. Huge grayish-white clouds poured from a car right in front of my home. The front end of the car was smashed in, and I saw her, a woman unconscious in the driver's seat. I panicked, and all I could do was yell at her to see if she would respond.

"Oh my God, are you OK?" were all the words that left my mouth. I couldn't move my body for a few minutes; I was in shock from what I saw as I stood there.

There was not even a whisper of a response back, not a "help me" or "please, I'm hurt," just the crackling sound from the electrical wires hanging from the pole. I could see sparks coming from the top of the pole that once stood tall as it slumped against another pole in front of it. Exposed wires crossed each other, making the area around the car dangerous.

I had to throw some clothes on and rush to the woman to make sure she got out before the car caught on fire or even exploded. Frantically rubbing my body dry on the verge of almost taking my skin off, I tossed the towel onto my bed and rushed into my closet. I threw on a pair of blue jeans and an old Van Halen T-shirt as fast as I could without causing bodily harm to myself in the process.

Terrible thoughts drowned my mind as I pictured running up to this woman and finding her dead. Visions of

91

blood and possibly even severed exposed limbs flooded my brain. I couldn't think straight, and as I ran down the stairs, I shook my hands rapidly to calm my nerves. I took in a deep breath just as I would do if I was nervous before taking an exam. It sure calmed my mind and helped me focus in the past, so why not now in this desperate moment?

I had no idea what had caused this accident. All I knew was someone was going to have to help the woman, and that someone was going to be me. Rounding off the bottom step, I skipped putting on a pair of shoes to cover my bare feet, swung open my door, and ran towards the car.

I couldn't have cared less as the rain once again began to soak my already wet hair. My goal was to reach this desperate woman who was sitting in front of my place with half the hood wrapped around her body and see how I could possibly help her. The thick, billowing smoke, which not too long ago had been barely coming out the hood, filled the night air around the car, making it very hard to see the driver.

Flapping my hands in a fanlike motion, I managed to carve a path just enough to visualize where the woman was inside the car. She looked like she was barely in her twenties as she lay there motionless, head stooped over with what looked like a slight gash on her forehead and blood running down the side of her face.

Oh my God, she's trapped inside. I have to help her, I thought. I yelled out loud, hoping to alert my neighbors in hopes of getting them to come out and help as well. I frantically reached for the driver's side door and pulled on the handle to open it, but it was jammed shut due to the impact of the accident. I banged on the window and screamed at her, "Are you all right?"

The woman inside, obviously shaken up, started to move and replied, "Help. I can't move." She began to panic.

"Hang on. Stay calm. Help is on the way," I reassured the young woman.

****

This was a perfect opportunity for Nicholi to inch his way around the bushes and make his way into Alexandria's townhouse and look for the envelope. He needed to be swift and quiet in order to not get detected. Nicholi figured he would get in and get out undetected, meet up with Bobby down the road, and this whole ordeal would be behind him. Handing Rozzito the papers himself would please his boss and help him regain the faith he so desired from him in hopes of being accepted into the Rozzito family.

Nicholi could see Alex trying to open the car door within the smoke. Slowly, with his back firmly against the outside of the house, he slid his body along, feeling the structure with his fingertips as he closed in on her front door, which was wide open. The rain was leaving puddles of water and was quickly making the grass soggy beneath his shoes. Each step closer to the door covered more and more of his shoes. It was now or never to rush inside and find the envelope while Alex was outside and distracted.

Nicholi moved to the walkway near her door and ran into the house, not realizing he was leaving behind a trail of muddy shoeprints that could later come back to haunt him if Alex were to see them. While Nicholi was searching high and low inside, Alex was trying to calm the injured woman down and knew she had to call for help.

****

Reaching for my BlackBerry, I dialed nine-one-one. The phone rang through several times before someone picked up. I had reached the local precinct and was connected with the night dispatch officer, Ryan Weston.

93

"Nine-one-one, this is Officer Weston. Please state your emergency."

"This is Ryan Weston?" I asked.

"Yes, this is Officer Weston."

"Ryan, there has been a terrible accident outside my home."

"Are you hurt, ma'am?"

"No, I am not hurt, Ryan. It's me, Alexandria Henson. A young woman in her twenties is trapped inside a car and needs help immediately." I looked around and now could see a few folks across the street looking through their window drapes out into the street right at us.

"Alex, I am going to have to put you on hold. Do not—I stress, do not—hang up. I will be back momentarily."

"Hurry, Ryan. I think she's fading fast."

Ryan put the phone down and quickly dispatched calls out to local patrol cars and the ambulance department in the area and came back to the phone.

"Alexandria, help is on the way."

"Thank you, Ryan."

I turned my attention back to the woman in the car and tried desperately to get her to tell me her name. I tried several times to get her attention, as she seemed to go in and out of consciousness. Knocking rapidly against the window that separated us, I could she was coming to as I shouted out at her. "Hey! Hello! Stay with me! Help is on the way. What is your name?"

The woman was dazed from the blow to her head. She opened one eye and slowly turned her head towards me and stated her name. "Uh, my name is Natalie...Natalie Ingram. Please help me. I can't feel my legs." Natalie was crying for me to help her.

"OK, Natalie, you must calm down. Help is coming. Can you tell me what happened?"

Natalie was obviously in much pain but managed to tell me that she was on her way home from her boyfriend's house after celebrating their first year together when she took a wrong turn down my street, and then out of nowhere, a blue SUV came at her head on. She attempted to swerve out of the way and hit the light pole; then everything went blank. Slumping slightly towards the steering wheel, she drooped her head down.

"Natalie, you're doing well. Stay with me, and keep talking to me."

Where were the patrol cars and the ambulance, for that matter? I nervously questioned myself. They should have arrived already. All I could do was to continue talking with Natalie, and reassuring her, my own nerves calmed down a little.

****

Meanwhile, Nicholi was coming up empty handed as he searched Alex's living room and kitchen area for the case papers. Tossing the cushions of the couch and tipping over Alex's favorite nine-hundred-dollar La-Z-Boy chair, which was given to her by her friend Daniele as a housewarming gift, Nicholi's ears became fully engulfed with hot blood that turned his ears red as a beacon from anger. He stormed into the kitchen and rummaged through all the drawers, yet there was still no sign of the envelope. His heart pounded in rhythm with the rain slapping the outside of the windows.

Suddenly his phone in his pocket vibrated several times. Reaching for his cell phone, he saw it was Bobby calling him. Nicholi rushed to the doorway and looked outside to make sure Alex was not coming back inside. The phone vibrated several more times before he flipped it open. Little did he know that what he was looking for was right next to his left shoe on the ground, wedged against the wall and front door, out of sight. Alex's backpack with the envelope was right there, but it eluded Nicholi as he looked outside and answered his cell.

"I need more time."

"What took you so long to answer? More time? We don't have more time. Mr. Rozzito wants us to head back to Vancouver, and he said we'd better have what he needs."

"I can't find it."

"You'd better find it, and find it fast, you little prick."

"Look, I'll call you when I find it. Give me more time. Stall him. You're the captain, right?"

"What do you mean, I'm the captain? Is that a joke, you little...?"

"Enough of the name calling. Geez Louise, relax. I was just saying you call the shots in the field since you're the captain. That's all I was saying."

"Damn right I'm the captain. Don't you forget it."

Nicholi turned the conversation away from him and talked Bobby into allowing him more time to find the papers, and it worked.

"OK, kid. Call me when you have it."

Hanging up the phone, Nicholi looked up at the stairs and decided it was time to venture up to the next level to see if Alex had the papers there.

****

I was still outside with Natalie waiting for emergency personnel to arrive. I saw a man across the street open his door and walk towards us. It seemed like hours waiting there when suddenly I could hear sirens coming down the street.

"Are you two OK?" the man yelled from across the street.

"Yeah, we are now. I can hear the sirens."

Just like that, the man turned around as if having little of no emotion over what was happening. He walked back through his door and closed it.

I raised my head above the top of the car, giving my neighbor a piece of my mind. "You've got to be kidding me. Seriously, you see us out here, you can see she's hurt, and you walk away?" I didn't know him since I had been living there for only a few months, but I felt he was being a jerk for walking away like that.

Patrol cars pulled up to the scene. Two officers got out and shone their flashlights in our direction. "Here! Over here!" I yelled. The officers approached the driver's side of the car, and I let them know that Natalie seemed to be OK but was in much pain.

"Who were you yelling at, miss?"

"Huh? Oh, nobody. Just a lousy f'in' idiot from across the street who refused to help and walked back inside his house."

"Are you hurt, ma'am?" one of the officers asked me.

"I'm all right. I was not involved in the accident. I live here in the Brownstone."

"Did you see what happened?"

"No, I did not see what happened, but I heard it."

"OK, step back." One of the officers pushed me back with his arm, but I resisted. "Miss, you are going to have to step back, or we are going to have to cite you for obstructing and delaying us from evaluating the situation."

"Obstructing and delaying the situation? Are you freaking kidding me? I'm the one who called for help!"

"Miss, step back before we make you step back. If you resist again, we will be forced to cuff you and bring you in to book you for questioning."

97

"This is not right." Tears formed in my eyes from sheer emotion. All I was trying to do was help this poor innocent woman, and I ended up being harassed by the police. "I know my rights. I'm a lawyer and know you can't do this to me."

"Look, miss, you may be a lawyer by day, but right now you are not a lawyer. Right now, you are citizen on the verge of being treated like a criminal. So please, I am only going to say this one more time…step back." The officer looked at me firmly while placing his right hand over his holstered weapon.

I was so beside myself in disbelief standing there. What had just happened to me? I was the first responder here. I was the one who called for help. No one else even bothered to help, yet I was being mistreated as if I was the one who caused this tragic accident. Little did I know, I did have a direct link to this accident. If Nicholi had succeeded in getting ahold of the case papers, this would not have happened. However, I had no idea what caused this young woman to hit the pole, let alone why it had happened on the edge of my home.

Ten minutes went by, and the ambulance finally arrived. The paramedic explained that they had had trouble accessing roads due to downed trees and power lines from the storm.

"Please help Natalie! She's trapped inside the car and can't move!" I yelled towards the paramedics some distance away from the car.

One of the paramedics reached inside the ambulance and grabbed a crowbar to wedge in the door to open it. With a few tugs and pulls, the door started to open, making a horrific sound of metal against metal. Natalie's legs were wedged underneath the steering wheel but didn't seem to be broken. Somehow, miraculously, Natalie had not suffered any life-threatening injuries.

"What is your name, ma'am?"

"Uh, Natalie."

"Natalie, we are going to attempt to move the steering wheel up and out of the way to free your legs."

Natalie nodded in agreement to the paramedics. Within a few minutes, the steering wheel was moved out of the way and Natalie's legs were free. The paramedics placed their arms around either side of Natalie and helped her out of the car and onto the gurney. For the next few minutes, the paramedics checked out Natalie's vitals as the officers questioned me about the accident. All I could do was stand there and pray that she survived this accident and they would stabilize her.

"Ma'am, we are going to need to take a statement from you."

"Sure, um, yes." I cleared my throat and wiped the tears and emotion from my face with my sleeve. I walked over to where the police officers were standing.

"Did you see the accident occur?"

"No. I had just gotten home after a long day of traveling and was in the shower when I heard a strange noise."

"What type of noise?"

"Are you kidding me?"

"Ma'am, please answer the question," Officer Dik asked me in a firm tone.

"I don't know. I guess you would say it was a loud thud of some sort."

"A loud thud like someone knocking on a door?"

"Huh, no, more like someone or something crashing into a pole, if you ask me, Officer Dick." Alex read from his uniform badge.

"It's not pronounced 'Dick.' It's Dik, with a long 'I' sound. I don't find your humor funny, and these questions are important, so, again, what kind of thud sound did you hear?"

"I'm sorry, my mistake on your name, but my mind is fried, and all I can say is a loud thud sound like a car hitting something, as you can see."

"Moving on," said Officer Dik, looking at me and motioning to move on after that question.

"Look, this is all I know, officer. I thought I heard a strange sound while my head was under the water, I stopped the water, and then I heard it."

"Heard what?"

"A horn blasting. I guess the thud noise might've been the impact of the car hitting the pole, but again, I did not witness it. But I heard the horn blast, jumped out of the shower, looked out my bathroom window, and that is when I saw a woman slumped over in the car and the horn going off, so I ran outside and tried to talk to her."

"Is there anything else?"

"Not that I can recall."

"So, you didn't happen to see a possible truck coming down the street and almost hit her car?"

"Now, how was I supposed to see that? I was taking a shower."

"Just doing my job, ma'am. You neighbor across the street stated he saw a strange truck, sort of like a blue Chevy Tahoe, sitting outside your place a few doors down, and he stated he saw someone looking up at your window and on the phone. So if there is anything you would like to add now, please do, because if you don't and we find out otherwise, you will be arrested for withholding evidence."

"First off, am I to understand I am a suspect in this accident? Is that what you are saying, officer? I can't believe this is happening to me."

"No, you are not a suspect. I'm just trying to figure out your neighbor's motive for mentioning this."

"Well, it could be a coincidence that some totally innocent stranger was in a car using a cell phone and parked outside my place. Sounds like this person was obeying the law by pulling over to make a call instead of driving while using his phone. As far as someone looking into my window, well, that would be hard since it is made of glass-frosted blocks."

"Thank you, ma'am, for your cooperation. Please step back again."

"That is all I know, officers."

Both officers then proceeded back to their patrol cars to fill out paperwork and call in their reports. My attention then turned to Natalie, lying on the gurney. I saw a chance to walk up to where she was being cared for by the paramedics.

"Natalie, you are a very lucky woman," exclaimed one of the paramedics. "Almost no one walks away from this type of accident alive, but you have without major injuries. You certainly have an angel watching over you!"

I reached out and grabbed Natalie's hand to comfort her. She turned her head in my direction and thanked me for helping her and let out a big sigh of relief, presumably thankful for being alive.

I asked the paramedic for something to write with. He scrambled around, searching his shirt and pants pockets, but he did not have a pen. He looked over at his partner for one, and she reached for her clipboard and tossed him the pen. "Here you go."

"Thank you."

The only problem I had then was that I needed something to write on and didn't have anything I could possibly use. I wanted to write down my number for Natalie. Looking around me as I searched my own pockets, I was coming up empty-handed. I could see the male paramedic was watching me as I scrambled to find something to write on. He happened to see something that I could use and alerted me.

"Hey, I think I found something that you might be able to use."

The paramedic pulled out something from his shirt pocket and handed it to me. Looking at what he handed me I noticed it was a pack of matches. The cover displayed a name, "Tawny's" or maybe "Tommy's," I think, but it was sort of rubbed out.

I wasn't sure if there was more to it, but it didn't matter. I just needed something to jot down my number on and give to Natalie. I tore off half of the cover and jotted my number down.

The paramedics began to lift the gurney up, and I wanted to make sure Natalie got my number, so I walked over to them, gave the note to her, and asked her to call me when she got to the hospital to let me know how she was doing. Once she was loaded into the ambulance, the female paramedic jumped in the back, saying words to calm Natalie and reassure her that she was going to be OK. Officer "Dick" closed the back doors and tapped on the vehicle to alert the driver to go.

Three chirps from the siren and the ambulance rolled away down the street as I watched. During all this commotion, I hadn't even realized that a flatbed tow truck had pulled up and had started to pull the car away from the pole. Soon it began to load the mangled car up onto its bed. I had been so focused on Natalie that I had blocked out all the lights from the ambulance, police car, and fire truck that had pulled up to take care of the cleanup.

I could not believe my bad luck between last night and now. My head felt as if I were swimming in circles, almost like how I felt after drinking those frozen mixed drinks on the ferry. Looking over the scene for a moment, I was in awe watching the firemen work as well as the tow truck driver, but as I stood there, I heard nothing. I was completely deaf, my mind blocking out all the noise. I just watched and watched until everyone had left the scene.

The pole that once stood in front of my house now lay on the sidewalk with police tape surrounding it in what looked to be an eight-foot radius. I guess the electric company wouldn't be coming until daylight since I didn't see them. I was beyond caring and needed to rest my mind and sleep.

Looking up at the night sky again, I could see distant light flashes as electricity shot across the horizon, bouncing off the clouds. I bet this storm wasn't done yet and there might be more to come. Gathering my wits, I headed back towards my house. The bottom of my pants was soaked, and mud on my feet squished between my toes from standing on the soaked semi-seeded grass.

As if a switch had been flipped, the sky opened up, and rain started pouring again. Looking up at the sky, all I could think of to say was, "Whatever, you win." I ran the last few steps up to my door and went inside.

****

Nicholi had come up empty-handed and saw that I was making my way back inside the townhouse. He scrambled to hide in the kitchen pantry, which was just big enough to walk in and close the doors. The small pantry door had slats that allowed for him to look out.

Oh my goodness, I was so overwhelmed with all that had transpired, I just wanted to cry. Leaning against my front door, all I could do at that moment was slide down to the floor, put my head between my legs, and embrace my head. This was not how I envisioned ending the Paris trip, especially my first day as a trial lawyer. What was I going to do?

I had had it all planned out in my head. I would go and have a great time with my best friend, Daniele, in Paris. We

103

would party and just be so carefree, two friends enjoying their time together and watching each other's backs. I had had no clue that it would end the way it had. I felt extremely drained. However, I couldn't think about that; I had the most important day ahead of me, and I should have time to glance over the case either on the ferry to Port Angeles or once I was on my uncle's Learjet. That would give me roughly an hour total between either ride to get what I needed and present the hearing in a professional manner. I was top of my debate classes in high school and law school.

I knew that I needed to drag myself upstairs and get into bed. Slowly, bracing myself against the floor and wall as I got up, I clicked the light switch off for downstairs, headed for the stairs, and climbed to the top of the foyer. Listening from behind the pantry door, the intruder waited until he couldn't hear Alex anymore before he quietly exited the pantry.

Standing at the end of her bed, I just fell backwards onto the bed. My head bounced against the plush pillow-top mattress clothed with satin sheets. My eyes finally in a restful state and sprawled out across the bed, I let out a sigh of relief as this part of my day came to an end, or had it?

I lay awake in bed, eyes closed; yet I could not fall asleep. Thoughts of Natalie filled my mind, wondering if this woman was going to make it. Flashbacks started to come and go from deep within my memory banks of when I was a little girl. Images from the past started to flood my thoughts, images so suppressed that they didn't make sense. .

In fact, those images were real and from my past when I was involved in a car wreck, yet I couldn't pinpoint them because I had blocked out that part of my life for so long. Seconds felt like minutes and minutes passed like hours as I lay there motionless. I had started to drift off to sleep, but I really wasn't asleep. Waking suddenly, all I could see was the ceiling fan spinning as sweat built on my forehead and face. My shirt was soaked right above my chest, but it wasn't from the rain. It too must have been sweat.

Opening my eyes and leaning my head towards my nightstand, I could not make out the alarm clock until I rubbed my eyes and refocused. It read three-seventeen as I glared at it for a moment. I had dozed off for only a few minutes, but it felt like an eternity. I wondered if this sort of thing had ever happened to anyone else and if I was waiting to wake from a nightmare. Yes, that's it; I must have been having a nightmare, and all this was just my imagination. Unfortunately, it was real, and I was living the nightmare.

I could hear heavy rain pelting the roof as if an angry sky never stopped altogether but had just eased off until now. *Are you kidding me?* I thought. I pulled the covers over my head to drown out the sound with no luck. Thunder sounds had come back, rearing their ugly noises again. One, two, three more crashes of thunder shook the entire house, causing me to sit up. Chills ran across my neck as if someone had stepped on my grave.

Within seconds, the storm intensified, and now I was really starting to get nervous. Suddenly another lightning bolt streaked across the sky outside my window and illuminated the bedroom.

"Oh God, not another one." I placed my hands over my ears as the thunder crashed like a judge's gavel hammering the court to obey order.

It was now evident that I needed to stay up all night and gather all the evidence to come up with a case so I would be able to cross-examine the allegations. I had no clue as to whom or what I was cross-examining since I had not read the files due to my laziness, let alone everything that had happened to me that day.

Now, if only I had had a strong cup of coffee, I could have stayed awake just long enough to make it through the rest of the day. Ha, something more like a personal intravenous drip bag would work for me! That's it. I couldn't fight it any longer. I was going to go downstairs and make some coffee! The question was, would it do the trick?

Grabbing my bathrobe from the back of the bedroom door, I made my way down to the kitchen. As I started down the stairs, swirls of wind bathed me, sending chills up and down my spine. After reaching the bottom of the stairs, I stepped in a puddle of water. Why were my floors wet? I reached for the light switch next to the fridge, and before I was able to turn on the lights, a strange yet somehow familiar voice stopped me dead in my tracks.

"Don't...Listen and you won't be harmed." The intruder had made his way out of the pantry into the living room and was looking around in the dark as I came down the stairs.

I screamed and fell on the stairs, catching the railing. I wanted to turn and run back up the stairs, but I couldn't. I was frozen in place from fear as I heard the intruder speak. Anxiety pulsed through my veins because I couldn't think of anything I could grab near me as a weapon. My fear quickly turned to anger. I demanded from this stranger in my house, "Who are you, and what are you doing here?"

Nicholi exclaimed in a commanding voice, "You know why I'm here!"

"Wait, does this have something to do with my case? You can stop this feeble attempt to scare me with some sort of sick, twisted initiation." I stood up and laughed. I was sure this was a practical joke by my new bosses to scare me on the eve of my new job.

"Quiet, you bitch!" Nicholi shouted at me.

DEADLOCKED: A Trial Beginning

Silence encapsulated the room as I stood still at the bottom of the stairs in the dark, wondering what was going to happen to me next. My heart was pounding against my chest, the sound of rain drumming against the kitchen windowsill in rhythm with my pulsating blood pressure.

"I have no idea who you are or why you are here. Please don't hurt me."

"I said shut up." Nicholi rushed towards me, got behind me, and placed a knife he had grabbed from the kitchen against my throat.

"Please don't!" I was scared and trembling as the coldness of the blade pushed against my skin. Tears flooded my eyes as I could feel the blade cutting into my throat as Nicholi held it tight against me.

"I said shut the hell up. Stop moving around. You know exactly why I'm here, and if you don't stop yakking, you won't see your pretty little face again." Nicholi was trying to make sure I was scared enough to quit talking by threatening my life. He had no intention of harming me; he just wanted to scare me into giving up the files.

"Give me the case files."

"Case files?" I replied, having no idea what Nicholi was talking about.

Nicholi panicked, pushing in my right leg from behind the knee with his leg, making me drop to one knee. He still held the knife firmly, following me down.

"You answer me wrong again, and it's over, Alexandria." Nicholi had made a slip of the tongue calling out my name.

"How do you know my name?" I was stunned, yet I still could not recognize the stranger behind the voice. I was certain I had heard it recently, but where?

He nudged the knife blade closer to me neck. I just wanted to get out of the situation. I broke down and said I would hand over the papers. "All right, all right, just don't hurt me, please. They're right over there."

"Over where?"

"Please, let me go and I'll get them, but I need to see."

"If I let you go, you do not try to run or do something stupid, or you'll end up dead. You got that, bitch?"

Nicholi removed the knife from my throat and forcibly pushed me down to the ground. He stepped back and told me to get the papers. Shaking all over, I crawled towards the front door across the rain-soaked floor, almost losing my balance, to where my backpack was. I started to fumble for the envelope. My hands were covered in water and mud.

"I need light to see what I'm doing."

"Fine, but don't look my way, or I'll stab you. Hurry up!"

I ran my hands over the floor and up the wall where I thought the light switch was. I stood up and flipped the switch. Right at my feet was my backpack. All Nicholi could see was my back as I bent over. As I opened the envelope, it appeared to me there were two copies of the case papers stapled together. I pulled out one of them and dropped the envelope. It fell behind my backpack.

"What are you doing? Pick it up and hand it over. I said hurry up!" I paused for a moment to let my hands simmer down from shaking so violently. "Relax," I said. "I have it right here in my hands." I turned my head in hopes of getting a glimpse of the intruder.

"Do not turn around. Come on, toss the papers over towards me and then turn off the lights and open the front door. Do not even think about running outside or you will get a knife in the back. Crawl back away from the door and close your eyes."

At this point, I felt like I could take this guy out and charge him, hoping he would drop his knife and I would turn the tables on him. But that moment vanished as quickly as it popped into my head. If he was going to run out the door, I was going to crawl to my keys that I remembered were on the ground. When he ran by me, I would scrape his leg in hopes of getting some DNA that I could give to the police to track him down.

"OK, I'm against the wall. Please, just go." I grabbed my keys as Nicholi bolted towards the door. As he passed me, I thrust my right hand out with the door key pointing like a blade and nicked Nicholi on his right arm. I managed to drag the key just enough to scratch him, catching some skin and blood as he stumbled out the door. He slammed his right side on the doorframe before running across the grass, slipping and falling on his ass. Scrambling to get up, he ran down the street.

I was in such shock and overloaded with adrenaline, I just sat there and didn't even bother to chase him. My ordeal was over, and I got what I needed. I still had a copy of the trial papers, and I now had collected evidence to use to find the intruder.

Chapter Seven
Foul Play

As I watched the rain pelt the threshold between my house and the steps down to the walkway, my BlackBerry kept ringing and vibrating. Slouched against the wall, I managed to lean towards the door and close it. I could feel the dampness and water on my other hand against the floor. My front foyer was rain soaked, and I didn't even care. Finally, the ringing noise from my phone stopped.

Climbing to my feet and flipping on the light switch, I could now see just how much water had come in along with globs of mud dragged in by me and that person who had just assaulted me for the damn trial hearing papers. I had to let someone know what had happened. I had key evidence on my house key that could expose this person. I knew just the person to call—Tomas. Vancouver Police Chief Tomas Rainer, to be exact. Tomas and I went back many years to when my Uncle Nicholas would bring me along when he visited his buddies at the precinct.

DEADLOCKED: A Trial Beginning

I first met him when I was twelve, and he took a rather fine liking to me. He always picked me up, hugged me, and called me his little daughter from another mother. I didn't really know what that meant at first, but after a while, I started to realize it was just an expression and accepted it. I had thought it was because I was a child relative of Uncle Nicholas's and it was his way of letting me know not to goof off there. Tomas always mentioned the same thing each time I came down to the precinct. Of course, that was after he had let me take a few lollipops from his jar on his desk. I so loved the watermelon and grape flavors.

I never questioned why we would go see the police; I just knew that my uncle had many friends there. I do recall sitting on the old wooden bench across the hall and a few feet down from Tomas's office. I could see into his office. My uncle would give me strict instructions to stay seated on the bench and wait for him while he and Tomas had a talk. I would just smile, lollipop and all in my mouth, and nod my head yes. It was strange, though; while sitting there with my feet crossed and swinging, other officers would come up to me, say their hellos, and tell me how wonderful my uncle was for helping out the community and the precinct. I had no clue what my uncle did with his money other than the fact that the finer things in life surrounded me, and I was quite happy since not too long before, I had just the opposite.

The funny thing is, I never really believed them, as they seemed to be putting on a good smile and a kind act, yet something was odd. In fact, it seemed fake, even as if they were paid to act that way towards me. I usually sat there for quite some time after my uncle walked into Tomas's office. I did notice that Tomas would always glance out into the hall in both directions, smiling at me once he saw me, and close the blinds from within the office.

Whatever Uncle Nicholas and Tomas were talking about, it obviously was important enough to be very private about it. If there was one person in the world I could trust and call other than my uncle, it would have been Tomas. I thought about calling the City of Victoria police, but after tonight's ordeal, there was no f'in' way. I loved living here but would avoid them at all costs.

Wow, I could not believe my eyes. The hand-scraped wood floor was just a mess. Muddy footprints were scattered everywhere, even on my Persian white rug in front of the fireplace. Looking around, I saw my couch and La-Z-Boy chair tossed about. "Are you freaking kidding me?" I blurted out to myself. The water and mud on the wood floor and rug didn't faze me, but seeing my nine-hundred-dollar La-Z-Boy recliner toppled over tipped the scale for me.

That was it! Grabbing my BlackBerry from the kitchen counter, I was furious. Scrolling through my list of contacts, I saw Tomas's number and clicked. The phone rang several times before I heard a slight "hello" coming from the other end. However, it wasn't who I was expecting. *Typical BlackBerry behavior,* I thought. I wanted to dial Tomas's number, but I dialed my best friend's, Daniele Ramos's, by accident.

"Hello? Who is this?" Daniele said as if she had been in a deep sleep and I had just woken her up.

I stood there quietly, as I knew I had just made a mistake. My hands trembled gently. My nerves are shot. I had to respond, but I couldn't quite get the words out. Daniele would be upset if she knew it was I who woke her up seeing as it was four o'clock in the morning. Oh my God, it was four in the morning! I could have cried just then, but Daniele responded again to my silence.

"Who is this?"

112

I figured she must have known it was me. Surely she had added me as a contact by now, but I remembered her saying while we were in Paris that she needed to but hadn't gotten around to it. That explained why she was asking who it was. I panicked and ended the call. I hated that phone. I swore I was going to get a Samsung Blue Earth as soon as this contract was up.

I just stood there holding my BlackBerry for a minute or two, waiting for her to call back, but she didn't. My backlight went dark, and silence filled the room. I could feel my skin shaking as the silence was more than silent; it was the loud, consistent noise everyone hears when sitting in a room with nothing happening. As I closed my eyes and took a short breath in, it happened.

My phone rang and scared me half to death. I dropped the BlackBerry to the ground, knocking off the battery cover. It rang and rang, vibrating in circles loudly against the wood floor and displaying an unknown caller. I instantly knew it wasn't Daniele calling back. The ringing kept on going and would not stop. Was I going answer it or not?

Maybe it was just a coincidence and whoever was calling was just a wrong number. Needless to say, I had to make it stop. Picking up my phone and the displaced battery cover, I answered.

"Hello?"

"You are alive only because we grant it. Say nothing of tonight to anyone, or next time your pretty little neck will be sliced from one end to the other. You will be watched."

The call dropped, and I could not stop staring at my wall with eyes full of fear. My ears started to get hot, and I knew my blood pressure was rising due to all this emotional stress. My mind was telling me to follow the unknown caller's demands, yet my integrity and wits were telling me I had to warn someone about last night and now.

The voice on the other end of the phone sounded nothing like the attacker earlier. It sounded much older and with sort a broken French accent. I couldn't wait any longer. I found Tomas's number and made sure this time I dialed it correctly. The phone rang only once before it was answered.

"Hello?" Tomas answered with a soft voice.

"Tomas?"

"Yes, this is Tomas. Who's calling?"

"It's me, Tomas, Alexandria."

"Alexandria, what on earth has possessed you to call me at this time of day?"

"Tomas, please forgive me. Something has happened to me, and I need to report it."

"What on earth has happened to you, child?" I could sense the rise in Tomas's voice.

"Tomas, last night, after I arrived back from my trip to Paris, some stranger was stalking me, and for the love of Pete tried like hell to steal something from me, and I have no idea why."

"Alexandria, what did he try to steal?"

"Well, you see, tomorrow…I mean, later today is my first time standing in front of a jury and judge presenting my very first preliminary trial hearing, and I think he was after the court papers for some reason. Not sure how he knew I would've had it on me, and I—"

Tomas quickly cut off Alexandria. "Alex...Alex, wait...stop. Don't mention the case in any way to me or I could be an accomplice to the case, and I don't even know what it is."

"I haven't even looked it over. I know, I know, not the typical Alexandria that you know. I'm usually at the top of my game."

"Well, I can understand if what you're telling me is true."

"Tomas, it's true. I was just harassed and attacked in my own home at knifepoint. I couldn't make the perpetrator out, but he demanded I give him the trial papers, and luckily there were two copies, so I still have a copy."

"You need to report this to the local authorities in Victoria."

"I thought about that, but I didn't. I called you, who I know and can trust. Can you have someone run a DNA test for me?"

"DNA test?"

"Yes. As the perpetrator was leaving, I managed to graze his right arm with my door key, and I think I was able to scrape some skin and blood onto it."

"For God's sakes, Alex. What the hell have you gotten involved in?"

"That's just it. I have no clue. All I know is I was stalked, saved by a stranger name Beauford, and attacked today, all for this trial case."

"Who's Beauford?"

"Oh, he's nobody, just some guy who happened to be there and took a liking to me while I was waiting for the ferry last night in Seattle. He's completely harmless and innocent."

"Does your uncle know about this?"

"No. If he did, he would be totally upset at me. You know my uncle; he barely allowed me to even go to law school let alone move away from Vancouver. I'm sure he's upset already since I didn't call him when I landed last night. I was supposed to take the family jet but decided to take the ferry instead."

"Let me see what I can do. I'm not going to promise you anything, but I will try. When you get done with your hearing, stop by the precinct and drop off the sample."

"Tomas, thank you."

"Don't thank me yet. We still might have to report this if this person has a rap sheet on him. I have got to go now because I'm being called in as a material witness this morning, and we all know that I despise being called in for anything, let alone being cross-examined by some new, young upstart lawyer."

"Well, thank goodness it isn't me. I would hate to have to go through that with someone I know and care about. What is it about?"

"Ah, don't worry yourself. It's just some confusion over false allegations against me. No worries. I've got this under control. Besides, I'm the chief. No one would even try to make a claim against me."

"Tomas, good luck, and I will stop by your office later after my hearing."

"Sounds good, Alexandria. Goodbye."

Hanging up on the call, I felt an ill feeling for a moment, but it passed. I needed to sleep and feel better now that I had told someone I trusted. I would have to make sure I read over the case and act like nothing had happened to me. I knew if I confided in Daniele about it over girl talk, I would feel so much better and be able to gather my wits to handle the situation.

****

Nicholi met up with Bobby down around the corner from Alex's home. Spotting the dark blue Tahoe sitting there with its lights off, Nicholi could see the exhaust rise from the pipe. Bobby was taking drags from a cigarette when he saw Nicholi approach in his side mirror. Raising his driver's seat upright using the electronic assist feature, Bobby observed Nicholi stumbling towards the Tahoe, holding his right arm.

Nicholi approached the passenger side of the Tahoe and tried to open the door as Bobby looked at him with an evil grin. The passenger side window dropped down slightly as Bobby greeted him, keeping the door locked.

"What the hell took you so long? You said you needed a few more minutes, but that was half an hour ago."

"Let me in. It doesn't matter. I'm here now. Let's go."

"Naw, naw, no. Toss in the envelope first; then I'll let you in."

"Come on, Bobby. I got it. Just let me in."

"First the envelope."

"Fine, but it's just the papers."

Nicholi stopped holding his arm where Alex grazed him, reached into his coat, and grabbed the rolled-up papers. He tossed them through the window opening and onto the passenger seat. Bobby closed the window, and Nicholi was left to see his reflection once again against the rain-soaked window. Without realizing it, Nicholi had stained the backside of the trial case papers with his own blood from his hand. Bobby lowered the window again and stared at Nicholi.

"This had better be your blood on these papers and not hers. If Mr. Rozzito finds out it's his niece's, you are a dead man."

"Relax. It must be mine. On my way out, I slammed into the doorframe and must have cut myself. The girl is fine. I asked for the papers, and she handed them over."

"Just like that? She didn't put up a fight or nothing?"

"No fight. I demanded the papers, and she gave them up."

"You'd better be telling the truth, Nicholi, 'cuz if you laid one finger on her..."

"I got it. I didn't touch her. The lights were off, and I demanded the papers, and she gave them to me. I think she was just scared."

"Oh, and why is that?"

"Because you, dumbass, almost ran someone over after you left her house. That driver tried to avoid you, and she hit a pole right in front of the girl's place."

"Whatever. She almost hit me. Besides, maybe she was drunk or something. Get in, and let's get the hell out of here. Mr. Rozzito has a chopper waiting for us, and we're to get back to the compound ASAP."

"Well, you'd better hope so, because there were cops and ambulances that showed up afterwards. That too is why it took some time. I couldn't find the papers, and well, I had to hide in her place when she came back inside."

"What, she went outside?"

"Yeah, that's how I snuck in…while she was outside trying to help that woman."

"Did she get a make on you?"

"No. She never saw my face. She came downstairs after a while, and I had to improvise."

"Impro-what?"

"Man, you are more stupid than I thought."

"Shut up, you punk." Bobby swiftly slapped the back of Nicholi's head, making him lean forward.

"Ouch! You freaking idiot. Improvise means to adapt to the situation. Dang, man, and you're the captain?" Nicholi reacted in advance to that remark to avoid Bobby taking another swing at him.

"That's right, kid, and don't you forget it." Bobby smiled and laughed as he turned the lights on, slammed the Tahoe into drive, and drove off, spinning the back tires and fishtailing the back end on the soaked road.

DEADLOCKED: A Trial Beginning

****

I was an emotional mess. Looking down at my hands, they shook from my nerves being shattered. I was going to crash and burn on my first day of work. This couldn't be happening. My townhouse was a wreck, and my mind was totally shot. I couldn't have cared less at the moment and just wanted to close my eyes and forget about it.

I didn't even want to climb the stairs to my bedroom. I was so physically exhausted, all I wanted to do was lie in my La-Z-Boy and sleep. I was so lucky to be alive. I could've been lying in a pool of my own blood, dying over a case that I had no idea what it was about. Tears slowly filled my eyes as I began to break down emotionally. Lifting my La-Z-Boy back up onto its feet and tossing my BlackBerry over onto the couch, I plopped my butt down in the chair and quietly cried myself to sleep. Before I knew it, I had dozed off for two hours as if nothing had happened.

Bobby and Nicholi made their way up north fifteen miles to Sidney International Airport where Rozzito's private Agusta A109 helicopter resided and was currently instructed to be fueled and ready to take off. Bobby and Nicholi were instructed to rendezvous with Rozzito himself at Anacortes Airport in Washington State just thirty minutes east of Sidney to hand-deliver the trial papers to him. Rozzito would then head towards Port Angeles Airport and wait for his niece to arrive. Alexandria had ridden aboard her uncle's private Learjet many times since moving to Victoria and now would be using the jet daily to and from Seattle. However, Alexandria had no idea her uncle would be there to greet her unannounced.

I lay there in the chair, dreaming of visions of my phone ringing and ringing. I had no idea why I would be dreaming that. Because the ringing was so lifelike, I woke frantically, eyes wide open. Looking around my place, I realized that all that had happened was not a dream, and my phone was ringing for real. But I had no idea where my phone was because it sounded a bit muffled.

Leaning over and pulling on the La-Z-Boy's lever to sit up, I could feel the right side of my ribcage pulling from stiffness. I now remembered tossing my phone onto the couch, slowly lifted myself out of the chair, and walked ever so gently to the couch.

"I'm coming, I'm coming," I yelled at my phone as if whoever was calling me could hear me. "Hello?"

"Alex, hi, it's me, Daniele."

"Hey girl, what's up?" I said, yawning as I tried to stretch without killing myself with pain. "Ouch!"

"What's the matter? You OK? You sound horrible."

"Well, I feel horrible, too."

"Talk to me, girl. Wild night of getting your freak on? Do I know him?"

"No, I wish that were the case, but it isn't. Hey, can we meet up for lunch later on today? There's something I need to mention to you, and I could use a little girl talk."

"Sure. When is your hearing over with?"

"Well, not sure, but the hearing starts at nine-thirty, and oh my God, it's after six. I've got to get ready, girl. Thanks for the wakeup call."

"Oh, OK. The reason I called was someone tried calling me last night and then hung up, and I was wondering if it was you."

"It was me. Sorry. I dialed your number by mistake."

"Alex, are you OK? Your voice sounds like you're in trouble or something."

"Listen, I'll explain everything later. I'm fine, really. I'll call you later so we can meet up for lunch, OK?"

"OK. *Entretien à vous une plus défunte Amie.*"

DEADLOCKED: A Trial Beginning

Daniele was showing off her French speaking abilities to me. What she was saying was, "Talk to you later, girlfriend." I kind of understood it as she hung up. What I needed was coffee, and I needed it now. That was what my mind was shouting out to me that very second, but first I needed another hot shower to help soothe my aching side.

I had yet to use my uncle's housewarming gift to me, a thousand-dollar coffee machine contraption. The only thing it couldn't do was sex, but supposedly it did pretty much everything else. Well, that was what my uncle swore. He loves fancy espresso machines and has to have at least three to four cups daily. I just want a cup of coffee, nothing fancy other than the occasional special creamers. This machine took up half my kitchen counter and looked like it was some secret weapon, if you asked me.

Standing there looking at this contraption, I just wanted to pull my hair out. I mean, come on, really? When did coffee become so complex? Shaking my head, I just turned around, walked towards my stairs, and stopped to look at my place. I could not believe this had happened to me. How could this be? It wasn't like I was involved in any criminal acts or anything like that. I am a stand-up young lady who had achieved a lot since leaving my uncle, yet I was feeling guilty as if somehow I had brought this on myself.

I still couldn't figure out why someone would go through the trouble of tracking little ol' me down. Maybe it didn't have anything to do with me and it was my initiation as a newbie lawyer. If it was my initiation, it sure felt more real to me then I would have imagined. Someone was playing their role out just a tad bit too far, but deep down inside me, I knew it wasn't a silly initiation. Whatever those trial papers contained must have had someone's blood on it for someone to go to that length to get ahold of them.

121

Luckily for me, I still had a copy that I planned on reading over once I got on the ferry to Port Angeles, but not so lucky for me if it got out that I was the one who had inadvertently given away confidential information. I did have a knife covering my neck by a thug threatening my life—which reminded me, I hope he hadn't left a mark on me. Not sure how I would explain that to anyone, let alone my uncle. I was planning on seeing him that Sunday, but I needed to make a mental note to call him that day. I couldn't imagine what kind of hell I was already going to get from him verbally for not calling him last night.

I looked at the clock on the wall and saw that it was approaching six-thirty, and I knew I had to shower, get dressed, and call a taxi service in order to make it to the harbor in time for the Port Angeles ferry ride.

Chapter Eight
Morning After

I made it to the top of her stairs, fell to my knees, and cried. Everything was all wrong. Suddenly, I felt as if I had lost grip on reality, and the last twenty-four hours was a nightmare I didn't want to remember. All I wanted to do was scream and let it out as loud as I could to expel the anger that raged inside me.

I wasn't prepared for starting a new life as a trial lawyer. I had been actually stalked, robbed, and emotionally raped by an intruder. Apart from that, my intellectual innocence had been taken from me as well as my inner self as I had been held at knifepoint and could have been killed.

I couldn't stay put even though I wished I could have just crawled into bed and pulled the covers over my head to make it all go away, but I couldn't. The fact was, what had happened to me happened for a reason, and I needed to stay calm. I had DNA evidence that I would give to Tomas later and would get to the bottom of this and perhaps find this person and press charges. I was better than this, and I needed to get my ass off the floor, get in the shower, and get ready for my day.

While I pulled myself off the ground and made my way into the shower, my BlackBerry vibrated several times on top of my kitchen counter. Several minutes lapsed as my phone rang again and again. No voice messages; just the message for two missed calls showed on the screen.

****

The person calling was none other than Alex's Uncle Nicholas. He was on approach to land at Anacortes Airport from Vancouver and wanted to call Alex to see how she was doing despite the fact that he was the one who was responsible for her trauma.

Nicholas was unaware that his niece had suffered more than just a simple encounter with Nicholi and wanted to call Alex, since she hadn't called him when she arrived home. He would have what she possessed containing information linking him to extortion, criminal activity, and involvement with money laundering and drug trafficking within the Mafia regime that spanned Canada, New York, and New Jersey.

This case included the name of the person who had made accusations against Nicholas. He needed the name in order to take him out of the equation in hopes that it would just get swept under the rug. What he didn't know and would find out shortly was that it was his old pal Tomas. Tomas had been the whistle-blower and had reported Nicholas Rozzito to the NSA and FBI in the States as well as to the CSIS, the Canadian Security Intelligence Service. His idea was to uncover this mafia crime lord at large in exchange for asylum.

Tomas had been paid off by Rozzito to look the other way for many years, but he had grown tired of it and wanted out. Nicholas had paid off the Vancouver Police Department and judicial staff. He had gone as far as paying off the Victoria

Police Department and had put in place one of his men to run the department. With the help of the New York and New Jersey capo families, he would connect and solidify his realm, even going as far as paying off the Coast Guard to look the other way when needed. In his mind, everyone had a price, and money always had a way of persuading even the most honest and righteous of men.

Tomas knew of all the illegal activity that Nicholas was involved in and had had enough. What he shared with authorities above him on both sides of the playing field slowly started the erosion of Nicholas's empire, and Nicholas was not going to go down that way. He had the money, the connections, and the weapons to fight back and would stand his ground. The only thorn in his side was Alexandria. He tried like hell to convince her to not get involved with the law, but in order to keep her from finding out, he paid for her to go to law school. *I guess,* he thought in the back of his mind, *if it ever rears its ugly face, I can persuade Alex to join me in preserving my regime.* However, he loved Alex so much and did not want her involved, but he couldn't stop her. And now, without her knowing it, she was about to open Pandora's box, and her life would be forever changed.

Nicholas ran his money laundering and drug trafficking out of his two Canadian fishing companies. Corsica Fish Packaging, located in Vancouver, British Columbia, right off English Bay, specialized in salmon and shellfish products, and the Adriana Fishery, located off the northern coast of Sidney, British Columbia, specialized in exotics.

Corsica Fish Packaging was not too far from the Rozzito compound that sat along the coastal side of West Vancouver off Piccadilly S. The compound had its own private beachfront and helipad. It was very secluded and heavily fortified with security to provide Rozzito the comfort he needed.

A mere nine-thousand-square-foot home with an Olympic-size swimming pool facing the water accented the gorgeous yard with his very own botanical gardens wrapped in a private wall of tall bushes. Not too shabby for a place that Alexandria called home during her childhood years.

She had been to both fishing factories from time to time as a child and really didn't care going there. The distinct odor of fish and guts always made her feel ill, and the nasty-tempered seagulls that let out a wrenching cry for constant food drove her nuts, not to mention slipping on the ice chips that seemed to be scattered throughout the loading dock area. She would have much rather stayed home or been off somewhere with her friends than spend time in those places.

It wasn't as if Alex had spent the time with her uncle. Nicholas would leave her in the care of the dock foreman to supervise her while he conducted mob business. Alex would stay as far away as possible from the revolting fisherman's wharf odors and would go off by herself until her uncle was ready to leave. This sheltered her from knowing what her uncle was really doing.

The best parts of the trips were the helicopter rides. Alex loved looking down and seeing all the ships and tiny boats leave wakes in the water, as well as the coastal lines zigzagging and curving in and out off the edge of the water. That alone made up for the awful trips and ghastly, disgusting sights of the fishing business. Besides, Rozzito always made sure to take her to her favorite restaurant before heading home.

Alexandria loved the Italian restaurant Mama Toscano's that sat along the western side of Vancouver in Horseshoe Bay. Alexandria knew this restaurant was family owned and family operated by her uncle and was strictly a legit business. Nicholas made sure that it had mirrored an old family villa restaurant his father had owned when he was a young boy in Sicily. This way,

126

it reminded him of home since his father's restaurant had been destroyed by a hurricane back in the summer of forty-eight. It also had killed his father, who had stayed beyond at the villa while others fled. Needless to say, it was one right he had, to honor his father.

Turning off the hot water from the shower stimulated me. I could feel the rush of my blood coming back to the surface as the heated steam escaped above my head. I felt clean and rejuvenated. Drying off my skin, I wrapped the towel around my head and reached for my robe, but to my surprise it wasn't hanging there like always. It dawned on me that it must have been on my bedroom floor because the night before in a panic, I had taken it off to rush outside where I found Natalie in her car.

"Crap. That reminds me; I need to call the hospital to check on her," I blurted out loud to myself.

I walked from the bathroom into the bedroom butt naked and realized that my bedroom window was wide open. Anyone and everyone could have seen me if they were across the street looking in. All I could do was drop to my knees, crawl over to the window, and shut the drapes. That really wasn't a good idea as my knees pinged with pain against the hardwood floor. I must have bruised them when I had fallen on the ferry.

Where the hell was my bathrobe? I couldn't see it as I looked around my bed. I must have tossed it somewhere out of sight. Managing to look like a fool, I squatted over to the window like a duck, stood up, and pulled both curtains together, only to notice I was being watched.

The neighbor across the street who had left me high and dry the previous night when I asked for help had just gotten a full view of my body from my waist to my head. He waved with a grin on his face. How was that for a morning greeting? I quickly grabbed both ends of the curtain and, with a hellacious force, closed them, almost pulling then off the rod. Great. I couldn't wait to hear about this on the local news. "Local Victoria woman waits in the morning sun, standing nude in front of her window as a young neighbor boy across the street gets his rocks off. Stay tuned as we uncover secret passions of the Brownstone."

Wow, what was I thinking? Why the hell was that boy looking into my window, and how many times had he noticed me naked in my room? I had to let his parents know what a little pervert he was. Before the taxi arrived in a bit, I would go over there and let them know. Besides, I had a few words to exchange with the prick anyway for not helping and walking away the previous night.

Funny, looking over to my right, I could see exactly where my robe had gone, right behind my sitting chair in the corner. OK, what to wear? What could I wear that said, "I am confident; I am a lawyer"?

I fumbled through my walk-in closet, skimming through many skirts and dresses, but I couldn't decide. *I know,* I thought. *I'll call Daniele. She'll know what I should wear.* Throwing on some black underwear and a tan bra, I made my way down to the kitchen only to notice my phone was vibrating. I missed a call. Shit, I knew it! It was my Uncle Nicholas calling again. He had called three times earlier and didn't leave a message. I knew I should have called him back, but I was so nervous and edgy right then, I needed my BFF. I dialed Daniele; her coaching would make me more confident. The phone rang several times before she picked up.

"Hey, what's up, girl?"

"You have got to help me. I've got a little less than a half-hour to get ready and make it down to the harbor, and I am far from being ready. My hair isn't done, and I have no makeup on. Help me, please." I raised my voice out of sheer anxiety and desperation.

"Calm down, Alex. We got this."

"Where are you?"

"Jim's Coffee House at Pioneer Square, standing in line....*Come on! Hurry up, grab your coffee, and move....* Sorry, Alex, you know me, running a little late for my case, and this handsome guy just turned around when I yelled at him in front of the line...Oh, wait, he's smiling at me...Now he's walking towards me. Wonder if he's single. Rats, false alarm."

"What? Wait, what happened? Daniele?"

"Why is it the extremely good-looking guys root for the same team? Argh, such a waste. So much potential to be had, just not for me. Damn, he sure is delicious, though."

"So he's gay?"

"Well, yeah, he's gay!" Daniele raised her voice, not realizing it until everyone around her looked up and the place went silent for a second or two.

"Why is it you somehow are drawn to gay guys?"

"I don't know, girlfriend. So, what are you wearing?"

"What do you mean?"

"I mean, what are you wearing right now? You naked or not?" Daniele once again was talking louder than normal, and the same people gazed at her. "Hold on Alex....*What? Can't a girl find out what another girl is wearing without you eavesdropping on me?* Geez, you would think I was the one who was gay."

"Well, you just broadcast that you were asking what a girl was wearing and if she was naked. That can be construed as you being a lesbian."

"Sorry, this girl doesn't swing that way, if you get my drift."

"Too bad," a young hot Latina girl behind Daniele leaned in and whispered in her ear.

"Who was that?"

"Oh my God, I just got hit on by a hot Latina girl behind me. I'm not sure if I should be flattered or disgusted."

"Well, you are the hottest girlfriend I know, and besides, you do look yummy all the time."

"Hey, back off."

"Relax, relax, just messing with you. Can you help me now?"

"Hang on, this line is too long. I'm going to have to skip the coffee and head back inside the courthouse. Talk with me as I walk."

"OK."

"So, what are you wearing?"

"Ugh. Black panties and tan bra at the moment."

"No. Ditch the bra. Black panties will conceal your goods, but tan bra speaks like you are a little innocent Amish girl."

"What? No!"

"Listen to me. You know damn well you're going to show some cleavage, and why not do it with some sassiness? Wear a purple or black or blue bra. That way, when the male gender in the room sees you, they will see that you have confidence by showing a little color with cleavage."

"I can't do that."

"Remember my first trial hearing, and I called you all excited and told you about how it went in my favor?"

"Yeah, you were off-the-wall excited. What does that have to do with what color my bra is?"

"Trust me, Alex. I wore a red bra that day and showed just a little extra for male viewing pleasure, and, well, it made them stumble over their words, and I looked like I was a pro.

The power of the female body speaks volumes when used in a certain way."

"I can't do that."

"You can and you will. Trust me, you will knock 'em dead, so to speak."

"Wait a minute, didn't you also go out that night with the opposite side's counsel…what's his name, Harry Laffter?"

"I told you that?"

"You did mention it."

"Well, turns out he was married and only told me after he dismounted and almost had a heart attack during sex."

"Oh, you are just a little hussy, aren't you?"

"Hey, no need to call me names. You're just jealous."

"Whatever."

"I tried to get you to hook up with that Frenchman at that party we went to, but no, you weren't looking for love. You wanted to stay focused because your new job was coming up."

"I didn't say that."

"Yes, you did, and come on, girl, he was smoking hot, especially with his abs flexed and his long hair that smelled so sensational…"

"Quit it…stop. He was only eighteen, for God's sake."

"Eighteen and legal!"

"You never stop amazing me, Daniele."

"Listen, I am going inside now. Can we talk later over lunch?"

"Yes, but wait…you haven't helped me pick out what to wear."

"That's easy. Wear the white two-piece Albert Nippon skirt suit from Neiman Marcus and a blue bra, but not the black panties. Change them to tan and wear the white Gucci heals. Got to go, girl. Knock 'em dead. Hugs and kisses. Talk later."

Just like that, Daniele was off the phone, and I was standing there in my closet. However, I felt better after talking to her. She always knew what to do in situations like mine. *Guess I'd better get ready and do my hair, put on my makeup, and get dressed,* I thought. It wasn't long before the time flew by. It was quarter to seven, and I was running late. I had to be down at the harbor no later than seven-fifteen or I was screwed and would miss my ride.

Throwing my makeup arsenal back into its bag and under the bathroom sink, I ran downstairs, grabbed my BlackBerry and backpack, and realized I needed to take the door key that had the DNA on it off of my keychain and get the spare key to my house. I didn't want to tamper with the DNA sample, so I just made sure I took it off nice and easy, placed it in a sandwich bag, and stuffed it in the side pocket of the backpack. My purse was still in it, so I walked out the front door and locked it. Then I noticed something wrong. I had forgotten the most important part of my outfit, the Gucci heels.

"Damn it."

Rushing back in to get them, I realized I had not covered up the knife mark on my neck. I grabbed a tiny white silk scarf and figured I would wear that over the wound to hide it. After managing to make it outside in one piece, it dawned on me how nice it was outside. What a change from the night before.

My BlackBerry read six-fifty-five on the screen. Fumbling through my contact list, I found the taxi service and started dialing it. I heard nothing but ringing.

"Come on, answer the phone, for the love of Pete."

Just as I said the words "for the love of Pete," someone picked up.

"Hello, thanks for calling the Victoria Taxicab Service. This is Pete. How can I help you?"

"Really? Your name is Pete?"

"Well, you just said you love me, so sure, why not?"

"Listen, Pete, or whatever your name is, I need a cab ride, and normally I would've called way far in advance, but I'm running late and just need a ride to the harbor fast, please."

"Ah, yes. Your number is bringing up A. Henson. You are Miss Henson, right?"

"That's me in the flesh."

"Yes, I can have a cab there in less than ten minutes. Will that be good enough, Your Highness?"

"Ha-ha, you are too funny."

"Will that be all, Miss Henson?"

"Yes, thank you."

"Well, have a good day. Goodbye."

Everyone seemed to be a joker lately. Ten minutes wasn't bad. Gave me time to put on my heels and wait by the curb. Great. I turned around to face the street, and lo and behold, pervert boy's father was coming out his door. He was looking at me, and I bet he wanted to say something to me. Go ahead...the way my day was going, he might just see what kind of a raging bitch I could be.

The look on his face was priceless as I just stood there. He knew I was watching him, and yet he displayed that poker face at me. What was he going to do? Was he just going to stand there and gawk at me, or was he going to make a move and walk towards me? Either way, I was in no mood for him, or he had better just give me a fake smile and go back inside.

Unfortunately, I saw he wanted to talk to me I saw as I came to the curb. He slowly walked down the steps from his house and headed towards me, eyes glued on mine. Well, maybe not. He stopped in front of his mailbox and opened it. Really? I wasn't born yesterday. The mail hadn't come yet. It is way too early. He was playing this out in his head as he went, it seemed. Nope, yep. For a second there, he turned to walk back towards his house and stopped. His manly ego must have gotten the best of him because he turned himself around, walked to the curb, and shook his head at me.

"I knew it," he said with a disgusted tone.

"Excuse me? Knew what?"

"You know what I mean."

"Actually, I do not. Why don't you clarify what you mean, Mr....?"

"Pichon. Edgar Pichon is my name."

"OK, Edgar Pitchun, what is it that you think you know?" Alex rolled her eyes.

"It is pronounced just like it sounds, Peeshun. It is French. Typical foreigners. You come over here with your corruption and filth, and look—you try to spread it to our youth, and you can't even get your pronunciations correct."

"Whoa...wait just a minute."

"No, you wait just a minute, you little hussy, or whatever you think you are."

"You need to back off, Edgar, and refrain from judging me. I am sorry if your son saw something he shouldn't have, but I did not do that on purpose."

"On purpose? What does it matter if it was on purpose? The fact is that you stood in front of your window exposed naked, and my son now can't stop saying the word 'boobs.'"

"Maybe you should tell your son to stop being a Peeping Tom."

"A Peeping Tom? No, no, no. You need to pack up your things and go back home to Montreal where that kind of behavior is, well, overlooked."

"You've got me all wrong. I am not a hussy, and furthermore, I am not from Montreal. I am from Vancouver, and I despise the fact that you are misjudging me."

"Look, I don't care how you make a living. One must work in order to pay the bills, but leave your work at work, and do not force it on the youth."

Man, was I getting steamed. My ears filled with hot blood that was about to burst out of my ears when Edgar's wife poked her head out and interrupted the conversation. She couldn't have done it at a better time, because if I had had a set of balls, I would have walked over to him, taken off one of my Gucci heels, and whacked him across the face with it for making such harsh remarks about me that weren't even true. But being the nice girl that I am, I bit my tongue as his wife spoke at me.

"Go home, pole dancer. We don't need you here. Stop taking our husbands from us."

"Pole dancer? Taking husbands?" Wow, she sure did have me confused with someone else. They must think I am a stripper or a call girl, but why? Because I accidentally flashed a kid?

"Look at you. All dressed up like a hussy. Dressed in white to pretend to be innocent, and those bright red shoes say it all. Edgar, stop looking at her breasts and come back inside. I told you not to go out here. For God's sake, maybe if you wouldn't act like you do, our son wouldn't be looking in some whore's window."

The tone of the moment fizzled as Edgar's expression went from judging to being judged. I needed some order-in-the-court action to cross-examine the false accusations these folks had against me.

"Edgar, I am truly sorry for what happened earlier, but you've got to believe me. It wasn't my intention. I am not a stripper or some call girl. I am just the opposite. I am a lawyer, sworn to defend justice and bring justice. I am in no way who you think I might be."

"Well, one would think differently if you ask me. I see you with that old guy from time to time."

"Old guy? You mean my uncle? He comes to see me every now and then. That's what family does. Why on earth would you even think that?"

"Sidney."

"What about Sidney? Australia?"

"Don't be messing with me, missy. Sidney up north. Tawny's right next to the airport."

"Edgar, I am afraid I have no idea about Sidney. Never been there and have no clue what Tawny's is, or any clue how my uncle and I seeing each other gave you the idea that I was a hussy or a stripper of some sort."

"Tawny's. The strip joint next to the airport. I see that old man go in there from time to time. They even say that the club has Mafia connections, and he is one of them."

"Oh my God." I started laughing uncontrollably. "My uncle going to strip joints in Sidney and being connected to the Mafia? That was a funny one, Edgar. I have no clue where Sidney is, let alone a strip joint there."

Just then, the taxi pulled up right in front of me, separating me from. I could not have asked for more perfect timing. That man and his wife were off their rockers pegging me for a stripper and my uncle, an upstanding, upscale businessman, a Mafia member. Please, my uncle may have some moments that are less than desirable, but Mafia? No way, not my uncle. He is the most loving and charitable person I know.

Throwing my backpack in the backseat and getting in the taxi, I stopped and looked over the roof of the car and left Edgar with my final statement. "Just tell your boy there's more to life than getting his rocks off by peeping on females. If you don't nip it in the bud, he is going to grow up and be a problem."

Climbing in the taxi, I smiled at Edgar, leaning over to the other side window as I told the driver to take me quickly to the harbor. The driver said, "Sure thing," punched the gas, and away we went. I was hoping for a better outcome today than what I was having to endure already. The ferry ride should allow me to relax some, collect my thoughts, and finally look at my case.

I had to admit it and agree with Edgar's wife—I did look slutty wearing a red bra, white suit, and red Gucci shoes, but I was taking Daniele's advice, and she was rarely wrong. Guess I was knocking them dead, so to speak, with my looks. A grin overtook my lips as the taxi drove to the corner and headed towards Government Street.

****

Bobby and Nicholi arrived just as Rozzito's Learjet was on approach to Anacortes Airport. Vincenzo, the A109 Agusta helicopter pilot as well as an old friend of Rozzito, was transporting Bobby and Nicholi to rendezvous with him. He taxied in from the only runway this airport had and made his way to the north end facing Oakes Avenue. Nicholi, looking out the window, could see Rozzito's Learjet descend and pass by them before touching down as smoke accented the runway beneath the tires.

Perfect timing, as they just made it before Rozzito landed. Being late was not in Nicholas's vocabulary, and if he had to wait, you surely would pay for it in some fashion. Vincenzo brought the helicopter to a halt and waited with turbines and rotors still running. There was no need to shut down because he would be taking off as soon as Rozzito had what he needed from Bobby. Bobby opened the side door and turned to look at Nicholi.

"Stay here. I'll hand Mr. Rozzito the papers."

137

"I can do it. I'm not scared of him." Nicholi was trying to act tough.

"It doesn't matter. I said stay here if you know what's good for you."

Bobby got out of the helicopter, closed the door, walked out from under the whipping wind of the rotors, and stood about fifteen feet in front of the helicopter to wait for Rozzito's Learjet to taxi in. The jet exited the runway and pulled in just to the side of Bobby. The front tire came to a halt as the pilot shut down the turbines. Bobby listened as the whining of the engines lowered by octaves. The door opened onto the stairs.

Gianna Bonifilia, Rozzito's personal stewardess, appeared from the hull of the plane and walked down the steps and over to Bobby. Gianna had been handpicked by Nicholas a year back. Gianna's father had been associated with Rozzito and was shot and killed while on one of Rozzito's fishing boats. Some said it was over a game of cards and the crew had had too much to drink and one thing led to another, but some said it was Rozzito himself because Gianna's father was allegedly stuffing his pockets with Rozzito's dirty money and not reporting the true amount. Gianna's father was captain of the *De Grasse*, Rozzito's largest French fishing vessel that worked out of English Bay. He had left a verbal will asking Rozzito to give his daughter a job, so Rozzito did just that. Gianna was not only pretty, but she also had smarts, and that pleased Nicholas.

"Mr. Rozzito will see you now."

Bobby followed Gianna into the Learjet as Nicholi watched from his seat in the helicopter. There was no way Rozzito would still be mad at him now that he had what he wanted. Maybe this would please him and Rozzito would give him another job. Nicholi hoped so in order to advance in the Rozzito family.

"Bobby, come sit, drink with me. Gianna, give my friend a glass of Barolo."

Bobby looked at Rozzito sitting in the middle of the plane, puffing away on a cigar. Sitting across from him was Donnie "The Wire" Bonnachi, Nicholas's former lieutenant and now underboss. Bobby had seen him only when he was recruited in as a capo. Donnie didn't care much for him because he wasn't family and was brought in as an indirect recruit since he had been a successful foot soldier for his family. Donnie always had a hateful look for him. Nevertheless, Nicholas always told his underboss to lay off and referred to Bobby as a good kid, and he had earned the right to be a capo. Still, why would he be here? Was he getting promoted, or was it something else? Either way, Bobby was a little nervous now.

"Mr. Rozzito, it's only seven o'clock in the morning. A little early for wine, don't you think?" Bobby said nervously.

"Sit...sit." Nicholas motioned Bobby to sit down in the seat across from him where Donnie was sitting.

Donnie smiled as he got up, stepping behind Bobby as he sat down. Gianna brought out a wine glass with just enough Barolo to wet the lips. Rozzito sat there with a gleaming smile on his face as cigar smoke filled the air.

"Thank you, Gianna," Nicholas said politely to Gianna as she looked at Rozzito and walked back towards the bar area. Bobby was on edge yet accepted the wine glass, smiled, and nodded to thank her as well.

"You know, this wine is made from the Nebbiolo grape variety, a full tannic red wine with a high alcoholic content produced in the Piedmont region of the world. It's required to be aged for three years before sale, a year in wood. Just like my soldiers, it takes time to make them great, just like wine; it has to age for some time before you can benefit from it."

"I had no idea, Mr. Rozzito; sounds like a great wine."

"Yes, Bobby. Go ahead, take a sip and tell me what you think, and please be brutally honest with me."

Bobby had a huge lump in his throat, feeling as if something wasn't right. He wasn't quite sure what Rozzito was getting at by having him taste wine this early in the morning. He had the case papers in his hand, and all he wanted to do was hand them over to Rozzito and get the hell out of there. Not to disobey the boss or look foolish, Bobby slowly raised the glass to his mouth. Rozzito glanced at Donnie, who was standing directly behind where Bobby was sitting, wrapping a thick, dull wire around both his hands.

Little did Bobby know that Donnie was about to surprise him. He closed his eyes and tasted the wine. Suddenly, Donnie reached over the back of the chair and Bobby's head just as Bobby removed the wine glass from his lips. Donnie placed the wire on his neck and pulled with just enough pressure to cause Bobby to struggle for air and squirm. Bobby dropped the rolled-up, bloodstained case papers to the floor near his feet as wine begin to dribble from the corner of his mouth.

Rozzito stood up. Looking down at Bobby's feet, he saw what he was looking for and bent over to pick it up as Donnie kept a firm grip on the wire wrapped around Bobby's neck. It wasn't looking good for Bobby; he was turning red in the face and fighting to gasp in some air.

"Bobby, Bobby, Bobby. You are supposed to be my captain, and yet here we are in this situation. You were supposed to set an example for the ones below you." Rozzito walked back and forth in front of Bobby, tapping the rolled-up paper against his left palm, as Bobby struggled against Donnie's grip.

"Tell me, Bobby, why should I let you live?"

Bobby, with his eyes barely opened and saliva forming at both corners of his mouth, mumbled the words, "Go to hell."

"What was that? I don't think I heard you." Rozzito had heard him just fine but leaned in, placing his right ear up next to Bobby's face.

"Please, Bobby, tell me why I should let you live."

"*Puisque vous êtes le patron!* [Because you are the boss!]" Bobby responded in his native tongue.

"No, no, no. I want to hear it in English." Rozzito waved his index finger as if to say no. At the same time, he gave Donnie a sign to tighten his grip by nodding his chin in a forward motion and then tilting his head back. Donnie knew exactly what to do.

Bobby's feet lifted off the ground as Rozzito waved Donnie off. Bobby coughed and gasped for air. Tears flooded his vision. He was getting a taste of what happened to someone who failed under Rozzito. As Bobby leaned his head down and the blood slowly reentered his throat area, Nicholas grabbed a fistful of hair at the back of his head, pulled his face up, gnashed his teeth, and grinned fiercely at Bobby.

"You're dang right I'm the boss!" Nicholas violently pushed Bobby's head forward as he released his hair.

"I'm sorry, Mr. Rozzito. It's that punk kid Nicholi's fault."

"I don't give a shit whose fault it is. You are the capo, and whoever is responsible for it beneath you doesn't freaking matter. You are to blame. You got it?"

"Yes, boss."

"Then start acting like my captain and handle it, and no, I don't mean taking it out on young Nicholi. I mean, handle it so he understands how important it is to do as I ask the first time. He needs to be able to respect the people above him. And when the captain can't control things, I guess I will start calling you Babbo instead of Bobby." Rozzito's lingo meant someone

141

whose services were not needed anymore; no one wanted to be called a Babbo.

"Mr. Rozzito, I got it."

"You'd better get it, or you will be broken." Rozzito again spoke in Mafia lingo, referring to Bobby being demoted.

"And another thing—this had better not by my niece's blood on these papers, or you will not see the light of day."

"No, she wasn't harmed. That's Nicholi's blood. He said he scratched himself on something and was bleeding, but he's OK."

"OK, enough of this nonsense. We'd better be taking off so I can meet up with Alexandria. Today is her freaking big first day as a lawyer. I just can't understand why she would choose that path, but hey, she is like a daughter to me, and I will do anything I can to see her succeed. Just hope this doesn't come back and haunt me, 'cuz if I go down, you go down, *capisce?*" Rozzito looked at Bobby as well as Donnie.

"*Capisce!*" Both Donnie and Bobby agreed out loud simultaneously as they exchanged looks.

"Gianna. Tell Miguel to fire up the engines. We are leaving for Port Angeles. I want to surprise my niece and wish her good luck in person."

"Yes, Mr. Rozzito, right away."

"Now, come here, Bobby, and pay me some respect."

Bobby cautiously and slowly rose to his feet, twisted his neck side to side to relieve the tension, and pulled down on his jacket to look presentable. Reaching into his pocket, he pulled out a sealed package full of dirty money that was a payoff from his business, and then leaned in and kissed Rozzito on both cheeks. Nicholas opened the money package, fanned it with his thumb, and then stuffed it into his suit coat pocket.

"I want you both to head back to the compound and wait for my return. I have a contract that I need iced. I want Nicholi to do it, and you are going to supervise him. He wants to prove to me he has what it takes to be a family member. This will be his shot. Now, go."

Bobby exited the plane as Gianna pulled the door up and closed it. Miguel Bonachelli, Nicholas's Learjet pilot along with copilot Angelo Delorenza, communicated with Anacortes's tower as the Learjet turbines revved up. The jet pulled ahead, turned forty-five degrees with a loud screeching coming from the twin turbines off the tail section, and taxied out towards the runway. Bobby watched as Rozzito's plane full-throttled down the strip and lifted off into the sky.

A sense of relief rushed over his body as a few moments ago, he thought he was going to be killed over Nicholi's mistakes, but he was spared. The only thing that bothered Bobby was he was a marked man now by Rozzito. If he didn't get back into his boss's good graces, he wasn't going to be around much longer. And he knew damn well he wasn't going to be just fired; he would end up as fish food, just as Gianna's father did. He knew too well that Gianna's father wasn't buried in the ground; he had witnessed Rozzito pulling the trigger that ended his life and having Donnie toss him overboard.

Bobby shook it off, turned around, and walked towards the helicopter. He raised his left arm and motioned Vincenzo to prepare for takeoff by circular his hand and finger pointing upwards. Sliding the door open, Bobby climbed aboard and closed it.

"Take us home, Vincenzo."

"You got it, my friend."

The A109 Agusta began to shake as the turbine spooled up to speed. Bobby laid his head far back in the seat and closed his eyes. Nicholi, anxious to know what had taken Bobby so long, couldn't stand it and had to bug him.

"So, what happened?"

"I don't want to talk about it."

"Wait, so is he pleased or is he pissed still?"

"I said I don't want to talk about it right now!" Bobby opened his eyes and gave Nicholi a look of disgust. He had to repeat himself twice before Nicholi backed off. The bruising ring that had formed around Bobby's neck was visible. Nicholi's eyes opened wide when he saw the mark. He slowly tucked himself back into his seat and looked out the side window. Nicholi knew something drastic had happened to him, and for Bobby to be timid and quiet now, it had to be something bad.

Chapter Nine
Emotional Distress

It wouldn't be long before I arrived at the harbor. The distance from my home on Chester Avenue to the dock was a little less than ten minutes, just enough time to pay the taxi driver and run down the stairs leading to the boarding area for the Port Angeles ferry with a minute or two to spare. There should have been no problem this time other than the fact that I was wearing high heels. That might have put a damper on things, but as I looked at my BlackBerry, the time seemed to be in my favor.

It was one minute past the top of the hour of seven, and that gave me nine minutes to be on board, just enough time to snag a cup of coffee before boarding, that is, if there wasn't a line. The taxi arrived just a tad ahead of schedule, like half a minute early.

My taxi pulled up behind another. I opened the door, grabbed my backpack, and proceeded to pay the driver. I normally paid a flat fee of nine dollars and fifteen cents, but to my surprise, today I was caught off guard when the taxi driver said, "That will be fifteen dollars and fifteen cents, ma'am."

"Fifteen dollars? What happened to the flat fee of nine dollars and change?"

"Compliments of the lieutenant governor."

"Yeah, well, I would like to share my thoughts on highway robbery to the governor's boss."

"Why, of course. Don't we all? But if you insist, you can find her in Westminster, and if you do, please give the queen my best regards." The taxi driver smiled sarcastically at me as he spewed out his humor.

"Ha-ha, very funny."

I dug through my purse only to find that I didn't have exact change. The smallest note I had was a folded-up five and one crisp twenty. A five note wasn't going to cover the ride, but a twenty would, though less than ten minutes of service sure didn't warrant a four-dollar-and-change tip. Maybe he would take it and have change.

"The smallest I have to cover this outrageous inflated fare is a twenty note." I foolishly handed it over before asking for change.

The driver took it, rolled up his driver-side window, and pulled away as I stood there in shock. This was the second time in forty-eight hours that a taxi driver had responded so rudely to me. There was no time to call the taxi service company and fight with someone over spilled change as that little distraction had cost me two minutes. I still had enough time to make it down to the dock area and get a cup of coffee.

Knowing that a cup would cost only a couple of dollars, I had it covered. Two loonies were tucked in the change part of my purse, and that would cover it. I was not about to take another chance of losing the five note even though that was merely my mind getting the best of her.

I looked down at the dock area and noticed the line of folks at the coffee stop. Shaking my head, I figured I would just go there, and if the line was too long, I would act like I was dying or something to get ahead in the line. That's how bad I needed caffeine. *No more drama*, was all I was thinking about as I made it to the coffee spot. The sweet yet bitter aroma of Arabica beans filled my nostrils as I let out a huge sigh of satisfaction. The lines were long but moved at a fast pace, and before I knew it, I was first in line. This coffee spot was no stranger to me; I always stopped here before boarding and knew the help really well.

"I'll take a bag of intravenous drip line of your best coffee," I said, being funny yet almost convincingly serious.

"Bonjour, Miss Henson. Good to see you. How was Paris?"

"Bonjour, Sofia. Paris was Paris, full of love. What can I say?"

"Well, tell me, did you find your love there?"

"No, no love there, but I did have a great time with my best friend, and as you mentioned, we stopped at Pigalle Place."

"And...?"

"Sofia, that place was not for me, as you suggested."

"Well, you did say you were lonely and needed to find love, so..."

"Oh, Sofia."

"What? Just because I am an old French woman doesn't mean I am dead. Hey, it is the city of love, even if it lasts only twenty minutes...no, more like five if you're lucky!" Sofia said, making a funny comment back to me as she giggled.

"You are a trip, girl," I said.

"So, the usual, then?"

"Yes, yes please."

I waited anxiously for Sofia to bring my favorite Italian cup of coffee. I pulled out my two loonie coins and handed them to Sofia.

"You know, I still can't get over why anyone would name a piece of metal a loonie. Guess they were loonie!" Sophia commented with a smirk.

"Sofia, you always make me smile and laugh. Thank you. I needed that."

Sofia handed me my precious cargo as I inhaled a deep hit of the full-bodied aroma that just overtook my senses in a wonderful way. Nothing better than this, except a little hint of cream and sweetener to give it the right pleasure of taste. Today was finally starting to look promising as I could hear people around me chatting and carrying on with their lives.

"Have a great day, Sofia. Au revoir."

"Au revoir, my sweet Alex," Sophia responded back, waving me onto my day.

I just loved her. She was so wonderful to all of her customers. What a great way to greet the morning, in my opinion. I could see the small ferries were very busy with tourists as I gazed upon the harbor. Seagulls cried out over the horizon. Many vendors were selling their artistic crafts as some played their instruments to songs that actually blended with the beautiful sunny day. Suddenly I was engaged with a mime in front of me, stopping me in my tracks.

"Excuse me, I must get to the ferry."

No response from the mime, of course. I was not really expecting this delay, so I tried to step around him, but he placed his hands up in front of my face. He started to act like there was a wall there and simulated a few feet to the side of me opening a door. Weird if you ask me, but I figured I would play along, so I stepped over and walked through this now-imaginary door.

As I stepped through it, he made a warning gesture with his hands and by opening his mouth wide as if the door was not tall and I had to duck. Without asking why, I did exactly what he wanted and ducked. Silly, as there wasn't a door there. After I was out of the imaginary door he pointed over my head as if to say there was something there. I turned my head and looked, but I didn't see anything.

I turned back around, and to my surprise again, there was the mime smiling and blinking his eyes and holding a beautiful red rose in his hands. He offered it to me.

"Oh how sweet, but I can't."

The mime turned his smile to a frown, made a wiping motion with his other hand, and silently began to cry. My heart dropped as I was taken over by his overwhelming act. It sure got to me, so I decided to accept his rose.

"Thank you. You are too sweet. " As I grabbed the rose, the mime clapped his hands quietly and pulled out a sign from behind him that said, "This rose is red and beautiful just like you!"

My cheeks became red as I became shy for a moment. The mime closed his eyes and leaned in for a kiss. This guy was either very ballsy or brilliant, but I wasn't feeling it and said, "Sorry, I must go." He stood there with a slight frown and shrugged his shoulders with his arms up as I began to walk away, but I stopped.

"OK, you got me." I walked back over to him, puckered my lips, and leaned in to kiss him. I kept my eyes open to see his response. He leaned in, too, but didn't touch my lips. His eyes lit up, and he even lifted one of his legs. He smiled and walked away. Too funny if you ask me, but I actually liked it. I was very nervous before this happened, and now I felt a calm come over me as I neared the boarding area for the Port Angeles ferry. Pierre was so right when he said this ferry was old. Funny how I looked upon it now with that in mind, yet she still was very majestic in her own way.

There was no waiting in line to board since many had already stepped aboard. No line was present as I walked over the bridge way and handed the port guide my ticket. Guess I had made it just in time as I can hear the engines powering up and see the men removing the huge ropes that kept her close to the dock.

"Phew! Guess I just made it."

"Have a wonderful day, Miss Henson."

"Thank you, Jeanue."

Walking up the ramp, I was greeted by deckhand Stephan. No Josh today, it looked like. I wonder if he had gotten in trouble for the other night since Pierre saw had him in action towards me.

"Miss Henson, you are looking rather chipper this morning."

"Morning, Stephan."

"Josh off today?"

"Josh does have the day off today. Some sort of order by the captain. Not sure why because Josh has never missed a day since he started, but I am glad to assist you in his absence."

"Oh boy, I hope he isn't in any trouble."

"Nothing like that. I guess he was working more hours than he was supposed to be, and the Maritime Gestapo don't like that, so he was ordered to stay home today."

"Oh well, that is a relief," I said, feeling as if I might have been the cause of Josh's absence.

"A relief? Why is that?"

"No worries, Stephan. I just wanted to make sure he was OK, seeing how he did act a little disoriented Wednesday night when I rode from Seattle to here on the *Victoria Cove*."

"Yeah, Josh has been working both ferries, and I guess he logged too many hours between them."

"Well, that would explain why he was on the last ride then. By the way, today is it. I am an official lawyer. I have my first big case this morning. I would be dishonest if I said that I wasn't nervous."

"Ah, you'll do just fine. Why, a gal like you defending justice makes me want to go out and get in trouble and have you represent me." Stephan being funny reassured me, and I smiled.

"Such a charmer. You always have the right words to make a girl smile."

"Just doing my job, miss Henson."

Stephan's words of encouragement provided a welcome sense of comfort. I honestly can say that I was a bundle of nerves that morning. I was not prepared at all for this case, and I just had had the craziest night I could remember. I didn't want to think of all that right now. I needed to get to the lounge and go over the case so I could at least show some effort on my part. Walking away and smiling back at Stephan, I made my way towards the lounge area.

Thinking silently to myself, all I could think about was my first words and actions. *Come on, Alex, get it together. You'll do fine. You were at the top of your class in law school. You won every mock trial case handed your way with ease. You will do fine.* Beneath my feet, I could feel the vessel was moving away from the dock. My journey as a newbie trial lawyer was almost upon me.

The one thing I liked about the Port Angeles ferry was that it had that old ship look and the essence of past times, yet there was a warming feeling about her. I made my way to the stern of the vessel and outside where I could sit at a table and watch the water while I relaxed. The place was open to the outside elements, yet it could provide cover with the new automatic awning that could withstand high forces of wind, which made it very pleasant with shade against the sunny day.

I loved my life and where I lived. I couldn't thank my uncle enough for allowing me to move here, since he fronted all the cash for my place and what seemed like an unending spending account. I was thankful he had let me pursue my dream of becoming a lawyer against his wishes, but today I would make history for myself. I just needed to make sure it was a good mark in history and finally read over my case. There was plenty of time between here and Port Angeles Harbor.

The Port Angeles ferry came about and trolled out, leaving the harbor in Alexandria's peripheral vision. The morning run to Port Angeles was only for walkers, which meant only pedestrians and bicycles could ride. The ferry was not used for transportation of vehicles during its first run. Being so early in the morning and with less weight, the ferry could make good time at a top speed of twenty knots for the twenty-two-mile distance, which normally took ninety minutes but more like an hour on a good calm day.

The two old diesel engines still had life in them as the ferry signaled her departure with smoke rising from her single stack. She had just had an overhaul that allowed each engine to push out a total of two extra knots of speed, giving her the advantage over her old, declining self that barely topped sixteen knots. However, today would be the proving ground as she made a trial run, hoping to shave off thirty minutes.

Waves began to form as the two big propellers rotated and churned bright blue water into a murky color. The captain blasted the horns, and the midshipmen rang the bells aboard the bow and stern. The Port Angeles ferry was still alive and kicking as she proudly passed the coastal land of Vancouver Island, making her way out to Rock Race Lighthouse. To one side of her was a wonderful view of Victoria and to the other, Johnson Bridge.

My nervousness seemed to dissipate as the morning sun covered my face and the natural scents of the water and air surrounded me. What a perfect day to put the last couple of days behind me. I dropped my backpack on the seat at my chosen table, which was close to the back of the ship. I walked over to the railing. I wasn't ready to sit down just yet. I knew I had to get busy looking over the case and just needed a few more minutes of this perfect view.

I figured once we passed Race Rock Lighthouse, the ferry would put the pedal to the metal, so to speak, and I would sit and go over the papers. It didn't take long before I finished my first cup of coffee and needed another one. I figured I would order one from the little cafe inside. At least I knew they carried only one brand, Seattle's Best, and that would do just fine. It was a bit strong as I recall, but it had enough punch to put some good pep in my tank. In fact, just thinking about it made me want to go get one right then to replace my empty cup.

My addiction to coffee was almost the same as an addiction to marijuana. Once I had a great hit, my body yearned for it. Truth be told, marijuana causes the brain to fire neutrons to the body, mellowing a person out and perhaps even making them hungry. For me, coffee indeed fires neutrons to my body, calms me down, and makes me focus more clearly. I can get that only with a true cup of coffee and not those so-called coffee drinks with made-up names by some young adult picking words out of a dictionary and jumbling them to sound fancy. Otherwise known as a college kid trying to make ends meet working as a corner street barista.

"Guess I'd better get a cup of coffee to go with my view."

"Would you like cream and sugar as well, madam?"

I jumped in place as I was caught off guard. I did a quick about-face and saw it was a working deckhand standing right in front of me. Odd thing was, he was dressed in an Old World outfit and not the normal attire I was used to seeing.

"Wow, you scared me. I almost leaped over the railing."

"My apologies to the lady. Shall I fetch a spot of coffee, madam?" The deckhand spoke in a deep, rich British accent that seemed overly forced.

"OK."

"I shall return in a horse length's time."

I stared at him with a bewildered look in my eyes. I felt displaced in time with this man speaking to me using an accent of past years. It was quite obvious I wasn't losing my mind, yet it was odd because when I boarded the vessel, all was normal. It didn't take long for the deckhand to return. My back was once again to him.

"Your coffee, madam."

"OK, you have got to be less subtle when sneaking up on someone."

"Sneaking? Why on earth, my lady, do you think that?"

"Seeing how you are being nice and all, I really appreciate it." Lowered my voice a bit and leaned in towards him. "But you don't have to play out whatever part you have been told to play. I am quite fine with you just speaking normally."

"Why, yes, my lady." He cleared his voice over several grunts. "Here is your coffee, sugar, and cream." He finished the sentence in a Jersey accent, far from his feeble British accent. "You happen to have a spare cigarette by any chance?"

"What? No, I don't smoke. You're not from around here, seeing as how I knew there was something different about your British accent."

"That bad, huh?"

DEADLOCKED: A Trial Beginning

"Horrible. If the queen knew, you would surely be hung out to dry for impersonating a Brit, and I bet fired, too, for smoking while on duty."

"Guess I'd better jump over the railing and into the wadda."

"You mean water?"

"Yeah, wadda. That's how we say 'water' back home."

"Well, I wouldn't go that far. You just need to work on your accent and try to refrain from asking folks for cancer sticks while you're on duty." I giggled a tad. "So, what's up with the accent and your outfit?" I looked around could now see other deckhands in the same getup.

"Oh, just some silly charade that the company has us doing today in celebration of the vessel testing out the overhauled engines. By the way, the coffee is free. In fact, all nonalcoholic beverages are free while you ride today. It's their promotional way of saying thanks for riding with us."

"Ah, spoken like a true American man, yet one who feels he has to play dress-up. Thank you for the free coffee."

"Touché. You got me there, and you are welcome."

"So, mystery man, do you have a name?"

"That depends on if you have a name."

"My name is Alexandria."

"Whoa, that name sounds like royalty. Wait, am I being watched by the queen's guards?" The deckhand looked around, pretending as if someone were watching him. He had raised his voice enough to gain the attention of folks near us.

"Shh. You're starting to freak me out, let alone the people around you."

"Sorry. Sometimes I play my characters out to much."

"Yes, I can see. So, do you have a name, Mister I Act Like a Fool When I Am Around a Pretty Girl With a Beautiful Name?"

155

"Well, you got me there. My secret's out. Don't tell my boss."

"Your secret will stay with me. Now, seeing how you have attracted some onlookers, sit down with me over here and try to take it down a notch or two." I smiled at him as we both walked over to the table where I had left my backpack and sat down.

"People back home call me Tony Bag a' Donuts."

"Sounds kind of mobbish if you ask me."

"Yeah, I get that a lot, but it's just a nickname my friends gave me back home in the hood."

"OK, you sure don't look like you're from the hood."

"Well, you know, we never lose it. We just grow up."

"If you say so, but really, Tony Bag a' Donuts? You have a thing for donuts or something?"

"You are direct, aren't you?"

"I'm sorry. I wasn't trying..."

"I'm kidding. Relax. My name is Anthony Capelli."

"Well, Anthony, nice to meet you." I reached over the table to shake his hand.

"The pleasure is all mine, Miss Alexandria. Guess I'd better get back to work before my boss finds me hanging out here with you."

"Tony...Tony! Stop distracting the guests and get back to work." Anthony's boss yelled out to him from behind us.

"Too late. Guess I'd better go or I might just have to jump overboard in the wadda and paddle to shore."

"Yeah, um, I don't think that's a wise choice seeing how we're passing Race Rock Lighthouse and the water is quite rough and the current would have you up against those rocks in no time. You would end up as seal food."

"Well, with that picture in mind, I'd best be shoving off, my lady. I surely do not want to end up as an appetizer for seals." Tony smiled as he quickly turned his horrible accent back on. He reached for my hand and raised it to his lips, offering up a gentle kiss.

Wow, this certainly was a crazy start to my day, yet I felt good about it, despite the strange encounter with the mime and now this deckhand. I truly appreciated the free cup of coffee...couldn't beat that. Looking down at my backpack, I knew the unavoidable moment had surely arrived, yet my mind was still wandering, and I just couldn't get it to focus on what I knew I had to do.

I figured if I just gave myself a few more minutes, I would be good to go and I would buckle down and skim over my case, catching key words that would help me while in session. I could wing it and probably get away with it. The Port Angeles ferry cleared the last water buoy that was temporarily serving a sunbathing hangout for several seals while being tossed side to side against the vast current.

I could hear the diesel engines gain momentum as the wake from her stern capped over with bright white color from the sun reflecting on it. The Port Angeles ferry sounded her horns as she pushed forward. The slight breeze suddenly became a stronger steady stream of wind, yet it felt good against my face.

Sipping my coffee, I couldn't help but notice to the right of me that a huge humpback whale had come out of the water and splashed back in as its huge tail submerged. I had never seen one before, and it was just beautiful. I kept on watching as I drifted off, remembering how I had come to live in the city of Victoria.

It was a busy couple of days the last weekend of June. I was so convinced I was going to live on Vancouver Island and had even prepared a speech for my uncle about why I should live there. My Uncle Nicholas wasn't so keen on it at first, but with my constant barrage of information about Victoria and why I wanted to live there, he gave in and took me there to look. Little did I know, he knew all about Vancouver Island, and was trying to keep me away from being close to his Mafia ties within that area.

At least in his eyes, after my relentless approach, he could keep an eye on me when he happened to be in that area and play it off as if there were no connections. In fact, he made sure at the very least that I lived in the most expensive place since I had grown accustomed to the finer things in life without even realizing it.

My Uncle Nicholas had molded me into who I am now, and that was his way of keeping the other part of his life hidden from me. He figured he would spare no cost to hide it and would do anything for me. For many years, I knew I was being spoiled and felt I had to give back, so that's what drove my passion to become a lawyer—to uphold justice—not to mention it came with a nice salary, but it would maybe help me secretly find out about my past.

I remember my uncle and me looking pretty much both days for a place and had almost given up when we came across the Brownstone off Chester Street. *What an elegant place,* I thought to myself, admiring the finer details of the brick, the wrought iron, the design, and the beautiful landscaping that enveloped the outside. I fell in love with it the moment I laid my eyes on it. My uncle motioned the limousine driver to stop right out front, and I couldn't wait to get out of the car and check this place out.

"Alexandria, slow down. Wait for your uncle. I'm not as young as I used to be."

"Oh, Uncle, you are just spoiled by having everyone cart you around. Come on, slowpoke."

Walking up the sidewalk, I turned around and said to my uncle, "Hurry, Uncle Nicholas. I want to see what's inside." I remember the joy I could see on my uncle's face as we reached the door, or was it the opposite? Hmm, I'd like to think it was a sign of joy since we had spent the last two days coming up empty-handed. I began to knock fiercely on the door with anticipation and was greeted by Ms. Marina Rosella.

"*Bongiorno*, Signore Rozzito and Alexandria!"

"How do you know who we are?" I asked, shocked. "Uncle Nicholas, you knew about this place, didn't you?"

"Yes, Alexandria, I did." Nicholas nodded his head to the side, making a gesture with his chin as if to say yes in his Italian body language.

"So what about yesterday and today?"

"Perhaps it was just time to spend with you. You have been very busy with school and haven't been home like you were when you were younger, and I...well?"

"Well, what?"

"I thought it would be good for us—oh, I don't know— to bond."

"Oh, Uncle Nicholas, I love you." I couldn't help but turn and run into his open arms, hug him, and turn around to greet the lady at the door. "*Bongiorno*," I said back as I kissed Ms. Marina on the cheek. My uncle always taught me that our Italian heritage was our proudest asset.

"You must be here to see the wonderful Brownstone, yes?"

"Oh yes, I am just absolutely blown away from just the outside and can't wait to see the inside!"

We walked in, and I was immediately overwhelmed with a sense of comfort and security. Everything was spacious and elegant, from the decorations on the wall, to the marble countertops, to the gorgeous living room complete with a fireplace! I couldn't help saying, as I turned and looked at my uncle with the biggest smile on my face, "*Mi piace moltissimo!*" which meant, "I like it very much."

Ms. Maria and my uncle engaged in conversation as I started to explore this magnificent new place, making my way past the living room and approaching the staircase. Heading upstairs, I stopped at the top and gazed directly in front of me into the huge master bedroom. Sunlight peered through the windows above the bed and filled the room with warmth. I can still feel the heat from the sun just thinking about it.

Off to the right was the master bath with a walk-in shower. The walls were decorated with early metro style art that was simple yet stylish. After exploring the upstairs, I headed back down to where my uncle and Ms. Maria were still engaged in conversation.

"So, Alexandria, what do you think?" Uncle Nicholas looked up at me coming down the stairs.

"Are you kidding me? I absolutely love it, Uncle!"

"Then it's settled. Welcome to your new home."

"Really?"

"Yes, child, this is your new home. *Divertiti!*" which in Italian meant "enjoy!" "You deserve only the best! You, after all, are part of the Rozzito family."

I was in total shock that day. I couldn't stop thanking and hugging Uncle Nicholas. The ride home on the plane was fast, and I couldn't wait to get back from my trip to Paris. Come to think of it, I guess I had known about Sidney. Well, at least from being at the airport. Funny how I had blocked that out. But still, the connection with my uncle, a strip joint, and the Mafia was not coming together, and I quickly dismissed it.

The wind had picked up even stronger, jolting me out of my stupor of daydreaming about the past. I looked around me for my BlackBerry. Wow, forty-five minutes had gone by while

160

I had sat there reminiscing. I wasn't sure, but I knew we had to be close to Port Angeles by now.

I had no other choice but to focus. I reached down and picked up my backpack, unzipping the top to reveal the copy of the trial hearing. Reaching in to grab it, I noticed a shiny object lying on the bottom of the bag. I had no clue as to what it was until I picked it up and realized it was a watch.

"Where the hell did this come from?" I asked myself out loud.

Examining it, I knew it wasn't just a normal watch, as it looked very complex and expensive. I had no freaking clue how it had gotten in my bag, let alone whom it belonged to. Turning it over and looking underneath it, I saw a small etching of three words reading, "Never say anything."

Strange, if you ask me. I had no idea what the etched words meant. Then it dawned on me. I bet this was Beauford's missing watch. Still, if it was, how did it end up in my possession? Hmm, well, maybe he had put it there thinking I would call him back. If that was the case, he wasn't so geeky after all and was one point higher in my book. That would have been rather cleaver of him, and you know, it worked if it was true.

Putting the watch back in my backpack, I finally glanced at the papers. Laying them out on the table and trying to secure them against the strong wind, I read that Judge Northrup would be presiding, a middle-aged man in his late 50s, firm but fair. Today was my first case in front of Judge Northrup. I had heard rumors of his strict court proceedings and didn't take lightly to counsel not being prepared. I learned that piece of information from Tomas.

"Great, guess I'm screwed, and I didn't even get to enjoy it."

The case read that the trial hearing was between international governments and maritime against the company named...just then, the unthinkable happened. A gust of wind swooped in, and right before my eyes, all the case papers blew away, landing in the open water as I tried desperately to catch them, falling off my seat. Well, that surely sealed my fate. I was surely screwed now! Guess I would be winging it for real. Sheer nervousness overtook my body as I overheard the loudspeaker call out what I thought was my name.

Lifting my head and looking around, I thought I was just hearing things. Could have been just wind playing tricks on my ears. I could not believe what had just happened to me. Lying on the deck, I watched my papers drift away, just as my new career was about to do. I knew better than to attempt to look over the trial case papers outside in the wind, but it was just so nice out and relaxing there...well, it had been a few seconds ago.

Now what? I had barely processed any information past the judge's name and the parties involved. I gathered I was representing the international governments and maritime plaintiffs' party, but I never made it to the place that mentioned who the defending party was or even the person representing them.

"Are you all right?" A nearby female passenger came running over to see if I was all right.

"I'm OK."

"Are you hurt?"

"No, no, just my pride. I feel rather embarrassed that I fell right of this chair trying to catch the papers I was reading." I said, still sitting on my butt on the ground.

"Guess you didn't see the sign that said to hang on to your personal property next to the door to the indoor lobby."

"Guess not. I was in such a hurry to get aboard and make it out here, I never stopped and realized that there was a sign."

"Yeah, I made the same mistake just about a month ago. Here, let me help you up." I held out my arm as the passenger helped me to my feet.

"Thank you."

"No problem. It tends to get windy out here, especially today since the ferry is cruising a bit faster. You sure you're OK?"

"Positive. Thank you again for your help. My bottom will recover from the fall. Luckily for me, today I will be standing."

"Will an Alexandria Henson please come to the ship's Customs and Immigration area?" the loudspeaker boomed.

"Well, guess I wasn't imagining it. That's me. Thank you again."

I said my thanks, grabbed my backpack, and headed inside to the Customs and Immigration area near the front of the vessel. I was clueless as to why I would be getting a phone call from the ship, if that's what it was, and not through my BlackBerry. Fumbling through my bag, I found my phone next to the watch and retrieved it.

That explained why I didn't get a phone call on my smartphone. The damn thing was off. I guess my spare battery wasn't holding a charge. Oh boy, just my luck because I would be needing it later to call Daniele for lunch. Shoot, maybe I could charge it on the ride from the harbor to the airport once we arrived in Port Angeles.

I didn't realize how hard it was to walk from where I was to inside as I never did walk outside on the deck when she was moving at top speed. It kind of made me feel lightheaded and nauseous as I opened the door to go inside. Funny how your peripheral vision gets out of whack when you're not expecting it, but I felt fine now. And funny how just being inside for that split second, my body adapted, and I couldn't even tell the ship was moving unless I looked back outside.

I wondered who would be trying to reach me. The only thing I could think of was that something terrible had happened. Overwhelming thoughts about something having happened to my uncle flooded my head…a stroke or heart attack, possibly from all the bad food he ate, especially the fried foods. I felt awful that I hadn't called him, as I should have. Reaching the Customs and Immigration area, I approached the man behind the counter.

"Hello, I am Miss Henson."

As soon as I mentioned who I was, the phone rang. The counter attendant lifted his hand to motion me to wait one minute while he took the call. I felt very impatient standing there, waiting for what seemed to be longer than a minute, wondering about my uncle. Not to mention, it seemed as if he was just carrying on a normal conversation on the phone—he was smiling and laughed a few times. When I couldn't stand it any longer, I rudely interrupted him,

"Excuse me? Hello?"

"Hold on one second," he said to whomever he was talking to. Turning his attention to me, he said, "Can I help you, ma'am?"

"Yes, I am Alexandria Henson, the one you just paged over the loudspeaker."

"Ah yes. We've been trying to find you for the last five minutes."

"Really? I just heard it, like, a minute ago."

"Well, someone called and left you a message. Some fellow named Marcus. He wanted me to give this to you. He said he had been trying for the last hour to contact you."

"Thank you. My phone battery isn't holding a charge." I held my phone up to show him like some idiot, as if he even cared.

"Yeah, never cared for a BlackBerry. You really should consider getting a Samsung phone. Heard they're much more reliable, especially with the longevity of the battery." He handed me my message from Marcus, my limo driver, I said, "*Merci!*"

"*De rien!*" The man behind the counter didn't even sound like he meant it. He looked away from me and went right back to his call as if I wasn't there. Whatever!

The message read, *Miss Henson, I will not be able to meet you at Port Angeles to bring you to the airport due to maintenance issue with the limousine; however, I have called a taxi service, and they will be waiting there for you this morning.--Marcus.*

Great. Another taxi service. Couldn't wait. So far, I was zero for two that day, let alone that I didn't have cab fare. Now what? I would just have to have one of my uncle's staff from the Learjet pay the fare. At least I would be able to keep my last five dollars for a cup of coffee before I went to the courthouse later.

Walking away from the counter, I passed through the upper seating area. I could see we were very close to Port Angeles as the coastal line was visible. The long stretch of land that would guide us into harbor was just about in front of the ferry. As windy as it was, I wanted to go back outside and walk the front bow deck area of the Port Angeles ferry as the others are doing. That way, I could enjoy what was left of my morning and see the harbor from this view. I guess I should have been more active in watching the scenery instead of sitting down in the area behind me as in the past.

It was so much more exciting from up here, of course, as long as it wasn't raining. That tended to put a damper on things. As we got closer, the water was busy with several types of small vessels, not to mention a few oil liners to the side of us moving at what seemed to be a snail's pace. It wasn't long before we passed the spot where smokestacks used to line the coast and reached the dock area. The horns blew several times, signaling our arrival.

The three flags stood proudly on top of the metal loading dock, waving fiercely against the breeze. The Canada, the United States, and Washington state colors saluted us as the ferry slowly maneuvered in with such precision, reversing the huge propellers while once again churning the water as it slowly made its way to the dock. It was so gentle, you hardly even noticed the ferry had stopped as the sound of metal ringed the air from the manmade connecting ramp stretching over and into the open back door where I would be exiting.

Wow, OK, finding my taxi was going to be a bitch. There must have been at least twenty to thirty different taxi companies lined up as far as I could see, just waiting for passengers to get off. I hoped Marcus at least had told them my name so I didn't have to go chasing a taxi down. Not that it would matter one way or another; I would make it to the airport.

I should have been able to charge my phone on the way to the airport seeing how this spare battery had failed me. I think my cable was still in the backpack. If not, then I was really going to kick myself in the butt. I swear, I felt like I was on a downward spiral and just waiting to crash but for some reason was stuck in limbo. I just needed to get past the hearing, meet up with my BFF, and the rest would be history. Well, not exactly. I still needed to file the report from Wednesday night's ferry ordeal.

DEADLOCKED: A Trial Beginning

I felt as if I was forgetting something, but I couldn't put my finger on it. I was sure it would come to me when I least expected it. Anyway, it looked like it was time to make my way off the ferry and towards the taxis. I sure wished the limo would have been there. I could really have used the space to put up my feet since I was going to be in those Gucci shoes all day. What was I thinking wearing such high heels? They made me at least two inches taller. I so wanted my Prada boots back. I had just barely broken them in before all hell broke loose. I was making myself sick just thinking of that horrible, horrible image.

I didn't realize exactly how many people were on board, but from the lines that had already backed up, it was going to be a little while before my feet touched land. I tried to think that today was just another day, but it wasn't. Today was a trial for not only me, it seemed, but for the ferry as well, which had seemed to make remarkable time across the water. I was glad I chose this as part of my traveling to work each day.

Nothing could replace this experience, just sheer relaxation…of course, without the drama of being stupid and losing the most important item that I just happened to need. I should have just read over the damn case when I had had plenty of time to do so. Sometimes I just wanted to kick myself for procrastinating. My uncle had tried on several occasions to convince me to take a short hop on a seaplane from Victoria to here as it would be much faster, but I would dismiss it and roll my eyes. Too much flying would make me feel unsafe. I was just getting used to flying in a private jet, which still seemed like a flying coffin equipped with luxuries and perks to me. "Nothing but the best for my little Alex," is what my uncle would have said if he had been here standing in front of me.

I had to admit, all in all, all the luxury was nice, but sometimes I felt a little less of it would have been nice, too, and that is why I liked riding the ferry. It brought me back to a normal level. Of course, now with Pierre's boat, it would be the opposite, but wow, the *Victoria Cove* not only meant fast, but it had a touch of class, too. I couldn't wait to ride her again and take it all in. Next time, I wouldn't just rush in and find a seat to sleep in. You never knew what you would encounter or whom you would meet who would change a part of you.

Finally, the line was moving. I felt a sudden rush of adrenaline again as I knew I was one step closer to my debut, and I didn't want to think about it. I was either going to sink or swim later on today. I wondered if the courtroom had life rings to grab onto if I started to sink, or perhaps a defibrillator to jump-start my heart when it stopped and I passed out from locking my knees. I was talking silly to make light of my situation as I inched my way towards the open door. It was kind of a nervous tic of mine I had developed in law school even though I had aced my classes. Still, I wondered if it was a genetic thing passed down to me by my parents. Someday I was going to find out what really happened to my parents and why I was placed in the godforsaken orphanage.

One thing that still boggles my mind is why after so many years, my Uncle Nicholas looked for me. What was the reason for him to find me and take me in? Not that I'm complaining, but I never could get an answer from him as to why. He always seemed to walk his way around it with his words. I wasn't his responsibility; I was my parents'. There had to be some sort of last will my parents would have left, yet I barely could remember what my dad or mother looked like. Somehow, the crash must have jolted my memory, and that is why I couldn't recall much.

I do, however, sometimes have dreams and occasionally nightmares of a horrific car crash, yet I don't recognize the car or the place. It just comes and goes, but I do remember one thing about my dad: his aftershave. For some reason, I have this strong memory of the smell of English Leather, so strong it was over powering. Strange, though—in my dreams, I'm smelling the English Leather, but in the nightmares, all I can smell is an overly sweet scent similar to Old Spice, and I always wake up before getting to see who it is. Uncle Nicholas wears Old Spice from time to time, and when he does, it makes me feel sick, but I think it's just because he puts too much on. Older Italian men overcompensate with cologne or aftershave to cover up something. Uncle Nicholas does it because he says it makes him feel important. Still, I'm not able to make the connection, so I just leave it be and never question him.

Making my way down the dock towards the parking area, I scanned for my taxi. One of them had to be mine, and I was hoping the driver at least had a sign with my name on it. It looked as if it rained there that morning. I smirked. Glad I missed it! Not a good combination while wearing my six-hundred-dollar Gucci heels. I would not be breaking any heels and tossing these babies over the side of the boat, no sir!

Vehicles were already lined up to drive aboard the ferry as dock personnel tried to make some semblance of order. Horns beeped from with the lines. Sometimes that made me feel good that I didn't drive on a daily basis, but I sure did miss my 530i E60. I kept it at my uncle's place, and whenever I got to go home, I made sure I drove her. My Uncle Nicholas, of course, had bought it for me as a small token of his love for me. Well, it was more like he already had it, along with seven other luxury cars besides the limousines. It just so happened he asked me to choose one. Naturally, I chose the Beemer! A girl has to look good while styling and profiling. That was Daniele's line, but fitting.

I could not believe my eyes as I walked towards the lines of taxis wrapped around the docking area on both sides of

Olympic Discovery Trail. It looked like every driver was holding up a sign with names on it. *This should fun,* I thought. I was glad I usually had the pleasure of Marcus pulling up in the limo and taking me to the jet.

I walked past several drivers holding signs that read, "Patrice Migone," "Sarah Belle," and "Lucas Rene," yet so far none were for me. I could feel the sun beating down on the back of my head as I strolled down the street in heels. The heat was making my clothes stick to my body, and I hate that feeling. I came upon an Indian taxi driver who just stared at me as I passed him. He was holding a sign that read, "Alissa H." Could this have been my ride? I decided to keep walking, staring back at him standing still there, waiting for his passenger to arrive. I came to the end of the street just before it turned left, and there were no more taxis in line. In fact, all but one was left, and it was the little Indian dude. This had to be my ride, so I headed back towards him.

I could feel the wetness building on the hair on my neck as I came back to the taxi driver. To my surprise, another woman had approached him, and it looked like they were verbally sparring. As I came upon them, I realized I was right. She had tried to hire the taxi, and the Indian driver was refusing. It made sense seeing how it must have been mine.

"Look, this taxi is empty, and I need to get to airport to make my flight, please."

"I am sorry, but this taxi is already reserved for someone else, so kindly back away."

"If I may be of some help..." I tried to intervene in the conversation.

"Look, please step back away," the driver said to me.

"I think you've got it all wrong." I again made an effort to break up the conversation.

"You heard the man. Back off, sister. This is my cab."

"If you hussies don't step back, I am going to have to go all Gandhi on your ass, so please step back so I don't have to."

"All Gandhi on my ass? Really? Is that the best line you got? Gandhi on my ass, wow! That doesn't even make sense." I was holding back from laughing. I couldn't believe this man had tried to use an ethnic reference on me and the other woman.

"OK, listen, it's obvious you're waiting for someone important, and that person is probably me, so let's just end this now because I'm getting hot and sweaty standing here, and I really, really don't need this. However, it's quite funny if you ask me, but that name is wrong. Don't you mean you're waiting for Alex Henson and not Alissa?"

"Who is Alissa?" the driver responded.

"Just what I thought. You were dispatched here by a man named Marcus right?"

"Yes, Marcus, yes, yes."

"I am your passenger."

"Good, good. OK, please, let's go."

I could see the disappointment on the woman's face as I opened the door and climbed in. The Indian driver had gotten back in the taxi and was about to pull away when I asked him to wait. "Wait, we can't just leave her here. She needs a ride, and I'm going to the same place."

"I am afraid I will have to charge double if she rides, too."

"Whatever. Just please roll down the window."

The woman had stepped back, and I knew she really needed a ride. I couldn't just leave because I knew she had to get to the airport, too. Besides, maybe since she needed the ride so badly, she would bail me out of my fare since I didn't have enough to pay him.

"Hey, let's make a deal," I shouted to the woman. "Since this is my ride and we're going to the same place, how about you pay for both of us, and that way we both make our flights and everyone is happy?" I turned my head around back into the taxi and asked, "Hey, driver, how much would it be for the both of us?"

"Forty dollars."

"Forty dollars? Isn't that a little steep for only ten minutes for two people?"

"Look, lady, I have a wife and three kids to feed. Take it or leave it."

"Hold on. Let me see if she'll go for it. What a rip-off, if you ask me." I turned around as the driver watched me from the rearview mirror, tapping his fingers against the steering wheel.

"Would you be willing to pay for both of us in exchange for the ride? The driver says forty bucks."

I guess she was OK with it because she grabbed her luggage. She struggled as she rounded the back of the car and to the other side. Her luggage was quite large, so if she put it in the backseat with me, it was going to be cramped. She opened the door, tried to lift the bag, barely could get it up, and tried to shove it in. She only got resistance, as the opening was too narrow.

"This isn't going to work, and time is of the essence," I said. "Why don't you get out and help her like a normal taxi driver would and put it in the trunk?"

"I'm sorry, but if I do that, I would throw my back out and be out of work. I have a wife and four kids."

"I know, I know, a wife and three kids to feed. You made that clear already. Hey, wait a second, you just said you had three kids, and now it's four."

172

"Yes, that is true. I have a child with another woman, too, so I have four kids, so you understand."

Yeah, right, was all I could think. I understood that I was being played for a fool. It looked like if I was going to make my flight, which should have been at the airport by now, I was going to have to help this woman with her luggage. Miguel didn't like burning extra fuel waiting on me; my uncle probably kept a tight grasp on how much fuel was being used and how much it cost.

"Fine, you sit there, and I'll help her. Pop the trunk. Can you handle that, or will you break a finger?"

"I can do that."

The trunk opened as the woman gave up trying to push the luggage into the backseat, where it wasn't going to go. I looked over at her and said, "Wait, let me help you put it in the trunk." I got out of the backseat and walked behind the car to the trunk. Opening the trunk, I helped lift the luggage into it. That thing must have weighed over a hundred pounds. We shoved it slowly into the trunk.

"What you got in there, sister, a dead body?" I joked as I caught my breath.

"Why, does it feel like one?"

"Um, well, I was merely making a reference to the weight of the luggage, that's all."

"Shh, don't tell anyone, but I did something terrible, and now I'm on my way back home."

The woman walked away and got back into the car. I hesitated for a second and poked the luggage to feel for an actual dead body before closing the trunk. *Great. What have I done? Did I just invite a killer to ride with me? What if inside that luggage is a real dead body. What is she going to do with it? Why not dispose of it rather than bring it with you? Why am I attracting this kind of thing?*

173

I got back into the car, and we drove off. For a few moments, I didn't say anything. I avoided eye contact with her, but she turned to me and introduced herself.

"Hi, my name is Kathryn Wells, from Rogue River Valley."

"Oh, hi. Alex." I hesitated to respond but did.

"Alex? Do you have a last name?"

"Yes, of course. Henson." I didn't want to reveal my last name in case she truly had killed someone. I felt it was best to not go there. "Rogue River Valley? Where is that?"

"Oregon. You know, that little state below Washington. The one people always refer to as the stepchild state. Or sort of like an older child wanting to still live with its parents sand mooch off them. Well, that's sort of like Oregon."

"I'm sorry. I'm not making the connection."

"No worries. It doesn't matter."

Suddenly, the taxi made a loud bumping noise as if it had run over something. It sent me out of my seat, and I grabbed the side of the door and whatever else I could grab onto.

"Oh my God, what was that? You really did kill someone, didn't you?"

"What? No."

"Then explain that noise coming from the back. You must have not killed that person all the way, and they're trying to get out." Scared, I moved towards the door to get away from her.

"Oh, girl, you really have an overactive imagination. It's just my luggage bouncing against the trunk as driver up there hit something in the road."

"Yes, yes, I hit a bump. Sorry. Please go on. Tell us what is in the bag."

"How about you pay attention to the road?" I said in a high-pitched voice.

"It's all right," Kathryn said to me. "If you can keep a secret, I'll tell you what's in the bag."

"OK, I guess." I still was not too sure I wanted to hear this.

"It's Tom."

"Tom? Tom, as in a man?"

"Girl, do I look like a killer to you? I could barely lift my luggage let alone kill some man. No, for goodness' sake. Tom is my pet python. My ex stole him from me and ran off to Port Angeles with my best friend Sally. That dang bitch double-crossed me, so I went after Tom. I couldn't care less about my ex and ex-best-friend."

"Wait, so what you're telling me is that there is a live snake in a suitcase and I just touched it?"

"Well, yes, and no, you didn't actually touch him."

"Wow. I poked your bag and could've sworn it moved, but I thought it was my imagination. Holy shit!"

"You can say that again. Tom is heavy."

"*Pavitra bakavāsa!*" The driver, looking back at us, repeated the words "holy shit!" in his native New Delhi tongue.

Kathryn and I looked at each other with eyes wide open, and within seconds we started giggling, which turned to hard laughter that made my stomach hurt. It was hilarious how the drive said it. It was truly funny. I think we offended him because he frowned at us with his eyes and started to pout, mumbling underneath his breath.

"I'm sorry. I didn't mean to laugh, honest, but the way you said 'holy shit' in your language just seemed funny!" Kathryn said as she opened her eyes wide smirking while looking over at Alex.

"Everyone makes fun of me. You will see. I will be a star one day as my voice is like when the beast met beauty."

"Uh, when what met what?" I did not see the relevance and responded awkwardly.

"Come on, you know, beast and beauty."

I looked at Kathryn. She too was confused and shrugged her shoulders. I had no idea where this guy was coming from, and it showed in my facial responses, but it suddenly dawned on me.

"I get it. You mean *Beauty and the Beast*."

"Yes, yes, I said that."

"No, what you said was..."

Kathryn reached over and grabbed my arm. She shook her head at me slightly to stop me from engaging him any further since it didn't matter. I looked back at her and rolled my eyes as if I thought this guy was a whack job.

"When both of them met, it was magic, yes?"

"Yeah, I guess you can say that."

"That is me. I come from my country to the United States of America to sing just like them. It was magic."

I couldn't help but smirk and laugh silently. I looked at Kathryn, and she was thinking the same thing as I was: this guy was talking about singing, yet he couldn't even speak the English language well. I didn't mean to, but I was stereotyping him and judging him without even hearing this poor guy sing. That was definitely not the way my uncle had raised me, and he would have been angry at me for my actions just now, but I couldn't help it. I was going to have to hear him sing to get past this.

"I try out for that show *American Idol* today when they come to town."

"Wow, don't you think you have to have a good voice in order to try out?"

176

"You don't believe me, do you?"

"Well, kind of not. I guess I don't see it."

"Well, hell. I'll even pay you an extra forty to hear you sing." Kathryn jumped in and tried to encourage him. "I can sure use another laugh. What's your name, anyway?"

"Sudhir Shindi."

"I don't think we need to hear you sing," I said.

"Oh, relax, Alex. Besides, we can use another laugh." Kathryn leaned in and whispered to me.

"So, yes? You like to hear me sing?"

"Deal!" Kathryn reached out with her hand and shook him on it.

"So, Sudhir, looks like we're almost to the airport. What are you going to sing for us?" Kathryn said leaned forward towards the driver.

"Dire Straits."

"Dire Straits? Oh boy, this is going to definitely make my stomach hurt," I said, leaning back in my seat.

"OK, Sudhir, what song?" Kathryn egged him on.

"I have a tape right here with just the music to 'Money for Nothing.' Yes, you ready?"

"I want my MTV song?" Kathryn said with a look of disbelief.

"Yes, yes." Replied Sudhir.

"Go for it." I didn't say a word as Kathryn gave him the OK to put the tape in and sing.

Sudhir put the tape in the cassette player, and the music started playing for a few seconds before he started to sing the lyrics to the song. He sang along to the music and sounded just like the singer. In fact, I couldn't tell them apart. That is how good he sang.

Wow, I was freaking floored. There was no laughing coming from Kathryn or me. We just looked at one another in awe as Sudhir blew us away with his voice. He truly was right, it was *Beauty and the Beast*, yet in this case it was his voice that was beauty and we were the beasts. He sang on and on with every line until the song finished. I couldn't move. I was frozen in my seat and speechless.

Then I heard claps coming from Kathryn. She was so excited and overjoyed that Sudhir's voice was spot on and that he sounded just like the lead singer from Dire Straits. I began to clap to with an overwhelming sensation, too, as my eyes got misty. I felt like a horrible person for prejudging Sudhir. This was such an inspiration. I wiped the tears away from my eyes. *Wow* is all I could think of to sum up his singing. The taxi pulled into the entrance to the William Fairchild International Airport, and Sudhir made his way towards the main gate. This is where my limousine would pull up near Uncle Nicholas's Learjet.

I could see the Learjet must have just landed as it was taxiing towards us. Sudhir put the car in park. I looked over to Kathryn and said, "Kathryn, it was a pleasure riding with you, and thank you again for covering my fare. I didn't really have money for the fare. I was going to ask one of my uncle's staff to pay him when they arrived in the jet. Here is my business card. If you ever need someone to talk to, give me a ring." I pulled out a business card from my purse and handed it to Kathryn.

"Lawyer. Well, that explains the way you're dressed."

"Too much, huh?"

"Just a tad, but you know what girl? You make the outfit work, got to hand it to you there."

"Well, thanks, Kathryn. Hope you and Tom live happily ever after, too."

"We will."

I closed the door, said goodbye to Kathryn, and walked to Sudhir's window.

"Sudhir, I just wanted to apologize for laughing at you. That was very immature and wrong of me. I'm sorry."

"That is OK. Make sure you watch the show this weekend. I will make it, I promise."

"I'll try, and I have no doubt you will blow them away as you did us. Thank you. You've made my day."

Sudhir dropped me off and made his way to another destination spot for Kathryn as I watched the Learjet pull up near me and come to a halt. Looking at the huge outside clock hanging above the terminal doors, I could see it was just about eight-thirty. The main door was unlocked, and Gianna lowered the door, revealing the steps on the other side. She waved to me in greeting as I walked over to the stairs when Miguel the pilot appeared and walked down the stairs.

"Ah, Miss Henson, good morning."

"Good morning, Miguel." I kissed both sides of his face, greeting him. "How're the skies today?"

"Smooth as a baby's bottom."

"OK, that sounds good to me. Quite a comparison there, Miguel."

"We will be leaving in about five minutes."

"Sounds good. Hey, does Gianna have her coffee going? I could use a cup right about now."

"Yes, already brewed to your liking."

"Excellent, Miguel."

"Oh, Alex, there is something you should know. Your uncle is on board waiting for you this morning."

"What? Are you freaking kidding me?"

"No, I am quite sure it's your uncle as well as his friend."

"His friend? Who? Which one?"

179

"Mr. Bonnachi."

"Great. I don't care much for him. Gives me the creeps. Something about his stare."

"The feeling is mutual, but nevertheless, your uncle insisted on seeing you since you never called him when you came back from Paris, and you never called us as we waited here for you."

"I meant to call him. I just forgot, and I am sorry. I just wanted to take the ferry from Seattle to home after that long trip."

"Well, no worries now. Just make sure you let us know in advance next time. You know how your uncle hates wasting money, if you get my drift."

"All too much."

"And by the way, *piace bella!*," which meant "you look beautiful."

"*Grazie*, Miguel. Don't let your wife, Lina, hear you say that around me. She might get jealous. Just kidding!"

Miguel took off his captain's hat and bowed for a second in front of me before walking towards the terminal entrance of the William Fairchild building.

"Hey, Miguel, what is his mood?"

"Meh. He seems fine, but he has had a couple of glasses of wine already. Don't worry, he loves you. He just wants you safe."

"*Grazie*." I thanked Miguel again as I walked up the stairs to the Learjet entrance. I smiled and greeted Gianna, who was standing there waiting for me.

Chapter Ten
Family Bonding

Clearing the patch of trees to the opening landscape, Vincenzo began to lower the A109 Agusta helicopter to Rozzito's landing pad inside his private courtyard. Nicholi and Bobby didn't even speak an ounce of words to one another the whole trip back from their excursion. The sun was just now rising enough to blind Bobby as he opened his eyes to see that they had made it back to the compound.

Rozzito gave Bobby instructions to lie low until he returned and to keep Nicholi close by because he would be meeting with both of them later on that day to discuss the contract that needed to be collected on. On the way over to meet with his niece, Rozzito had discovered that the one person he trusted the most had betrayed him and jeopardized his criminal regime.

"OK, boys, time to get off." Vincenzo looked back at Bobby and Nicholi to let them know it was now safe to depart the helicopter.

"Finally!" Nicholi pulled his door open and jumped out.

Bobby did the same from his side as Vincenzo powered down the Agusta. Walking around the front of the helicopter to catch up to Nicholi, Bobby wanted to make sure he wasn't going to take off anywhere.

"Hey, Mr. Rozzito wants us to lie low here at the compound, so no running off, you hear me?"

Nicholi didn't respond. Bobby hated being ignored and started to walk faster towards him, shouting at him this time.

"Hey, I said Mr. Rozzito said to stick around here and not go anywhere, so you'd better do as he says." Bobby grabbed Nicholi's arm to get his attention.

To his surprise, the little punk wasn't even listening because he had on earphones, listening to music. Nicholi reacted to Bobby in a violent way, pulling back his arm and turning around as if ready to brawl.

Bobby reached in and pulled one side of the earphones off, restraining Nicholi with his other hand still firmly around the arm. Nicholi tried to retract, but Bobby held him and yelled, "Can you hear me now?"

"Take it easy. Chill out."

"No, you chill out. That's what Mr. Rozzito has requested for both of us to do, so no going off right now."

"Look, I have to go wind down a bit with my buddies. Relax, I'll be back in an hour or two. Besides, Mr. Rozzito won't be back for some time."

"Yeah, well, you'd better, or it's your ass on the line. Don't think because you finally got what he was asking for that you're off the hook. He wants to meet with us when he returns and wants to speak to you. Where did you get that music device?"

"I've had it. It's mine."

"Yeah, right, you've had it. You jumped off an f'in' moving boat into the water and this device survived?"

"Yeah, it did. What about it?"

"You took it from her place, didn't you?"

"No."

"Let me see it." Bobby pulled it out of Nicholi's coat pocket, and seeing that it looked very new, he turned it over. It had an inscription on it that read, *"Per la mia bella ragazza, amore zio Rozzito."*

"You little shit, this reads, 'To my beautiful girl, Love, Uncle Nicholas.'" Bobby was getting agitated at Nicholi for taking Alexandria's personal belongings.

"Get rid of it. If Mr. Rozzito catches you with it, you're a dead man."

"All right, calm down. I will. Back off."

"Just you don't go too far, and be back before he gets here."

"Tell me, mister, I cut your thumbs off and shoved them up your nose, what he wants to talk about. You realize that your signature move is really amateurish?" Nicholi was acting all cocky towards Bobby, trying to get his goat by insulting him.

"I see what you're trying to do, you little pissant mother fucker! Not going to work. You're trying to get my blood pressure up. Not going to work, kid."

Nicholi started to grin and laugh at Bobby as well as Vincenzo, who happened to be walking by both of them.

"Shut your mouth!" Bobby yelled at Vincenzo.

"Easy, now. You know he's just trying to get you pissed off. Looks like someone needs a nap."

Bobby's blood pressure had risen so far from the insults that he went to kick a statue that was next to them in the courtyard out of frustration, but he ended up missing completely and slipping on the freshly watered grass, falling on his butt.

Nicholi, Vincenzo, and other staff members of Rozzito belted out laughing.

This infuriated Bobby as he tried to get up and slipped again, plunging his face into the grass. Nicholi waved his hands at him, said goodbye, and walked inside. Jonnie, one of Rozzito's foot soldiers, happened to be outside and witnessed this act. He walked over to Bobby and offered to help him up. Bobby, embarrassed, told him to leave him alone as he stood up by himself.

"What you all looking at? Don't any of you repeat what you just saw!" Bobby was screaming towards Vincenzo and the others as he tried desperately to make himself look presentable as the capo. He pushed Jonnie aside as he made his way towards the house. As Bobby entered the house and closed the door, they all started to laugh out loud because it was funny seeing their captain acting stupid.

Bobby, on the other hand, had had enough and turned back around, reached down, and pulled a little .22 caliber out of his ankle holster and went back outside to say his piece. The door swung open as he bolted outside, pointing his gun and popping off a few rounds towards the ground.

"Yeah, not so funny now, is it? Stugots!" Bobby looked around, calling all of them pricks for laughing.

No one made a move as Bobby stood there waving his gun around, reminding them who he was and for them to respect him.

"Thought so," said Bobby.

Turning around, Bobby walked back in the house and slammed the door. Nicholi had left the house and headed into town to meet up with some friends, which would be revealed later on not to be a wise choice.

****

I boarded the plane, greeting Gianna. Looking towards the center of the plane, I didn't see my uncle, only the top of Donnie's head.

"Hello, Gianna. Where's my uncle?"

"Perhaps using the little boy's room." Gianna turned around to look for Rozzito, too. "Would you like a cup of coffee before we take off?"

"Oh yes, please. You read my mind."

"I'll bring it to you after you're seated."

"Thank you, Gianna."

I smiled at her and walked towards the middle of the plane, past Donnie as I placed my backpack on the ground in front of the seat kitty-corner from him. For a moment, before noticing me, Donnie was wrapped up in reading the *Vancouver Sun* newspaper that he had brought aboard.

Sitting down, I could tell Donnie had not noticed me yet and figured that was a good thing. Something about him just made me feel icky inside, and I was quite glad he had his eyes glued to his newspaper. Getting myself situated before takeoff, I decided it was best to plug in my BlackBerry to charge it. I bet I had a few voice messages that I'd missed. Gianna walked up to me with my hot cup of coffee and set it on the built-in side table.

"Oh, thanks, Gianna." I cupped the coffee with my hands and leaned in to smell the aroma.

"Mmm, now that smells good."

"*Grazie.*"

Donnie, realizing that I had come aboard, raised his head above the top of the newspaper and then began to fold it down as he welcomed me. I could see he was looking at me and tried to keep focused on the cup of coffee as he said hello.

"Ah, *Bongiorno*, Miss Henson."

"Hello, Mr. Bonnachi."

"I hear from your uncle that today is a big day for you, yes?"

"Yes, today is a very big day for me. Um, have you seen my Uncle Nicholas?"

"I see your manners have not changed as you have aged. Always changing the subject."

I didn't care to respond and decided to mix my coffee with the fresh creamer and sugar instead in hopes of avoiding much dialogue with Donnie. I knew he wouldn't just sit back and ignore me; he always felt compelled to make it known he was around you.

"So, Alex, tell me, do you have what it takes to be a lawyer?

Just then, Gianna stood between Donnie and me, smiling at me. It was time to depart as Miguel had made his way back aboard and the main door was closed. I knew she was standing there to distract Donnie from engaging me for a few minutes so we could take off.

"We're ready to take off, so please make sure you have your safety belts on."

Silently, I mouthed her, "Thank you." She blinked her left eye and made her way back to the front to sit down. It looked like my uncle would have to wait until we were in flight to join us. At least if he was here, Donnie wouldn't even try speaking to me.

I watched Donnie sit back in his seat, yet his eyes focused on mine, and it dawned on me why I didn't care for him. His eyes squinted and twitched every ten seconds or so when he would focus on me. I wasn't sure if that was a tic or a disease that he had, but I sure didn't care at all for it. Just then, Captain Miguel Bonachelli came across on the intercom.

"Welcome aboard again, Miss Henson. On behalf of Mr. Rozzito and my staff, we welcome you and look forward to

186

serving you each day. We should be airborne momentarily, and the flight duration should take only roughly thirty-five minutes. Sit back and enjoy the flight. *Ciao!*"

We taxied out onto the runway and waited for a few minutes as I looked out the side window. There was a plane ahead of us waiting for takeoff. From what I could see, it looked like an old dual prop plane, huge in size. Within seconds, I saw black smoke shoot out both of the engines as the plane revved up and slowly crept away from us down the runway. Miguel rounded to the left, positioning us for takeoff.

I just wanted to close my eyes and relax. Taking off was not my favorite part of riding a plane. Donnie just stared at me with a grin on his face. A second later, I looked to my side and saw we had started to move. As the engines got loud and pushed me back in my seat a bit, we hurtled down the runway and lifted off the ground. This sucker was fast getting in the air. It was going to take me a few rides to get used to that.

It wasn't long before we leveled off. I could see in Donnie's eyes that he still was looking for an answer to his stupid question, so I decided to go against my better judgment and reply to him.

"I think I will be able to hold my own, if that answers your question. I was top of my class."

"Perhaps. You do know that your uncle despises..."

"Despises what?" Nicholas had appeared from the lavatory just as Donnie was about to tell me that my uncle didn't like the fact I was going to be practicing law, but Rozzito interrupted him.

"Uncle Nicholas!" I was so glad to see my uncle. I stood up and hugged him.

"Ah, my wonderful niece, who happened to almost give your uncle a heart attack wondering about you."

"I'm sorry. I meant to call you, but it was late and my phone wasn't working."

"Yes, but that was two days ago."

"I'm really sorry, Uncle Nicholas. I just had a lot going on."

Donnie clenched his teeth and didn't say a word. Nicholas gave him the head nod for him to get up and go to the back of the plane so he could be alone with me.

"Just remember, I love you and just wanted to make sure you were safe. I got a call from Miguel Wednesday night stating you had not arrived, so I began to worry."

"I took the ferry from Seattle to Victoria. I just needed some alone time."

Nicholas looked at her since he knew exactly where she had been but pretended to be concerned. "Are you OK?"

"Yes, I'm fine. Why do you ask?"

"I received a call from Tomas the other night saying that someone had crashed in front of your place, and you called him but not me. You know that hurt me."

I felt betrayed by Tomas as I specifically had asked him not to say a word to my uncle about the crash and break-in, but maybe he didn't know about the break-in. I could see in his eyes he was upset, but I felt if I leaned in and hugged him, he would forget about it, so I did. He responded by hugging me back as well, and I thought for a second it was behind us, but it wasn't.

"Are you in some kind of trouble?"

"No, why do you ask that?"

"What's that scarf around your neck for?"

I had totally forgotten that I had wrapped a scarf around my neck to hide the cut mark the stranger left on me from his knife. I tried quickly to think of something to diffuse this, but my Uncle Nicholas caught me off guard when he had asked me something totally not even close to what happened.

"Is that a hickey?"

"Yes. Yes, it is, and I didn't want to alarm you, so I covered it up." Wow, did I just get lucky. However, I knew what was coming next.

"You know how I feel about you and boys."

"I do, but I think you're going to like this one. And in fact, this weekend he's coming over to my place for a get-together with a friend, and I wanted to later on come to your place in Vancouver so you could meet him."

"I'd rather you didn't."

"Oh, Uncle, he's harmless. He's kind of geeky. Beauford is a microbiologist."

"What the hell kind of name is that?" Uncle Nicholas spit out his words as I almost choked on my coffee. It almost came out my nose because I had thought the same thing when I had first heard his name.

"I felt the same way, too, when he told me, but I really like him. So, I really would like you to meet him."

"Maybe some other time, Alexandria. This weekend, I have an important business meeting."

"OK, I just thought we could spend some time together since I've been gone for a couple of weeks. I love my new place, but I miss home."

"I thought this is what you wanted. You argued with me to be on your own and to pursue college, even though it isn't the kind of degree I wanted you to earn."

"Yeah, I know, Uncle. It's just that it's finally becoming a reality and well, I'm kind of nervous and scared."

"I told you how I felt about your becoming a lawyer, but you insisted on it. I even went as far as putting in a good word for you against my better judgment."

"You always told me to aim high, so I did. This is what I want to do, and thank you for providing me the means to do so. I guess its just pre-jitters, cold feet."

Gianna walked up and politely interrupted our conversation to see if I needed my coffee topped off. Looking down at my cup, I decided I'd better not.

"Thanks, Gianna, but I'll pass. I'm good for now. I'm sure I'll get a cup before I head into the courthouse."

Gianna just stared at me because she had never known for me to pass on coffee, but I was already wired beyond my means.

"Is there something wrong with it?"

"Oh no. I just feel if I drink too much, I might overload and pop!"

"Well, we surely don't need that. Are you finished with your coffee, then?"

"Not yet. Still nursing this one. Thanks, though."

Gianna smiled and looked at Nicholas. He nodded his head to let her know he didn't need anything, either. She walked back towards the galley. It was true; I was a little nervous, but that was mainly because I wasn't prepared for the hearing. Stupid wind, stupid me.

I must have said it out loud, as Uncle Nicholas responded to me, saying, "What was that, Alex?"

"Uh, nothing, just talking to myself." I turned my head towards the window.

"So, today is the big day. You ready?"

I didn't answer him and just sat there moving my lips from side to side to side. "Ready? That's a big word," I eventually said.

"What's the trial all about?"

"I have to admit, I have no clue. Not like me, huh?"

"Oh, Alex, tell me why not."

"It's a long story, but on the way over here, I was sitting outside on the ferry and was about to read the case, and the wind came in and blew the papers overboard. All I got out of it was the judge's name. Guess I'm not as perfect as I thought I was."

"That's all right, honey."

Nicholas felt relieved when he realized that there must have been two copies of the trial papers and he now held the only copy that revealed his snitch. A devilish grin started to form on his face, but he quickly withdrew it.

"I'll just have to go in and wing it and pray that it works."

"Listen, it's your first day. I'm sure they will understand, and maybe they will delay it since you aren't ready."

"Well, that would look terrible on my part. No, I must try my best anyway."

Nicholas was quite happy that Alex wasn't prepared and had no clue about the case and his involvement with allegations against his criminal business. Inadvertently, he had gotten his way. Just a little help from Mother Nature had helped seal the deal.

The Learjet had begun its descent when Miguel came back on the intercom. "We have started our descent towards Seattle and should be on the ground in less than twenty minutes."

Wow, this flight didn't take long at all. I could see through the clouds now as I looked out the window. The land and water were very visible. Donnie made his way towards us. He leaned in to whisper in Uncle Nicholas's ear. I could see him looking at me the whole time and made me feel that terrible feeling again. What was with this guy? I knew he was one of my uncle's friends and business partners, but man, he sure put off a persona of a bad guy, if you asked me. My uncle nodded his head as if to say yes and then waved Donnie off with his hand before turning his attention back to me.

"You're going to have to excuse me, Alexandria. I have an important call to take. I'm sorry, but you must understand; your uncle is a busy man these days."

"Oh, OK. I understand." I stood up and hugged my uncle, kissing him on both cheeks as he caressed my face.

"Good luck today. Call me over the weekend and let me know how it turned out, yes?"

"I will. I'll try this weekend. I'm pretty busy myself with being invited to a party back in Victoria."

"That's right, you did mention something about attending a party. Hmm, anyone I know?"

"I don't think so. Just some older guy I met on the ferry on my way back the other night. Seems he owns it. His name is Mr. Gustave, a very nice person. Anyway, he invited me and a guest to his party on his yacht, and I thought, why not?"

"Never heard of him. Well, be careful. You can never be too sure." Rozzito responded, as he knew exactly who Pierre was.

"You're such a worrywart."

"You're my little niece. Uncles are supposed to worry."

"That's why I love you so much. Now, go before they hang up on you."

"Yes, you are quite right. You must stop by soon at the restaurant so I can have them serve up your favorite. *Ciao,* Alexandria." Uncle Nicholas kissed me as he walked towards the back of the plane to his private office with Donnie falling behind him. Donnie turned around before closing the door and winked at me. Chills ran up and down my spine as I shook it off and sat back down. I could see we were moments away from touching down as the Seattle skyline was just below the left wing. Miguel banked left and lined up for approach.

Gianna came by to collect my empty coffee cup. I smiled at her, and she smiled back. I noticed that my uncle had left rolled-up papers with dried blood on them lying against the back portion of his seat. I went to reach for them because my curiosity got the better of me. Something about the papers seemed all too familiar as I tried to get a closer look, but I couldn't since Gianna picked them up, looked at me, and then turned away, concealing them. I could have sworn they looked like court papers.

Chapter Eleven
Butterfly Affect

    Seattle's harbor was buzzing with vessels coming and going. We were low enough now, crossing over the water that stretched from Bainbridge Island to Harbor Island, where I had taken the ferry home last Wednesday. The plane started to bank right. Looking down now out the window at the water, I spotted the *Victory Cove* leaving Seattle and heading out into Puget Sound. I would really have liked to be there instead of on the plane, but it was time to earn my rightful place as a lawyer and see if what I had been taught was worth it all.

    Vibrating sounds from my BlackBerry lying on the table startled me. I could see my phone displaying a hundred percent charge on the screen as I unplugged it, thank God. It was Daniele; she had sent me a text message wishing me good luck. I needed all the luck I could get. Too bad there wasn't any fairy dust to sprinkle on me so I could fly away or a magical potion to drink to give me knowledge of all things. I guess I was stuck being an adult. Such a rip-off, growing up. Whose idea was it for people to get older and take on life? We should have the option to stay young.

Thoughts flooded my head as we leveled off and touched down. A few short taps of the brakes and the sound of reverse thrusting, and we were slowing down to a crawl. I began to shake my hands rapidly while breathing in and out, hoping to slow my heart rate from being nervous all of a sudden. I wondered if Daniele could possibly have gotten someone to e-mail me the trial papers. At least that way, I could have had some sort of idea of what to expect. I could barely hold my BlackBerry as both my hands shook, but I managed to reply back to her asking for help.

She was either going to say yes or she was going to yell at me for not being prepared. She was a perfectionist, and I couldn't imagine her thinking I wasn't, not to mention I had lost confidential trial papers not once but twice. A minute later, my phone began to vibrate again as I held it.

Yes, she had been able to swindle someone to send them to me, and I should be getting a copy in my e-mail within the next ten minutes. I would owe her big time for it. She would talk more over lunch. *Boy, did I dodge a bullet, sort of,* I thought as I closed my eyes and kept them closed until I felt the plane stop.

I could see out the window that my ride was there as Michael my driver waved and smiled at me. Waving back, I unbuckled myself and stood up. I looked back behind me, hoping to see if my uncle would come out the door, but he didn't. I would have liked to have said goodbye, but I knew my uncle was busy. I gathered my belongings and headed towards Gianna, who was standing at the opened door and ready for me to depart.

The cockpit door was open, and I could see Miguel as well as Angelo, his co-pilot, talking amongst each other, probably about airplane stuff. I walked up to Gianna and leaned my head into the cockpit. I wanted to say thank you to them both.

"Thank you two for such a smooth flight."

"It is our pleasure, Miss Henson. Will you be joining us later today?"

"Yes, I should be down with my case this afternoon and should be ready to board to go home around five-thirty as long as it goes smoothly. I have a few errands to take care of before Michael brings me back here, but I should be ready then."

"Good, good. We have a busy schedule today with Mr. Rozzito, but you can count on us being here at that time."

"Thank you. Well, wish me luck."

Both Miguel and Angelo wished me luck, and Gianna smiled at me while saying, "Break a leg." I looked at the stairs and my heels and said back to her, "Let's just hope these heels don't break, girl, or that might come true for real." I stepped down the stairs towards my limo. Michael had already opened the back door and was waiting for me as I walked over to the car. I checked my e-mail to see if a message had arrived with my case, but nothing.

"Good morning, Miss Henson."

"Hey, Michael, good morning."

"So, today is the big one, huh?"

"Yep, today is the big day. Not sure I'm ready, though."

"It's your first day. You'll do fine."

Smiling at Michael, I climbed into the backseat as he closed the door. Getting into the driver's seat, Michael rolled down the privacy window and asked where I would be going. I felt like telling him anywhere but where I needed to be, but I told him King County Courthouse. I looked again at my BlackBerry as if something had changed since the last time I looked three minutes ago, but the light still blinked green, and the time now showed nine-twenty-two. Just a little over a half hour before my debut.

"Come on. Come on!" I was staring at my Blackberry, talking to it.

"Is everything al; right?" Michael responded as he watched me yell at my device.

"Sorry. Must look a little weird for someone to be yelling at her phone."

"Well, some might think so, but your secret is safe with me." Michael, trying to make me feel better, offered up a little humor.

"Thanks. I was hoping for an e-mail that I'm waiting for, and if this damn green light would turn to red, it would make me feel a lot better."

"Have you had your morning coffee? I see you don't have one in your hand."

"I've had several cups, but I could go for cup of Seattle's Best."

"Well, I'm fresh out of that, but if you check the cooler, I have a few cold bottles of Poland Springs."

Water is not my thing, but since that was all that was available for me at the time, I decided to grab a bottle. Something about bottled water or water in general just seemed too boring to me. It didn't take long before we started to see Seattle out the window as the limo made its way in and out of traffic.

I could see the skyline of downtown in the distance. Standing tall against the backdrop of mountains was the iconic Space Needle, a symbol of Seattle. Majestic the city was, the crown jewel of the Pacific Northwest and home to more than half a million people. Also, known as the gateway to Alaska, Seattle is a vibrant city full of life. Off to my left, I could see the world headquarters of Amazon.com sitting high atop Beacon Hill.

A former Marine hospital in the 1930s dominates this landscape. Seattle has lots of history tied to her, and one more event would be added to it once I was done with my hearing. Like that would be counted as history, but in a way, yeah. Moving further along up the road, I could see the Landmark Sears Building, which now is the world headquarters of Starbucks Coffee. I love my coffee, but nothing beats a good ole' cup of Merl's Devil's Blood. I certainly didn't need any of that fancy hard-to-pronounce foo-foo coffee. "Ha-ha," I laughed to myself out loud thinking about it.

"What's so funny?"

"Oh, nothing, just thinking out loud to myself. I was thinking about coffee as I was looking at the Starbucks Headquarters."

"I know, I know. I'm obsessed with coffee." I looked at Michael's eyes looking back at me through the rearview mirror. He shrugged his shoulders and paused for a second.

"You know, they just purchased Seattle's Best."

"No way. They'd better not ditch the brand. That is my coffee. When was that?"

"Just this past April, I guess. I read they're keeping the brand, but they own all the stock of the company."

"Wow."

"Guess the owner is trying to be like Bill Gates."

"Who?"

"You know, the Windows guy."

"Window guy?"

"No, not a window guy…Windows, the operating system for your computer."

"Oh, that guy. Ha, I thought he got into a fight with that Apple guy and died."

"Are you for real?"

"What, that didn't happen?" Michael just looked at me in disbelief. I was sure that was what happened.

"You really do need some coffee. You're talking gibberish. Both guys are still alive and kicking. However, I have to agree I like the Apple computer better than PC. Just two guys fighting for territory. Sooner or later, one will win."

"I don't care much for PCs, but my uncle bought me a PowerMac G5 silver-looking tower and huge monitor for my apartment, and I just love it. Does everything I want it to do. Besides, I hear horror stories about people's PCs crashing all the time. That would just infuriate the hell out of me."

"Sounds like your uncle hooked you up. I like Mr. Rozzito. He treats me well. Just sit back and enjoy the ride. I'll let you know when we get close."

I couldn't help but feel a sense of wonder and excitement, as we get closer to my destination. Just then, my phone vibrated. Yes, a new e-mail. Daniele had come through with the e-mail attachment. It was the e-mail I was waiting for. I opened it and began reading it.

The trial hearing was set to commence at ten o'clock Pacific Time at King County Courthouse off Third Avenue in downtown Seattle. Parties would be sworn in, and the hearing would take place with the Honorable Jacob Northrup presiding. According to the deposition, the case involved the International Maritime Organization versus the English Bay Fisheries for money laundering and drug trafficking across international waters. The preliminary hearing had already been conducted, and...

Dang it, that was all that was there. Wait a second; the preliminary hearing had already taken place? I was coming in on a trial hearing? Oh my God, this was bad. I had no information on preliminary, let alone who the defendant was?

Who was I defending? I tried to see if there was more to the e-mail, but I had already hit the "more" selection and exhausted the e-mail.

"Stupid BlackBerry e-mail. I swear, your days are numbered."

"You sure it's the smartphone and not whoever sent it to you?"

"It's just me, Michael. I'm nervous and lashing out at my phone again. I got enough to get me going, better than nothing at all, but I just realized there was a wrench thrown into this case—me!"

"You know, right outside the courthouse, there should be a Seattle's Best stand. I think you need to stop there." Michael smiled and laughed at me. I smiled back in agreement. I figured this case wasn't ordinary, and coffee would be my lifesaver. I thought I might be a coffeeholic. I wondered if they had similar meetings as Alcoholics Anonymous for people like me that are addicted to coffee.

"Miss Henson, we are five minutes out."

"Thank you, Michael."

I was panicking slightly, and my heart started to beat faster. I began to think over what I was going to say for my opening statement, trying to reassure myself that I would do fine, even though my gut was telling me otherwise. I was not sure why my new employer, Winslow and D'Entremont, had thrown me into the wolves' den by having me, a newbie lawyer, come in on a case that was going to trial. I figured it would be a tough case, but never in my wildest imagination would it have been this.

It wasn't like I could call them now, seeing how it is less than twenty minutes away, and explain to them what had happened. I was quite sure that would be terms for letting me go. I'm sure my uncle would even be upset at me for getting kicked off the case and fired. In one breath, he might be happy because he didn't really approve of my choice to become a lawyer, but in another, it was his recommendation that got me the job. It would be like wiping my feet on his face, disgracing the family.

English Bay Fisheries, it said. Hmmm. I knew my uncle ran one of his fishing businesses out of that bay close to home. I wondered if he had heard anything about this. I hoped he wasn't involved in this. That for sure would get me fired for association by crime, even though I wasn't connected. Great, just what I need added to my already heightened stress level today.

Michael exited off Highway Five and turned left on James Street towards Third Avenue. I had never been here, but it looked as if I would be entering the building from around the corner of Third and Jefferson. Michael turned left onto Third Avenue and pulled in to the front of the courthouse.

"This it?"

"Yes, Miss Henson. According to the GPS, this is your destination, and I have been here before, too."

"OK, looks massive to me."

"Relax and break a leg today."

"That's the second time I've heard that today. Let's just hope that doesn't come true."

"Would you like me to get the door for you?"

"No, I've got it."

"If you look at the window to your right, you will see the little Seattle's Best coffee stand. I suggest you stop there."

Smiling at Michael, I opened my door and exited. Michael told me to call him when I was ready to head back to the airport later, and he drove off. Looking around, I could sense my surroundings as I heard beeping noises from horns and brake noises from city buses stopping. Many people were walking about, trying to get to or from their destinations, and here little ol' me was standing still. I guessed I'd better get on over and get some java power before venturing inside. Stepping off the sidewalk and into the street, I didn't look, and a horn blast startled me.

"Sorry!" I waved and smiled at a sheriff's deputy sitting in a patrol car that had almost just hit me. The deputy rolled down her passenger side window and decided to let me have a piece of her mind.

"Are you looking to get hit? Didn't you see that sign right there?" She pointed at the sign as I looked in that direction. "It says look before crossing. Didn't your momma ever teach you to look before crossing?"

"I'm sorry, really."

I couldn't think of anything else to say but sorry as I crossed over and watched the deputy's evil eye as she drove past me. I knew I was at fault for carelessly stepping into the path of the car, but seeing how I had grown up with no mother, the deputy's comment seemed more of an attack. Still, the deputy had no way of knowing that, and I should have been paying attention.

This was not going to be a good day. I could feel it my stomach. *Relax, Alex, focus and breathe in and breathe out.* I felt much better after taking my own advice and walked towards the coffee stand. No line. That was different. I was so used to having to wait in line anywhere I went. This was nice.

"Hello. Would you like to try one of our cold coffee specials today?"

"No, just a cup of hot brewed coffee."

"You sure, because we have Iced Caramel Mocha as well as Frozen Caramel Mocha."

"No, just..." I was cut off as the young man behind the portable counter ignored me and went on about more items.

"We are featuring our Mint Chocolate Mocha drink, iced or frozen, for a dollar less today."

"No, I just want a..." I just stood there looking behind me as people started to line up. I figured I wasn't going to get a word in and just let him ramble on. Besides, he had to run out of drinks to talk about sooner or later.

"Are you going to order?" A slim, short, geeky guy in glasses standing behind me was getting impatient.

I turned around and said, "I'm trying to, but this guy is just rambling on. Sorry."

"We also have iced and frozen Caramel Pretzel Mochas as well as Classic Hot Latte."

"All I want is a hot cup of coffee. Can you handle that?" I was now annoyed because I felt I was holding up the line.

"Well, why didn't you say so in the first place?"

"I did! It doesn't matter. Can I please just have a cup of plain Jane coffee?"

"No need to lash out at me, girl. I just work here, and I don't need this abuse and name-calling."

"Abuse? Name-calling? You have got to be kidding me. All I want is a Seattle's Best basic, no-frills, hot cup of coffee that I can just put a little cream and sugar in, that's all."

"Geez Louis, fine. You're in luck. It's free today. Enjoy your plain coffee. Here you go. Next, please."

Was it me, or did I have a sign on my forehead saying, "I'm stupid. Please treat me like it"? All I wanted was just a simple hot cup of coffee before I headed inside. I never thought that would be such a chore to get. Wow, you would think that with all those different types of coffee, you would get confused. I know I was. I had to put down my backpack for a second to add the sugar and cream off to the side on the condiment table.

I pulled out my BlackBerry to see what time it was since it must have been getting close to ten. It read nine-fifty a.m.

Shit, I had to go! Grabbing my coffee and fumbling to find the garbage can to toss in my used condiments, I decided to leave them at the table and make a mad dash to the courthouse. All of a sudden, I heard a voice behind me say, "Miss, you forgot your backpack."

Crap, I am a total idiot. Turning to acknowledge the person calling at me, I didn't notice the young man who had been standing behind me in line walking right in front of me, not paying attention and drinking his coffee, and then it happened. WHAM! Everything went into slow motion for a moment. I turned my head around just in time to see my coffee cup leave my hand and hit the ground, spraying coffee everywhere.

My first reaction was to make an effort to catch it and possibly ruin my suit as I hit the ground, not to mention sprain my ankle and twist my heels. My instinct instantly took over and told me to back up to avoid getting any coffee spilt on me. Looking down and checking for any coffee stains, I breathed a sigh of relief when I determined that I had somehow miraculously managed not to get a single drop on my suit or Gucci's. Thank God for that!

I snapped back to reality, saying, "Hey, watch where you're going next time, mister!"

The young man retaliated at me with, "Listen, lady, if you were paying more attention, this would not have happened. If you had just ordered your coffee, you would have been gone by now."

I was about to bark back at this snotty young punk, but I bit my tongue and paused for a second. "Listen, I would love to stand here and argue over who did what, but I'm late for my trial hearing."

Walking away from him as he stood there looking at me, I went back to retrieve my backpack and made a run for the courthouse entrance. Gucci heels or not, I was not going to be late. Crossing Jefferson and up to the front door, I reached for the handle and froze. I suddenly realized that this was the moment that all lawyers dream of, their first big case.

Taking a deep breath to calm myself down, I looked up at the height of the door, pulled back on the large handle, and made my way into the main level of the building. Making my way towards the elevators, I noticed off to my left two officers were seated at the information desk.

"Good morning," I said.

"Good morning, ma'am. Do you need help?"

"Can you tell me on what floor Judge Northrup will be presiding today?"

"Room H-203."

"Oh, OK." I looked puzzled since I had no idea where room H-203 would be.

"You must be a newbie."

"That obvious?"

"Yep, sure is."

"Don't listen to Officer Calloway," said the other officer. "He does that to all new lawyers if he's never seen you. He's just trying to act tough. Be nice to her, Ben." Officer Shelly Clarke, Officer Calloway's counter partner, stood up for me and told me where to go. "Take the elevators to your right. Push the eight button. Get off, hang a left, and walk down the hall until you see room H-203 on the right. Can't miss it. There is a sign outside the courtroom displaying the case parties and judge presiding."

"Thank you."

I smiled and said thank you to Officer Clarke while glaring at Office Calloway. I made my way over and onto an open elevator. I reached over and pushed the eight button. Just as the elevator doors were about to close, a hand came protruding through the doors, and I heard, "Hold the elevator."

To my dismay, it was the young man who had bulldozed me over just minutes before, spilling my precious cup of coffee.

"You!" I exclaimed with a slight hint of anger.

"Get over it."

"Get over it? You just about knocked the stuffing out of me. What were you thinking?"

"Thinking? I wasn't thinking; I was drinking."

"I saw that. You weren't watching where you were walking and ran into me."

"Well, if you would've just remembered to grab your bag, we wouldn't be having this conversation now, would we?"

I just stood there feeling angry. I wanted to choke the crap out of that little fucker but didn't. The elevator stopped at floor five and opened. A group of attorneys came in, pushing between him and me, talking loudly and rudely. I tried to move closer to the corner of the elevator.

The men proceeded to talk about their time at their favorite watering hole—Sully's Ale House last night and how this one female bartender got a little friendly with a few of them and ended up working a little extra out back on her knees for extra cash. I couldn't take it anymore and had to say something.

"Why don't you boys grow up? Acting like animals, getting off talking about nasty things you did with a female bartender." I ripped into them as I noticed most of them sported wedding rings. "I bet if your wives knew, you wouldn't be so happy amongst counsel. You would be needing a lawyer."

All I got back at first was silence and ten eyeballs looking down at me. Luckily, the elevator stopped at the sixth floor, the law library floor. All of them got out except one, and he stood there slightly in front of me in the middle of the floor. The doors shut as he turned to me and said, "What's your problem? Jealous it wasn't you?"

"Hey now, back off. No need to talk to her like that."
The little punk-ass kid had just stood up for me. I was shocked, to say the least. I did not see that coming.

"Thank you." I looked over at him as he nodded back at me.

"Whatever, dude."

Finally, the elevator reached the eighth floor, and all three of us exited. The nasty-minded lawyer looked back and just looked me up and down before walking away. I was quite glad he had left as I thought about giving him something to remember me by. And it wasn't me on my knees. He would be from my high heels shoved into his crotch for being so rude and disgusting. I hoped I never had to see him again as I exited and made my way to the left, looking for room H-203.

I couldn't have been more wrong as I approached, walking past H-201 and H-202. The nasty lawyer had turned directly into H-203, where I was going for my hearing. Maybe he was the defendant's lawyer. Oh, that would wild, as I would find a way to give him a piece of my mind. The little geeky guy wearing glasses had turned the opposite way as we exited the elevator, so I figured he was either attending another hearing since he looked like a lawyer, too, the way he was dressed.

A brass easel stood outside room H-203. White letters on it stated the parties involved in the hearing, the judge's name, and the time of the session. It read, "International Coastal and Maritime Crime Division as Plaintiff versus The English Bay Fisheries Local Five Zero Nine FWOC." I assumed FWOC stood for Fishing Workers of Canada as defendant, with Judge Jacob Northrup the presiding judge, to commence at ten o'clock today, Friday, July Twelfth, Two Thousand Three.

Looking up at the clock on the wall, I saw it is already five past ten, yet the judge wasn't there yet, and folks were still going in. So much for punctuality. I was late but wasn't. I didn't hesitate this time and walked through the door and headed down towards where I would be seated. The room wasn't glamorous as I had imagined. It was just like my mock classes in college except there were no wooden benches lining the floor outside the lawyer's boxing ring. These chairs reminded me of theatre seating and looked comfy.

I could see the chairs that were rolled up underneath the tables where I would be were not so comfy. They looked like old library wooden chairs on metal casters. I guess that was fitting, as I wouldn't be seated that long. However, it made me feel sort of relaxed as I looked around at the folks in the room and realized how stale it smelt. It must have been the liquid used to keep all this woodwork shining on the railing and chairs, especially in the judge's area. Smelling that for the next hour was going to drive me bonkers.

No one was at either table. I must have been the first counsel to arrive. I couldn't help but look around for the asshole in the elevator, but I didn't see him and sat down. I pulled out my BlackBerry, pen, pencil, and writing pad. In college, we only did preliminary runs on beginning hearings. This should be interesting, to say the least.

Chapter Twelve
Half Baked

I dreaded the thought that I might not convince the people inside this courtroom, let alone myself. Watching the seats fill up with strangers, I spotted the jerk from the elevator. He was standing halfway in and halfway out of the doorway to the room, chatting on his cell phone.

The people coming in seemed to be a mix of business attire and causal looking. I was not sure what to expect, but I knew one thing; as much as I hated water, the ice-cold pitcher sitting in front of me was inviting. My throat felt like it had been scraped with sandpaper. It wasn't just my imagination. Reaching for the pitcher, I started to pour myself a glass when someone walked up to me.

"This seat taken?" I looked up and noticed it was the young man again.

"Oh, um...no."

"I didn't realize you were counsel for the defendant, FWOC."

"FWOC? No, no. I'm here representing the plaintiffs."

"Then I guess you might want to go and sit at the other table seeing as how we are going against one another."

I looked around the courtroom. I had not even considered what table was the right table to be at and my nerves must have taken over. I had just sat down. It wasn't like there was a sign with a huge arrow pointing down at each table with a description. I just figured it was the right one.

"I'm sorry, my mistake. Lots going on, and I guess it didn't occur to me that this table was for the defendant."

"Well, that explains why you bumped into me."

"Hey, now, you bumped...never mind. I'm moving." I was just thinking this kid was OK until he made that remark.

Grabbing my BlackBerry, pen, pencil, and notepad in one hand, I moved to the other table furthest from the jury benches. I went back to get my backpack. Turning back around, I noticed the jerk on the phone looking down at me with a smirk on his face. He began to walk towards me. *You have got to be kidding me,* I thought to myself, hoping he was representing the FWOC side and not the International Maritime Crime Division. To my dismay, I was wrong, and he walked up and sat right down next to me.

"Well, little darling, looks like you and I will be getting to play with each other after all."

"Grow up, you sick-minded, perverted freak."

"Whoa. I sense some hostility in your voice. I like that."

"Yeah, I bet you do, and I am not your little darling."

"Easy, *Chica.* We can do this the easy way, or we can do this the hard way. Either way, we're on the same team, it seems, so just follow my lead. Sit back and try not to stare at my ass when I'm standing in front of you, OK?"

"The only thing I am going to be staring at is your ugly face." I tried to make a comeback but fell short of the words I wanted to say and could come up only with "ugly face."

If it hadn't been for the elevator encounter and seeing what kind of a slime ball this man was, I might have thought differently because he did have a nice butt and was rather good looking, yet I knew underneath all that was nothing I wanted.

"Feisty, that's good. Makes for a good recipe to bring down these bastards. If you ask me, it's a no-brainer and should not even be going to trial."

"Why is that?"

"Organized crime!"

"OK, so because you think it's organized crime that's to blame for this case, it shouldn't go to trial? That doesn't prove guilt or innocence, only speculation."

"Whose side are you on? You're supposed to be representing this firm. Did you not get the trial papers to read over before today?"

"I did."

"Then you should know that this is not a normal trial hearing. This is the big time. Who are you, anyway?"

"Alexandria Henson."

"I've heard about you."

"Heard what?"

"Shh, here we go."

"All rise! The Court of Seattle, Washington, is now in session, the Honorable Jacob Northrup presiding."

"What is today's docket?"

"Today's docket number 11289 in the matter of the case between the International Maritime Crime Division against the English Bay Fisheries Local Five Zero Nine, Fishing Workers of Canada. Allegations of money laundering, drug trafficking, and murder involving participation by organized crime families across United States and Canadian Territories. The preliminary hearings have already been heard, the parties are sworn in, and the jury has reconvened for this trial hearing."

"Thank you, bailiff. Please be seated." Judge Northrup glanced over the courtroom as he instructed everyone to take a seat.

"Counselors, please step forward before we begin."

"What's going on?" I wasn't sure why the judge had asked for us to come to him before the hearing even began.

"Just his style. He likes to have a powwow before we begin. Makes him feel superior."

I followed the other two men towards the judge, as the room became deathly quiet. Leaning in to hear him, the judge looked at all of us and said, "Is there a reason why this type of case is in my courtroom today? I've read over the case and this is clearly an international case and not within US jurisdiction, " said Judge Northrup starring at the counselors with a firm eye.

"Um…according to the Jurisdiction of the Federal Courts Rules and Policies it makes perfect sense that this be held here." I blurted out unconsciously to the judge.

"She with you, Mr. Beacon?" The judge covered the Mic and leaned closer towards us.

"Yes, Your Honor. Miss Henson is new to the trial and is co-counsel. She has been added to the case by my firm."

"Hmm, I wasn't aware of anyone being added. Will she be adding anything to the case today?"

"No, Your Honor. She is here merely to observe and learn."

"Then I would strongly advise your co-counsel to contain her tongue."

"Yes, your Honor." Said Timothy looking over at Alex rolling his eyes.

"Learn? I was merely providing you a direct answer to why this case could be taken place here instead of across the pond." Alex again spoke up with directness.

"Miss Henson, I am going to go out n a limb here and assume since you went through Law School you know the rules, am I correct?"

"Yes…you are correct."

"I wasn't asking for an answer. I am aware of the rules and policies and since I am the one wearing the black robe, I say what goes on in this room. Speak only when called upon. If you are out of order, you will be banned from this courtroom and subject to contempt of court. I don't care for any funny business here, understood?" Judge Northrup looked at all of us one by one, but mostly focused on Alex.

It is clear that he asked me a question. The look on my face has got to be priceless. What the hell did I do? I am only here to observe and guess its best to zip my lips. Without hesitation I made a gesture as if to zip my lips while he starred at me before sitting back in his chair hesitating for a second before shaking his head.

"Mark it down that I will allow this court session to proceed and Miss Henson to be present to observe. You don't have any more surprises I should know about, do you, Mr. Beacon?

"Not at the moment, Your Honor."

"Let's have a clean fight today. No punches below the waist."

"Timothy, I know your grandfather was a great lawyer who represented our wonderful state of Washington, God rest his soul, but if you think I am for one minute going to tolerate any funny business from you just because your last name just happens to be Beacon, son, you are sadly mistaken. Do I make myself clear?"

Timothy just nodded as if to say yes. "Still, he is a good man, Your Honor, and my granddaddy is not dead, just not practicing law."

"Hmm, quite right you are. But you do understand me?"

"Yes, Your Honor, I do."

"And you, son, what's your name?"

"Andrew Peanus."

I started to laugh under my breath as this guy's last name couldn't be funnier, but it was, and I tried to hold it back. Even Judge Northrup turned his head slightly, copping a smile. I felt bad for him now. I wouldn't want my last name to sound like a male part of the body. I actually wanted to say I was sorry for earlier, but I didn't. It looked like this judge wasn't playing around. It was a good thing this situation happened to turn around and benefit me, and I would not have to speak today.

"Really? My last name is that funny to you? It's pronounced 'Pee-nus,' emphasis on the 'nus' sound, not 'nis.'"

Andrew defended his God-given last name with anger forming on his face. Still, it was a word that hit home and, well, made me laugh. It wasn't my fault he had a last name that sounded similar to a male body part. I hoped for his sake he performed better than his last name.

"So be it."

The courtroom overheard the judge's last statement as he uncovered his hand from the Mic accidentally and began to spawn giggling noises. Judge Northrup looked up, grabbed his gavel, and slammed it several times, saying, "Order in the court!"

The room quickly hushed. You could have heard a pin drop; only silence and the ticking of the clock on the wall rang through the room.

"Go back to your tables, and let's get this done. I have tee time at one p.m."

I turned around and walked back to the table, followed by Timothy. I looked at him as he motioned to me that he had this and winked at me. I had just found out that this man was related to Timothy Beacon, a highly distinguished attorney who had represented the gay community of Seattle back in the late sixties but soon was disbarred for being caught up in a sexual scandal himself involving a well-known male prosecutor, speculated to have been linked to the Mafia.

I remembered reading about him in my law history class, but from what I gathered from all the witnesses and the provided material, he claimed he was framed but still lost his license to practice law, and the prosecutor soon fell off the map, disappeared, never to be heard from again. Some say he was secretly involved in organized crime as well a member of the Collado family, best known for gambling, extortion, strip clubs, and ties to a number of Russian organized crime syndicates that plagued Seattle in the late sixties. Others said he was gay and was taken out of the picture, as homosexuality was not tolerated in the Mafia regime.

Who knows? But I felt I was being set up myself and didn't like it, just a feeling deep down inside that I was missing something. I saw Timothy looking at his papers as he put them down, then turn to face the jury to begin.

"Mr. Beacon, you may begin any time now." Judge Northrup was getting a little agitated that Timothy seemed to be stalling.

"Yes, Your Honor." He cleared his throat. "Good morning. My name is Timothy Beacon the Second, lead counsel on behalf of the International Maritime Crime Division and the prosecution. We are here today because previous allegations have been made against the English Bay Fisheries and said workers of the FWOC, allegations that have deep roots and ties within the organized crime operating out of the United States and across international waters into Canada."

"Objection, Your Honor. Prosecution is making speculations."

"Objection?" Timothy said. "Allegations have already been proven in preliminary hearings. Your Honor, I am just reminding the jury of said allegations already established since a few months have passed. I'm sure there is no harm in it. Certainly Mr. Peanus can understand my intentions."

"Overruled. Continue on."

"Such allegations of money laundering, use of drugs openly in businesses in English Bay, and murder have eye witnesses. We have eyewitness accounts of using Canadian harbors as operation points to load drugs on board fishing vessels operating out of the bay as well as other international harbors and our very own Seattle Harbor, as well as traveling across international waters with the intent to distribute in exchange for large sums of money. To further these notions, the same vessels are also linked to crimes using a portion of the Alaskan Pipeline as well to move money and drugs into Russia under the cloak of oil in conjunction with working with Russian organized crime syndicates."

"Objection, Your Honor. Speculation and move to strike. On what grounds is this true? Seems to me the prosecutor has been watching too many Hollywood movies, perhaps."

Laughter came from the crowd of onlookers behind the prosecutor's table.

"Quiet!" Northrup tapped his gavel once to silence the crowd.

"Your Honor, this is far from speculation. I am stating fact. Perhaps I have been watching too many movies lately, but that is irrelevant. We all watch movies."

"Get to the point fast, counselor."

"Your Honor, I would like to enter into evidence photos taken from eyewitnesses showing that these allegations are in fact going on in some of the businesses around the English Bay area and other places as Evidence A."

"Bailiff, please bring those to me. Do you have copies of the photos that the jury and the rest of us can see?"

"Yes, Your Honor. If I may, give me a second while I connect the video to my laptop. I will bring them up on the overhead screen so they may see them."

"Very well. Proceed."

"As you can see in this first photo, we have two men talking between themselves and standing near a fishing vessel, exchanging what appears to be a package of money."

"Objection. Oh, come on, it could be just two men exchanging a gift. How's that classified as money laundering? Again, move to strike, Your Honor."

"Sustained Mr. Peanus."

"If we zoom in on the photo, you can clearly see that the two men are not just normal men. In fact, one of the men seen here is wearing a uniform of the Vancouver Police Department while another man, if we just zoom a little closer, resembles the lead man from one of Canada's organized crime families. And as you can see, if we zoom in just a bit further, we can make out this man who happens to be Bobby Sidermo."

"Objection, your Honor. Prosecution is pinning this as a connection to the English Bay Fishery companies on what grounds? A cop and two men who may look like thugs? Possibly just a friendly conversation between buddies exchanging a gift? I see no connection to the fishing businesses."

"Wait a minute. I thought you just said there were 2 men, not three." Alex once again blurted out with out warning.

The judge hammered his gavel several times before directing his attention to Alex.

"Miss Henson, was I not clear in what I stated? Do you have a hard time understanding simple requests?"

"No your Honor."

"Then I will only say this one more time. Do not speak until I say so, is that clear?"

"Yes."

"Yes what?"

"Yes your Honor."

Judge Northup turned and looked at the bailiff, who happened to be smirking from all this commotion before making his ruling.

"Overruled."

"Come on, really."

"I said overruled, Mr. Peanus. You do understand that I have the last say here. Prosecution is just merely pointing out what is clearly in the photo. You will get your chance to state your defense. Continue on."

"Thank you, Your Honor. The connection is quite simple, to be honest, and with the next photo, you will see. This first man in this photo is the same man in the previous one. His name is Bobby Sidermo, a notorious man known best as being related to the Montreal organized crime family. He is said have held the level of capo, otherwise known as captain. The other man is Sammy "The Chainsaw" Delgado, who is believed to be connected to the Jersey organized crime syndicate, wanted for extortion, illegal operation of gambling, drugs, murder, and so on and so on. So, can you see my connection between these guys?"

"How does this have anything to do with the allegations against my clients, the FWOC?" Andrew asked.

Judge Northrup tapped his gavel to get the defending lawyer's attention. "Mr. Peanus, if you have an objection, then state it. Otherwise, kindly refrain from interrupting. Mr. Beacon, answer defending counsel's question so we can move on."

"Well, Your Honor, jury, and people inside this courtroom, these two men, as you can see in this next photo, are clearly demonstrating to some of the FWOC based out of the English bay fisheries how to stuff drugs inside large fish and pack them on ice. Then those drug-stuffed fish are loaded on these vessels. We have blacked out the vessels' name due to the fact that we can't prove that the names used are real."

"Objection. No valid proof that those fish are the same fish being loaded, and how is this related to the murder you speak of?"

"Overruled." Spoke the Judge.

"I will get to the murder in a bit, but first let me provide you my proof."

I was just sitting there watching Timothy conduct himself, and I had to say, he was not the same person I had just met on the elevator. He knew his stuff, and I was intrigued to see him in action. It seemed so far to me a no-brainer. The photos seemed to be displaying a connection; however, our opposing counselor seemed to know only how to say he objected.

"Call your first witness, Mr. Beacon." Northrup was already showing signs of not being pleased since this wasn't going, as a trial should; however, he was allowing this half ass trial to continue.

"The prosecution calls Mr. Hugo Jacques. Mr. Jacques is a former forklift driver for the local Five Zero Nine, forced into retirement last year due to accounts of being not able to work after sustaining an alleged on-the-job injury."

The bailiff stood in front of Mr. Jacques, asking him to swear on the Bible as I looked upon them. I had never been up close and personal to an oath being recited other than when we simulated that in class.

"Do you swear to tell the truth, the whole truth, and nothing but the truth, so help you God?"

"I do, so help me God." Hugo removed his hand from the Bible and gave a quick glance over to Timothy and me as he slowly made his way to the witness stand.

Unexpectedly, the unthinkable happened. Timothy's cell phone started to vibrate on top of the table next to me. This interruption was not pleasing to Northrup or the jury. Timothy looked over at me as if asking me to answer it, so I did.

"I'm sorry, Your Honor. I must have forgotten to turn off the ringer. I do apologize."

I answered the call, but no one responded. Looking over at Timothy, I shook my head no to let him know no one was there, but he seemed puzzled as he walked over and grabbed it from me. I couldn't believe what was happening. Judge Northrup looked at me as if I had done something wrong. Looking around the courtroom, I could see the jury whispering amongst themselves just as the crowd of folks sitting behind me were.

I scanned the room and then stopped. I couldn't believe whom I saw sitting in the back row in the corner. It was Tomas. *Why is he here?* I thought as our eyes connected. He gave me the nod off as if to tell me not to stare at him, but I stood up as he looked away, trying to ignore me. Then it happened. My BlackBerry vibrated loudly as Judge Northrup pounded his gavel and shouted out, "Order in the court!"

This was not good. I looked at the judge and said, "Sorry," as I glanced at my phone. It was a restricted number, and I quickly made it stop ringing by lowering the sound until I couldn't hear it anymore. I had forgotten to silence it when I entered the courtroom; it has just totally skipped my mind.

"Are you two done disrupting my court?" Judge Northrup was not at all pleased with what had just happened.

I shoved my BlackBerry under my notepad as I watched Timothy still conduct his call. He was arguing with the caller, and Northrup hammered away again with his gavel to regain control.

"Mr. Beacon, you realize you are about to be in contempt of court if you don't hang up the phone and get back to your witness."

"I'm sorry, Your Honor. This happens to be a call I need to take. It's an emergency. Please excuse me. My co-counsel will take it from here."

Had I just heard him right? He had an emergency call, and I, who had no freaking clue about this case, was now lead on this trial? You had to be joking me. *Come on, Alex, now is your time to shine! Show this jerk you can do it. Piece of cake. Just wing it, just like you said you would do. No, sit back down; you have no idea about this case. Shut up. Yes, you do.* The voices seemed to get louder and louder as I shouted out, "Shut up!"

"Is there something you would like to say, Miss Henson?" Judge Northrup looked at me as Mr. Peanus smiled. It must have been amusing to him as well as the people in the room, but it wasn't for the jury. They stared at me, waiting for my response. Looking over to where Timothy was, I noticed he was gone. I was left there on my own to continue.

"Well, Miss Henson?"

"I apologize, Your Honor. It's just..."

"Just what, Miss Henson?"

Everything that I could have thought of to go wrong was going wrong. I was now lead on a trial case that I had little to no information about and was about to make a total fool out of myself in front of everyone there. I would have been ready if I had just read the dang papers when I had had the chance. I would have known this wasn't a preliminary hearing and was now a trial, and I would have read over both parties' sides.

"Miss Henson, you do realize that if you can't go forward, this trial will be declared a mistrial due to incompetence, failure to comply with my court rules, and obstruction to provide proof against the defendant, and we will be forced to have the jury nullify this case?"

"I do, Your Honor."

"So, is it your intent to waste the time of this court?"

"Um...no."

"Then take your place and question the witness!"

I wanted to cry, but I didn't want to give the jury, the judge, or the defendant the satisfaction, so I took in a deep breath and turned towards my notepad. My hands shook as I poured a glass of water, spilling some it on the table. I was quite sure everyone's eyes were glued on me. I couldn't question this witness, let alone myself. I knew what I had to do. It just bothered me that Tomas was there to see me fail. Turning around, I gave them my excuse.

"Your Honor, I have to admit I am caught off guard and am not prepared to question any witnesses, let alone understand the nature of this case. You see, I don't have the trial case papers."

"What happened to them? Didn't you get them weeks prior to the case?"

"Yes, I did. However, something happened to them before I had a chance to read them. I was going to read them, honestly; it just never happened. I am truly sorry for not being prepared, and if it pleases the court, I would ask to be taken off this case as well and take full responsibility for my actions and whatever punishment is deserved."

"Miss Henson, do you take me lightly?"

"No, Your Honor."

"Are you trying to make a fool out of me?"

"No, Your Honor."

"Are you going to tell me next that your dog ate your case papers? Please tell me that isn't what happened. Please tell me this isn't a dream and that we all are not really just hanging out on the playground as kids."

The courtroom lit up with chatter from the crowd behind me, waiting to see me hang myself, as Andrew Peanus called for a mistrial. Judge Northrup was beating his gavel so hard, he snapped the handle from its head. I watched it roll onto the ground and under my table. The room became deathly quiet once again. I stood there frozen. My legs felt heavy, and I thought I was going to pass out from locking my knees.

"Everyone quiet down. I have called order in the court. Well, Miss Henson, is this a dream, and are we back in middle school, or is this for real?"

"This is real."

"Exactly! This is real, and this case is real, and we are adults, adults in a profession that depends on questions and answers that balance the justice from the injustice. Are you following me?"

"Yes, Your Honor, but..."

"No, no buts, only actions. Based on the nature of today's proceedings and mishaps, I am not going to call for a mistrial, Mr. Peanus, because of Miss Henson not being prepared or whatever excuse she has. It is irrelevant at this point. I am hereby releasing this case out of my court and transferring it to the Canadian Supreme Court in Vancouver seeing as how this is more of an international case than a US case. There, Mr. Peanus, you will not have an excuse for your client not to be present. You'd better make sure that whoever they are appears. That is an order."

"Yes, Your Honor."

"Let them handle this so-called trial. As for Miss Henson, she was simply here to listen and learn. However, since lead counsel has decided to excuse himself without my permission, I am releasing him from the case, and you, Miss Henson, are now going to be the prosecutor. Is that understood?"

"I guess so."

"You guess so? You don't get to guess, only provide factual information. I hereby adjourn this session and transfer it to the Canadian Supreme Court in Ottawa to resume on Monday of next week, allowing Miss Henson a few days to get up to speed. You may step down, Mr. Jacques. Let it be recorded that this case will not be a mistrial. That is all."

"I object!" Andrew was fighting for the mistrial because that was what Rozzito had sent him there to do based on knowing Alexandria had no clue about the case. It would have been a no-brainer except Northrup felt compelled to give Alex a chance for this case.

"There are no objections, Mr. Peanus. My decision is final. I don't have the time to sit around in my court with a case that isn't ready and that doesn't belong here. Miss Henson, meet me in my chambers in ten minutes." Northrup looked at the bailiff to signal that he was leaving, tapped the gavel block with just the handle, and then threw it on the ground.

"All rise." The bailiff called for everyone to stand as Judge Northrup left the courtroom. He whispered to one of the bailiffs standing next to the door as he exited, "Thanks to these clowns, I will make my tee time after all."

I was beside myself as I stood there watching the judge and jury leave. All of them looked at me as if I were the one on trial. Can the judge actually transfer the case? Everyone else behind me started to make their way out the doors until only one person was left, Tomas. Tomas made his way down to me and held out his arms to hug me. He knew I was being set up and could tell I was frazzled and dazed from what had just happened.

"You OK, Alex?"

"I don't know, Tomas. What just happened?"

"Not sure, but I think you just got played by your own team. You are very lucky you weren't in contempt of court, or I would be trying to get you bailed out of jail. Listen, before you go, give me the key you mentioned. I will have someone here with the Seattle PD run the DNA test for you. We can talk later."

"Tomas, can the judge actually transfer a case from the United States to Canada?

"Apparently so."

"Tomas, why are you here today? Is this the case you were summoned for?"

"Yes, but I can't talk about it right now. I need to tell you something, but it will have to wait. I will be here for the rest of the day with my family staying overnight."

"Where? I could meet you later before I head home."

"No, I have a big dinner tonight. My wife and I are celebrating our thirtieth anniversary with our kids tonight at some fancy Italian restaurant downtown called Guido's Ristorante."

"I could meet you after I talk with the judge. I'm quite sure he is going to give me a lecture for my actions and I might be a while, but I can meet you."

"No, we can meet for lunch on Monday. I'll be back in Seattle then, and I'll tell you what I need to tell you then. Listen, you'd better go before the judge sends out his posse looking for you. You have the key?"

"Yes, right here." I reached into my backpack and grabbed the baggie that had the key and handed it to Tomas.

"OK, now give me a hug. You sure you're OK from last night?"

"I'll be fine. I was just shaken up. I'm going to call Royal Jubilee Hospital and check on that woman, Natalie, who was hurt and hopefully go see her."

"That would be nice of you."

Chapter Thirteen
The Chamber

Judge's chambers are not to be taken lightly if you ever see the inside of one. In my case, I had no choice. I was handed a free ticket to the chamber. I did it to myself as the dice rolled and my lucky numbers didn't come up. Not reading the trial case when I had the chance had changed my course in this vast sea of the judicial realm. I felt as if I were playing a game of Monopoly and landed on the Chance spot. My card, however, was to go directly to jail and not to pass Go. In my case, I was sentenced to the office of Judge Jacob Northrup, and there was no chance of collecting two hundred dollars.

The door was open, and I was the only one present. I guess he had to be coming soon. I hoped so; I was starving. I thought for sure I was going to pass out from being famished. I knew I should have grabbed something on the plane ride over, but I was too nervous. I figured coffee would hold me over. Boy, was I wrong. At this pace, I was sure my blood sugar count was way too low because I felt funny.

Wow, this office was spectacular, from the twelve-panel wood walls to the decor throughout it, almost fit for a queen. No expense was spared in here for sure. The judge's dark gray high-back office chair seemed small behind his huge desk that was surrounded by the American flag on the right and the Canadian flag on the left on the wall. To add character, law books lined one wall, stretching from floor to ceiling.

Brass ladders attached on side rollers on the bookshelves sealed the deal with antique chairs displaying a touch of a flower pattern on the opposite side of the room, separated by a dark cherry table with a brass-colored lamp sitting on top. What caught my eye the most was that there was no sign of dust anywhere in his office, and there as a lonely book placed on the table next to the lamp either by the judge as if he might have been reading it or merely placed there for ambience.

Corruption of Blood by Robert K. Tanenbaum was the novel, and it looked quite used from the look of it. It was a novel written by a former chief of the New York City DA's Homicide Bureau and the late seventies House Select Committee on Assassinations. However, this book portrayed two investigation crossing paths, including all the usual suspects you would find in such a great novel composed by a one-of-a-kind author, a former DA going to work for the Select Committee, dragging with him an investigator. Cards were dealt and played, and the former DA was now marked as a slime ball for actions he performed, leaving no choice for his wife and child, but to leave him.

The story be told, the wife volunteers to organize the evidence of a Select Committee member in hopes of clearing his late father's name from being labeled as a spy, which led to his being fired from a government position after the Second World War. Connections with Mafia capos and foot soldiers, former CIA personnel and assets, as well as past and present Russian spies and none other than Lee Harvey Oswald intertwined as the plot unfolded as to who killed President John F. Kennedy.

My uncle had this very same book in his library. I knew that for a fact as I swear I saw it on his desk the previous month. Weird, as it looked to have a similar torn-off corner on the front cover. I wanted to pick it up and see, but why would a novel my uncle owned be here in Judge Northrup's chambers, as he had never been here let alone the judge and my uncle crossing paths.

The urge to know drew me in as I started to walk towards the novel, tripping over my own backpack and almost twisting my ankle. I braced myself on his desk. "That was a close one," I said out loud to myself. I couldn't imagine what was taking the judge this long to arrive; surely it had been more than ten minutes. Yet at that very moment, I was focused only on that novel and had to know. I knew deep down inside it was far-fetched, and I was about to pick up the novel when I was startled. The side door to the judge's chambers opened and then closed.

"Mm hmm. Miss Henson, please take a seat," Judge Northrup said in a firm voice as he walked over and closed the main door to his office. "Do you know why I have called you in this morning, young lady?"

Nervously, I responded by stating, "Yes, I do, Your Honor. I was not prepared to take lead in this morning's proceedings. I know that looks bad seeing how today was my first...is—" I was immediately interrupted by Judge Northrup.

"Miss Henson, the law dictates that I have authority over these proceedings, and I expect all counsel to come prepared and ready to examine each party involved."

"Your Honor, I—"

Judge Northrup quickly cut me off again and said, "Stop and listen. Two things bug me more than anything in my courtroom. They are counsel who is unprepared and cases that give me headaches, both of which were evident this morning."

"I know. I am sorry."

"Be quiet and listen to me. I should have you taken off of this case immediately for your blatant lack of effort to be prepared."

My back and butt seemed to be consumed by the chair since I felt as if I was being sucked in backwards as I prepared for the worst.

"Miss Henson, you are smart enough to know that I am not your average judge. I do believe in the process of the law and expect nothing but the best from all of my fellow constituents."

"I totally agree with you."

"Then why on earth would you step foot in my court unprepared?"

"If I may add to my defense, Your Honor, I had every intention to be prepared, but every time I went to do it, something got in the way. I know, I know, this sounds like an excuse, but I really do apologize, and it won't happen again."

"You'd better believe it won't happen again, or you will surely lose your license and be stripped of your fancy Harvard law degree."

"Seattle University."

"Excuse me?"

"I received my law degree from the Seattle University, Your Honor."

"I don't care if you got it out of a Cracker Jack box, Miss Henson. You step foot in a courtroom unprepared again and waste my time, any other judge's time, and the taxpayers' time, you will not only be disbarred, but the only thing you will be doing for a living is flipping burgers and crying for your mother. You got that?"

"Yes, Your Honor."

"Do I make myself clear?"

"Crystal, Your Honor."

"Good. Now, before I arrived, I made several calls and had the case moved to Vancouver to recommence on this coming Monday at ten o'clock sharp. Since the defending side had no representation from the English Bay Fisheries, I have made a court order to subpoena all parties involved, and if they fail to comply, they will be arrested and forced to attend. This falls under the Canadian Supreme Court with Judge Lucas Oliver presiding. If you think I am hard on you with my remarks, play the same game you did today and you will see how I am puppy chow compared to him."

"I understand, You Honor."

Just then, my BlackBerry rang. I could see Judge Northrup wasn't at all pleased. I tried to ignore it, but whoever was calling was being persistent. Several rings went by before the judge motioned me with his eyes to either answer it or silence it. Reaching for it, I saw it was an unknown number.

"I am so sorry, Your Honor. Please give me a second to see who this is, and I will tell them I am busy."

The judge motioned with his head to go ahead. I answered the call, turning my head to the side. "Hello? Who is this?" I whispered, covering my mouth.

"Hello, Alex. It's Beauford. Did I catch you at a good time?"

"Not exactly. How did you get my number?"

"You told me to look you up, so I did, but I got your answering machine and your message said to contact you on your cell if not home, so here I am. I can't stop thinking about you."

"Aw, that is sweet, but now is not a good time. Can I call you back later today?"

Judge Northrup kept looking at the clock on the wall and signaled me to hurry up because his time was way too precious to be sitting there listening to me on the phone.

"Oh, OK. You got my number?"

"No. Listen, how about you just call me back in a few hours? We can chat then, OK?"

"Sounds good. Hope you've been thinking about me, too."

"Yes. Now, hang up. I've got to go. I'm in the middle of a meeting with a judge. I must go."

"Oh, shoot, my bad. OK." I abruptly ended the call or Beauford would have gone on and on. I switched the ringer to off.

"Everything all right?" Judge Northrup asked, staring at me from the other side of his desk.

"Yes. Everything is fine. Just some guy I met. No need to get into it with you."

I could see he was less than thrilled about what had just happened. He shook his head side to side and began to speak again.

"Make sure you get up to speed and use all the resources that you can. Check the archives and cross-check your material before next week. Check with Sally, my assistant. She can get you access to the files you need in the file vault across the way in the administration building. She is on the fourth floor. Just tell security I sent you. Oh, since you are native Canadian, this will probably draw news media as well, so be prepared to act professionally and answer professionally. Good luck."

"Thank you."

"It's Friday, and I am almost late for my tee time. That is all I have for you. Are there any questions you have for me?"

"Just one, Your Honor."

"OK, go ahead, but make it fast."

"Where did you get that book on the table?" I pointed at the table behind me.

Judge Northrup looked over my shoulder and noticed the book lying on the table. He got up and walked over to it, picked it up, walked back to his desk, and placed it in one of his desk drawers before responding to me.

"Just something I am planning on reading. I must have left it there this morning. It was a gift to me from an old friend. Why do you ask?"

"Just curious because I know it is written by a former district attorney turned author, and it looks to be intriguing."

"Yes, indeed." Judge Northrup responded to me by making eye contact without blinking for several seconds before excusing me. "You may go now."

I grabbed my backpack before standing, then turned around and walked to the door. I opened the door and glanced back at Judge Northrup as he sat there with a slight smirk on his face. I exited and closed the door.

****

Judge Northrup opened the desk drawer and removed the novel, opening it up halfway. The back half of the book had been hollowed out in the middle of the pages, revealing a generic USB thumb drive and a thick roll of Grover Cleveland's with a sticky note attached to it and the initials N.R. written on it. He pulled out the roll of cash and kissed it and then grabbed the thumb drive and shoved it into his pants pocket before tossing the book into the garbage can next to his desk.

It seems Judge Jacob Northrup wasn't who he seemed to be, and no one suspected him. Was he a slime ball and involved in something he shouldn't be? What did the roll of cash with the sticky note and thumb drive have to do with the novel? Whose name belonged to the initials N.R.? Guess no one would know unless he got caught.

Vibrating noises from my bag went off. The ringer on my phone was still set to off as I pulled it out of my backpack. Daniele had sent me a BlackBerry message saying to meet her for lunch at Cafe Bengodi, a little taste of Italy at the corner of Cherry Street and First Avenue, at twelve-fifteen. I guess she figured I would be out of court by then. Luckily, due to this unfortunate incident, I would be able to meet her. My BlackBerry showed it was forty minutes past eleven.

There was no time to meet Sally, Judge Northrup's assistant right then. It could wait. I needed my girl time now and to feed my hungry tummy. I could just go see Sally after lunch. It wasn't like I was on a time schedule now. Well, sort of…I had to be back at Port Angeles before six in order to make the crossover to Victoria. Looking at my BlackBerry, I knew I had plenty of time to meet with Daniele, grab some files, and call Michael to pick me up. I'd better send her a message back letting her know I was on my way.

"Leaving now... meet you in a few," is what I typed as I walked towards the elevators.

Standing there for a few minutes waiting on the elevator, I figured it would be a perfect time to check on Natalie. This elevator seemed to be working in reverse as it was taking a long time to get to the eighth floor. I didn't know the phone number for the hospital, but I figured I could look for it using the browser icon on the phone, but that would have taken too long and frustrated the heck out of me. I had tried it before with no luck. As much as I figured it would be a long shot, I decided to dial four-one-one in hopes of getting the number.

Finally the door opened, and I was almost trampled by people getting off as I quickly tried to enter. Figures, it always happens to me, yet I still tried to get on without looking first. So much for the call…lost signal as I entered the elevator. I would just have to try again once I got outside.

DEADLOCKED: A Trial Beginning

The elevator made it to the lobby with no stops as I exited and walked towards the main doors. Walking past the information desk, I could see Officer Calloway sitting there, watching my every step. His eyes focused on me with a dead stare. The only thing I could think of to do was to look over at him, smile, and blow him a kiss, but that would have just pissed him off. I figured I had already caused enough damage that day, so I decided to ignore him and exit the building. This was a man I would have to see every day, and I didn't need that added drama.

What a beautiful day it had turned out to be. The sun was shining, and a warm breeze welcomed me. The time now was eleven-fifty-five. *Better move it; don't fail me know, Gucci,* I thought.

Chapter Fourteen
Affirmation

My feet were not used to being subjected to this ungodly forty-five-degree angle forced submission. I like shoes and love to shop for them. I just never like how sometimes they make you uncomfortable. I could imagine my little toes suffocating and starting to feel numb. Truth be told, I hated this pair of shoes. It was Daniele's idea for me to buy them. I wanted something with a little less incline, but she insisted it would make me feel taller and force my posture to shine. She wasn't kidding; it did both. I just wasn't ready for the pain, but the look and color of them sold themselves. My freaking calf muscles were aching something fierce. I wanted to rub them so bad, even if it was just a few seconds, just enough to take the edge off.

Maybe I could get Beauford to rub them this weekend since my legs had already captured his mind. Call it a little weekend teaser. I giggled as I rounded Cherry Street and walked towards First Avenue. I was actually looking forward to seeing Beauford again, and the very thought stimulated my body. I felt chills once again run up and down my arms. Thoughts of Wednesday night came to mind, of me standing underneath the umbrella, the rain encapsulating both of us. My body had not even been an inch away from his, and I could vividly remember the sound of my own heartbeat and the warmth of his body.

"Watch where you're going, lady!" I had drifted off for a second as I was walking, almost colliding with an oncoming man riding a bike, causing him to veer off the sidewalk and almost taking out a light pole.

"Sorry."

Just walking on the sidewalks in downtown Seattle was dangerous enough. Adding daydreaming to the mix would just be suicidal. I couldn't believe I had done it again. Thinking about Beauford seemed to intoxicate me like a drug and fog my mind. Something about this man made my heart skip, and I couldn't wait to see him again. Of course, I would have to control myself and not let him think I was that into him, even though I was and even though I had thought about sleeping with him.

"Hey, girl, come on. You daydreaming?" I could hear Daniele's voice as I refocused, reaching the cafe at the corner of First.

"Something like that." I hugged Daniele and kissed her cheeks.

"So, how was your first day as a trial lawyer?"

"Er, let's get something to eat first, and I'll tell you while we eat."

"Oh no. I know that look. Sounds like we need to skip this place and head to a bar!"

"I would love to, but I have to eat and get back to the administration building and collect some files."

"Well, I know what you need, then. You need some good old-fashioned Italian pizza."

"You sure this place is safe to eat?" I had never been there before, and from the outside, it looked uninviting.

"Relax, girl. It's not like you're going to catch an STD from being here. This place may not look like anything on the outside, but the food is amazing. I had to reserve us a table ahead of time. Kind of cramped inside, but you'll like it."

"Not too sure, but if you say so, I'm game. I'm so hungry, I could eat a whole cow myself."

"With that white outfit? We might need to get you a full-body bib." Daniele looked at me and laughed.

"Ha, you mean a full-body condom. That way I can eat and be protected at the same time."

We both giggled as we entered the cafe. The aroma quickly caught me as I took in a deep breath.

"Now, that's what I am talking about!"

"Welcome to Cafe Bengodi. Do you have reservations?"

"Yes, two under Daniele Ramos. I called earlier today."

"Ah, yes, follow me, please."

"Are you sure it's safe in here? Look at the tables with plastic-looking lawn chairs." I noticed the cramped feeling of the tables close to one another with cheap-ass-looking chairs. I felt sort of uneasy about dining at this cafe.

"Stop worrying, Alex. Trust me, the food is to die for."

"Let's just hope that doesn't become reality."

"You need to relax and take a deep breath. Don't judge the cover before you had a chance to read the book. I'm telling you, it is safe, and the food is awesome."

"You're right; I'm sorry. I'm just not having a great day so far."

"Nonsense. You're with your BFF now. We'll order, and then we will talk about it. Haven't I always been there for you?"

"Yes."

"Good. Now, look at the menu and find something."

"Wow, there are so many items to choose from. What do you usually get when you come here?" I couldn't make up my mind because all I saw was a sea of words.

"I just go for the gusto and order a wood-fire-oven-baked pepperoni pizza."

"Sounds yummy but not conducive to white clothing."

"Oh, Alex, mangia!" Daniele was telling me to not worry and just eat a little, telling me to relax and let go of the fear of getting it on me.

"Easy for you to say; I'm the one wearing white."

"Just remember to open your mouth before taking a bite." Daniele looked at me, smirking.

"Ha-ha, very funny." I looked back at her, shaking my head with a smile and returned Daniele's gesture by flicking her on the chest.

"Ouch, girl, don't bruise the goods. Going to need these puppies in perfect condition for the weekend."

"Hot date? Anyone I know?"

"No. Let's just say, thanks to you, I have sort of an arrangement to fulfill, and perhaps it may lead to something else."

"You shouldn't live your life between your legs, Daniele."

"Hey, if you wouldn't have lost your trial papers, we wouldn't be having this conversation. Besides, I figured, why not use it to my advantage?" Daniele looked at me, blinking her eyes.

"Oh, so it's my fault now? I see."

"Just because you're still a virgin, girl doesn't mean I have to be."

"Shh, don't say that out loud. Everyone is looking at me now. I just want to wait for the right guy, that's all."

"Honey, by the time that happens, the second coming of Christ will have come and gone. That heart-shaped tattoo of a lock and key on your inner thigh, girl, won't keep your virtue for life. It's time someone unlocked it and set you free."

"Whatever. Just order the dang pizza, will you? Make it a large, and we can split it." I shook my head while giggling. I knew Daniele wasn't too far off from reality. It was my way of protecting the most precious gift I had to offer, but maybe she was right. Maybe it was time to unlock it and live my life.

I reached into my purse to pull out a twenty when Daniele gave me the eyebrow raise.

"Put that away. My treat for your first day on the job."

Daniele raised her hand to signal the waiter to come to our table to take our order. He saw her and walked towards us. "Are you ready to order?"

"Yes, my friend, I will have a large pepperoni pizza with extra pepperoni." Daniele always had to have as much topping as could be. However, I was thinking about the grease and how embarrassing it would be if it got on my white dress.

"Fine choice, indeed. Will either of you be requesting something to drink as well?"

Daniele looked across the table at me as I nodded my head. I didn't care what we drank as long as it wasn't water. She ordered two glasses of Coke, and that was fine by me.

"*Grazie, mio bel signore!*" Daniele replied back to him with a kiss, saying, "You're welcome; our pleasure." The waiter walked away with a big fat grin on his chubby face. I swear, the guy looked like Chef Boyardee the way he was dressed from head to toe. Daniele could never resist a man that talked sweet to her.

"OK, so spew it out. What happened in court?" Daniele couldn't wait to hear how my lovely embarrassing first day on the job had gone.

"You really want to know?"

"Come on, girl, don't hold back. This is me you're talking to."

"Horrific!"

"Didn't show enough cleavage, huh? I told you to use it when needed. Works for me all the time."

"No, no, nothing like that. You are crazy, girl."

"Then what?"

"After I texted you to see if I could obtain the trial papers, what I was able to read from my e-mail was nothing I was prepared for, not to mention I was already freaking from not being prepared from the start."

"Oh my, what did it say?"

"You know I can't tell you. It's classified."

"Classified my ass! It's just the two of us. Tell me!"

"Fine, but I swear, if you mention this to anyone, I will haunt you this weekend. I will visit you subconsciously while you're getting it on with what's-his-face, and you will see my face and not his."

"Oh wow, girl, I just lost my appetite."

"Hey, I'm not that ugly."

"Oh shut up. I was kidding. You're a fine, sweet, sexy, off-the-chart woman," Daniele joked around while she began to suck her own index finger.

"Ewe, stop that."

"I'm kidding. Relax. Tell me!"

"Fine. Well, long story short, according to the papers, this wasn't a preliminary hearing, and in fact, it was already at the trial stage, and I guess my presence there was merely to be co-counsel and to learn."

"Wait, so you weren't speaking today?"

"Wait, it gets better. I was told by Judge Northrup I was allowed to sit in on case and observe and learn, and lead counsel would present."

"Northrup? I hate that motherfucker. Oops, sorry!" Daniele had blurted out loud, grabbing the other folks' attention in the cafe.

"Are you crazy? You just said a bad word in public."

"Ewe, please, girl, like they have never heard the two words out loud before."

"Why do you hate him?"

"One word: slime ball."

"Hmm, well, I didn't get that impression. What I got was that he's a hard ass and a strict judge," I whispered, leaning in to Daniele.

"He's far from that, honey. In the last month since I have been a lawyer, that man has tried and tried to make a pass at me, touching my arms. Creeps me out."

"Wow, I never would've guessed." Just then, the waiter came up to the table with the two Cokes. Both of us quickly leaned back in our chairs.

"Here you go. Two Cokes, and your pie will be out in just a few minutes."

"Thank you," Daniele responded to the waiter, grabbing her Coke and straw and sucking down on it. "And to top that, I heard he's seeing some mysterious woman who seems to have him wrapped around her finger. When she calls him, I've seen him turn into a weak little boy."

"Would love to meet the woman who makes him submit," I said, laughing.

"So go on."

"OK, it turns out the lead counsel from our firm, Timothy Beacon, was about to question a witness from the case, and all of a sudden, he gets a cell phone call and has to take it and excuses himself from the courtroom."

"No way. I know Timothy. Absolute heartthrob." Daniele seemed to go off into a daze, tilting her head to the side and up.

"Really? Is there anyone you wouldn't sleep with?"

"Yes...no...Maybe." Daniele stared at me, blinking her eyes rapidly and smiling.

"Anyway, he leaves, and the judge orders me to take over as lead."

"You have got to be joking. You're not qualified."

"Well, I wouldn't say I wasn't qualified. I was top of our class. Beat you, didn't I?"

"Yes. You know what I mean."

"So, there I was, standing, shaking, and totally caught off guard. I almost fainted by locking my knees."

"Oh, you poor thing. You see, if you would've just used those puppies, you would not be in this predicament." Daniele reached over the table and returned the poke against my right breast.

"Dang, girl, you've been working out. Those things are so stiff, you're going to poke someone's eyes out. Let me touch it again."

"Stop it. Quit it!" I playfully swatted Daniele's hand away from my chest.

"And...?"

"Judge ordered the case be transferred to the Supreme Court in Vancouver and for me to be lead prosecutor."

"Holy shit!" Daniele lowered her voice as she glanced around the room.

"SC. Wow." That was the shorthand term all lawyers used for Supreme Court.

"And to top it off, this little wannabe lawyer, Andrew Peanus, the defending counsel, was trying to get the case thrown out as a mistrial due to Timothy walking out and my not knowing anything about the case."

"Never heard of him. Wait, did you just say...?"

"Yes, the poor guy has a last name referring to a guy's package."

"Focus. Yeah, yeah, go on."

"Well, Judge Northrup wouldn't call for a mistrial, and the case is moved to Canada, where on Monday I will be cross-examining witnesses."

"Wow, you are going big time."

"I know." I showed a little sign of being scared and nervous on my face. "Who'd have thought little ole' me from West Vancouver would be lead on a trial case, let alone on my first-ever case as a lawyer?"

"Well, don't let it go to your head. Be yourself, and use those things if needed."

"You are too funny, girl." Just then, the waiter arrived at the table with our pizza.

"OK, ladies, here is your extra pepperoni pie. *Mange!*"

The smell rising from the pizza was mesmerizing as I grabbed a slice and bit into it. Daniele was right; this food smelled and tasted like heaven. Cafe Bengodi's motto of "A little taste of Italy" was spot on. I had never tasted a piece of pizza this fresh, mouthwatering, to say the least. I carefully took another bite, making sure none of the sauce dribbled onto my white outfit. Daniele's cell phone rang. She threw down her slice and reached for it in her purse.

"Hello?"

"Are you with her? If so, excuse yourself before responding."

"Hey, I've got to take this call. Do you mind?"

"Oh no, go ahead. I'm enjoying this slice of heaven."

"Hey, don't eat all of it, now," Daniele joked as she made her way outside the cafe.

"What does she know?"

"Not much other than the fact that the case is being moved to the Supreme Court in Canada."

"What? This was supposed to go away."

"She said it was going to be a mistrial, but for some reason, the judge didn't allow that and had the case transferred to Canada."

"*Figlio un cane!* That son-of-a-bitch kid."

"Who? You referring to Andrew?"

"He was sent there to represent me on my behalf. I told him to not say anything. I bet he did."

"Well, Mr. Rozzito, no offense, but you should've been there. I am assuming since the case was not a mistrial, you will have to appear in court, or you will be subpoenaed to appear either by will or force."

"No. Alexandria must not ever know I am a part of this case. If she finds out, she will know I was the one who had her parents whacked and sent her to the orphanage. If it weren't for the fact that I was next in line to be who I am today, this would never have happened. My sister's husband, Salvatore Vitelli, head of the Rozzito crime family, was named successor to the throne by my father, Giuseppe Rozzito, who was don before he was killed in a hurricane. He wanted to turn this family regime into weak advisory, ending organized crime in Canada, and I was not going to let my family name die in vain. Besides, with Alex and her parents out of the picture, I was set to take my rightful place on the throne and inherit the three-billion-dollar empire that would've gone to Alexandria on her tenth birthday.

"You just keep tabs on my niece like I paid you to do and report back to me. I'm quite sure the one and a half million American dollars for your role is insurance enough for her to not find out you have betrayed your friendship and the fact I rescued your mother from being the whore she was with the French ambassador in Washington and gave her a good life that you now enjoy, yes?"

Tears started to form in Daniele's eyes, and she said nothing back to Rozzito. She truly loved Alex and didn't want to betray her, but she had no choice. Nicholas Rozzito had bought her and her mother's freedom, as well as her new cushy job as a litigation attorney. Daniele's mother secretly worked for Rozzito as his full-time *comare*, his mistress, in exchange for both of their lives.

"I didn't hear you."

"I understand you," Daniele said, wiping the tears from both her eyes.

"Good. Now, run along and remember, if she finds out, well, you can take a guess what will happen to you and your mother. No one will ever find you again." Rozzito ended the call as Daniele stood outside, her back to the window. Alex looked towards her. Daniele regained her composure before turning around and heading back into the cafe.

Something wasn't right. I could tell Daniele had been crying, but why? I watched her come back to the table, smiling, yet I felt it wasn't real. Whatever was said on that call had made her cry, and I wanted to know why.

"Everything all right?"

"Yes, why do you ask?"

"Clearly, something is wrong. I can see you've been crying."

"It's nothing."

"Obviously it's something. You want to talk about it?"

"Look, I said it was nothing!"

"OK, sorry. I didn't mean to upset you."

"I'm sorry, Alex. It isn't you. Hey, listen, I'm going to take off early. I've got lots of work to do before the weekend. Promise me you'll call me later and tell me more about your case?"

"Sure, OK. You want any pizza to go?"

"No, I've lost my appetite. You take it." Daniele walked around the table to where I was sitting as I stood up to hug her. "I'll try to call you on Sunday. Big day tomorrow."

"Oh, that's right. Your boyfriend is coming to see you."

"Well, I wouldn't exactly call him my boyfriend, but yeah. He's supposed to call me soon."

"'K girl, call me. Love you."

Daniele quickly left the cafe as I stood there watching her leave in a tizzy. I was not sure what had just happened, but I didn't like it. Daniele had never acted that way before, and I was worried about her.

Chapter Fifteen
Arbitration

Money, the root of all evil: a biblical reference that tends to rule many people. In Daniele's case, it was a double-edged sword that became her evil. Forced to live a lie and deception, she succumbed to her role of being Alexandria's friend over the years as ordered by Nicholas Rozzito. Nicholas's deception was right on track. Alexandria had no clue her uncle was head of a Canadian Mafia family, let alone the one who had carved her very path of life and stolen what was rightfully hers.

Rozzito's helicopter could be seen from over the horizon as Bobby waited for his arrival. Rozzito had called Bobby right after he hung up with Daniele, requesting him and Nicholi to be ready because he had a job for both of them to carry out. Bobby nodded his head, as he knew this was a perfect place to be since young Nicholi had gone against Rozzito's orders and was not going to be present when he arrived. Bobby figured it was time to get rid of this young punk trying to worm his way into the business. He disliked him. Still, for some reason, Rozzito liked the boy and saw something in him that no one else did. Rozzito seen it as a way of raising the boy he never had but raising him the way he felt best, the Mafia way. Hell, half the job was done because Nicholi's persistence to please Rozzito came out of want and desire to be there, and Rozzito favored him over the rest of crew, which drove Bobby nuts, making him feel very vulnerable.

Miguel brought the helicopter over the beachfront property and slowly brought it down on the landing pad. Bobby patiently waited for his arrival, sporting a big fat smile. Nicholi's absence would now send Rozzito into a rage, and Bobby would get his satisfaction of taking him out. At least he hoped those would be the words coming from Nicholas. Miguel touched down safely, exited the front seat, walked around to the other side, and opened the door for Rozzito. Bobby walked towards him, meeting him halfway.

"Where's Nicholi?"

"I don't know, Mr. Rozzito."

"What do you mean, you don't know?"

"Like I said, I don't know. He left."

"Left? I gave you strict instructions to wait here, and once I returned, I wanted to meet with you both. Can't you do anything right? *Stupido stronzo!*" Rozzito gave Bobby a stern look as he took out one of the black gloves he kept in his coat pocket, smacking Bobby across the face, calling him a stupid ass.

This infuriated Bobby. He clenched his teeth and did the unthinkable. His temper quickly rose as he violently shook his head, pulled out his gun, and pointed it at the front of Rozzito's head. Babysitting was not his thing, and the last forty-eight hours had just about pushed him over the edge with this kid. He just snapped.

"Who the fuck do you think you're dealing with?" Bobby yelled at the top of his lungs, drawing attention from the foot soldiers in the house as well as Donnie, who was still inside the helicopter.

Rozzito stopped in his place, tilted his head from left to right, slowly cracking his neck before turning around and facing the end of the Bobby's .38 Special. Foot soldiers ran out the back door, weapons drawn as Bobby pulled out another pistol and pointed it in their direction. Rozzito's hired snipers perched on the roof locked targets on Bobby. Bobby could see the red little circles collected over his heart area as he became more agitated.

"Easy now. Let's not do anything hasty and have a bloodbath."

"No. I am tired of you protecting that little prick, and I am tired of you taking it out on me." Bobby waddled in place as his adrenaline was at full power, .38 Special drawn on Rozzito and his spare drawn on the foot soldiers. He made sure to move his arm around, covering all of them.

"Is this what this is all about?" Rozzito looked at Bobby, grinning, and took a step forward.

"Don't you make a move?"

Bobby repositioned the pistol on Rozzito and pulled back the hammer with his thumb, alarming the foot soldiers and snipers. Rozzito used both his hands to signal them to hold their fire. Donnie crept quietly Bobby towards from behind him, wrapping his signature wire around both fists.

"Bobby, Bobby, Bobby. Is this what you really want? You know if you shoot me with one bullet, you will end up looking like Swiss cheese, making a mess of my garden, and you know how I feel about my garden. I expected more from you as my captain, Bobby."

Bobby looked around the garden nervously as he realized he had snapped and saw all the weapons drawn on him. He sensed someone was behind him and glanced over his shoulder, as Donnie was about to take him out with the wire. Bobby quickly placed the end of the barrel of the gun in his right hand on Donnie's forehead, catching him off guard.

"I swear to God, I will blow both of you away. I may die, but so will you!"

Rozzito signaled to Donnie with his hands to back off. Donnie pulled back away from Bobby. Rozzito looked around and realized it wasn't worth dying that day over something as silly as a boy and ordered his crew to stand down.

"Put the guns away, Bobby. You see, I ordered them to stand down. Relax. We can work this out."

"No, as soon as I withdraw, you will have them kill me. Besides, they all hate me, anyway."

"Perhaps so, but that is good, Bobby. You are capo. You are supposed to be hated and feared. What happened to the Bobby I knew when I found you?"

"Nothing. I am right here, Mr. Rozzito."

"Then start acting like him and put those guns away."

Walking through the front door, Nicholi had returned and noticed the house was strangely empty and quiet. No servants were around, as usual. It was as if everyone had taken the day off until he noticed that everyone was gathered near the back looking out the windows. Nicholi walked closer to see what all the commotion was. His eyes opened wide.

"What the hell? What's going on?"

"Bobby has lost his mind," a servant responded.

"Lost his mind? Looks like the gunfight at the OK Corral."

"Yeah, well, it doesn't look good. It could get very messy if he doesn't put his guns down."

Nicholi figured it would be best to go out back and see what the deal was but hesitated for few seconds. He sure didn't want to get iced unintentionally by someone. Still, he made his way out the back as he saw all the firepower pointed at the three standing in the middle of the garden.

"Whoa, what's going on here?" Nicholi said, standing behind Rozzito's foot soldiers and adding his two cents to the scene.

"Seems to me you're the cause of this," Bobby said, looking over at Nicholi, who seemed to have appeared out of nowhere.

"Me? What did I do?"

"Bobby said you left the compound against my instructions," said Rozzito. "Is that true?"

"I only went out to meet with some of my buddies for something to eat. Been a rough couple of days. Sorry, Mr. Rozzito. I wasn't gone long."

Rozzito looked at Bobby and nodded his head as if to say he understood his frustration. Bobby withdrew both pointed weapons and holstered them. Nicholas ordered his men to stand down once again, and this time they did. However, Donnie still had his wire wrapped tightly around his fists, and he began to drip blood from the wire cutting into his skin.

"You see, everything is OK. Let's forget this happened. I have a job for both of you. Relax, Donnie. Put that away, for the love of Mary. What's the matter with all of you? Jesus, we're supposed to be family, not enemies. Let's go inside. I've had a long day already. Enough of this nonsense. I'm working with a bunch of fucking retards."

Donnie unclenched his fist and pulled out a handkerchief to wipe the blood of his hands, but he stayed focused on Bobby, making sure he didn't pull his gun back out and actually pull the trigger on Rozzito or him. Slowly, Bobby brought his blood pressure back down. He walked past Rozzito, bumping Nicholi with his shoulder as he walked inside. Donnie walked past Nicholas, who grabbed Donnie's arm.

"I want you to ice that Oabatz SOB when this case is behind us. I can always recruit another capo. Perhaps Sammy Delgado from Jersey."

"With pleasure!" Donnie grinned in happiness at Rozzito as he kissed each side of his face before walking in the mansion.

Rozzito stood there shaking his head and mumbling underneath his breath before going inside and grabbing Nicholi by his coat. Nicholi reacted by flinching while trying to escape Rozzito's hand. "Get inside and meet me in my office. Go find Bobby and tell him as well. I have had enough of this bullshit between you two. It ends today."

"Yes, Mr. Rozzito." Nicholi walked away, scared. He knew Rozzito wasn't kidding around.

I could have sat there all day trying to finish the pie, but my stomach was starting to hurt from stuffing myself. Besides, it must have been getting late, and I needed to head back to get the files and be on my way home—not to mention, I was worried about my BFF. I sat back in my plastic chair, trying to reposition my stomach in order to get some relief.

What I needed to do was get a to-go box and get back to the administration building. I still needed to call the hospital to see about Natalie, and I was waiting for Beauford to call back. I looked at my BlackBerry to see if I had missed his call, but no messages. Flagging down the waiter, I was able to get a to-go box small enough for at least four pieces. I figured I would munch on them over the weekend at some point.

Nicholas sat down in his office chair and sighed. Having dissension in his ranks was not a good thing, especially his captain pulling a gun on him. Still, he needed Bobby to make sure young Nicholi carried out the contract he was about to hand him. On top of his desk was a box of His Majesty's Reserve, known as the Rolls-Royce of cigars, a gift given to him by a hired connection who worked for the Russian Mafia KGB and infiltrated as a spy inside the United States Central Intelligence Agency right before the Cold War ended.

Too bad he ended up mysteriously vanishing off the face of the earth. Rozzito smirked as he cut the end of one of the cigars, flipped open his late father's lighter, and puffed a few times to get the cigar going. O-rings of smoke rose to the ceiling. As he waited for his two clowns to meet him, Rozzito flipped the top of the lighter open and closed repeatedly.

Nicholi had managed to track down Bobby, who was in Rozzito's bar lounge room mixing a drink of Crown Royal Canadian whiskey and Goldschlager cinnamon schnapps. Bobby figured that after what had just happened, it was better to wash it down and try to erase it.

"Mr. Rozzito wants to see both of us in his office."

"Tell him I'm busy." Bobby slammed his drink down, tilting his head back then up rapidly, wiping his mouth with his sleeve.

"You tell him yourself."

Bobby mixed up a second glass and was about to slam it when he stopped and saw that his hand was shaking out of control, jiggling the few ice cubes he had in the glass. Nicholi walked slowly towards him, hearing ice clink against the glass, but he stopped a few feet from him. He wasn't about to be attacked by Bobby again as he had been in the Tahoe.

"You all right?"

"What's it to you?"

"Nothing. Just looks like there's something wrong with you."

"Yeah, you!"

"Me? What did I do?"

"Disrespect!"

"How so?"

"I'm the fucking captain, and you, you are nothing." Bobby gnashed his teeth together, slammed the alcohol down, and threw the glass at Nicholi, missing his head. It ended up smashing against the wall.

"What the hell, man? You've lost it."

That was all Bobby needed to hear. He turned and made a dash at Nicholi, grabbing both of his shoulders and running him into the mirrored wall with extreme force. Nicholi's head bounced against it, cracking the glass. Nicholi was caught off guard and was dazed from the blunt trauma to the back of his head.

"Look here, you little punk-ass. I have spent the last seventy-two hours babysitting you, watching you fail at every turn."

"Take it easy."

"SHUT UP! You don't have the right to tell me what to do." Bobby, still with a tight grip on Nicholi's shoulders, pushed him against the wall a few times more.

"Whatever, man."

"I'll give you whatever. You're nothing, you hear me?"

"Go screw yourself, you washed-up, sorry excuse for a capo."

Bobby drew his .38 Special and forced it into Nicholi's mouth, taking his right arm and bracing it across his chest and pushing in with force. Nicholi was now in the predicament he was trying to avoid, yet his mouth had gotten him there. A few foot soldiers heard Nicholi being slammed against the wall. The shouting of both drew their attention and ran into the bar. They saw Bobby manhandling Nicholi. Nicholi tried to turn his head, but Bobby shoved his pistol further down his throat. Just then, the words, "Let him go," could be heard coming from the entry area of the bar.

"Fuck you. Back off. This kid is mine." Bobby had no idea who it was that said the words until he saw what looked like Donnie's image reflected through the cracked mirror.

"Respect? Seems to me you've forgotten the meaning, and you should be the one braced up against the wall."

"You don't understand." Bobby shook his head, looking in the opposite direction of Donnie.

"I understand all too well. Look at me when I'm talking to you! I've earned that right!" Donnie shouted at Bobby with authority as he wrapped the wire around his fists once again. "Let him go, now."

Bobby looked at Donnie and knew he meant business. He slowly turned his head towards Nicholi. Seeing the tears that flooded his eyes as Nicholi stared at him, Bobby released his grip and withdrew his pistol. Nicholi fell to the ground, coughing several times to gasp for oxygen as Bobby backed away with his hands slightly raised and cocked back.

"Now, both of you get your asses up to Mr. Rozzito's office," ordered Donnie. Donnie helped Nicholi to his feet and gave him a poker-face stare before ushering him on, nodding his head in the direction of the hallway. Donnie didn't even blink an eye as he watched Bobby leave the bar area.
"Ah, yes. Who's going to be my bartender? I'm all wired up and thirsty now." Donnie smiled at the foot soldiers standing there. They both looked at Donnie's hands wrapped in wire before one of them decided to get behind the bar.

It didn't take long for Nicholi to get to the outside of Nicholas's office. He knocked ever so gently against the open door. Rozzito waved him in as he puffed away on his cigar.

Bobby came along a few short seconds later, and Rozzito ordered him to close the door.

"What's going on between you two?" Rozzito rocked back and forth in his chair as he directed his question to them both. Bobby started to speak but was silenced.

"Don't say a freaking word out of your mouth. You sit there and listen." Bobby lowered his eyebrows, looking back at Nicholas pissed off.

"And wipe the scowl off your face." Rozzito flew out of his chair to his feet, pointing directly at Bobby. Nicholi giggled. "And you, you little prick. When I say stay put, you fucking stay put. You go that?" Nicholi nodded his head without speaking, pissing Rozzito off even further. "I didn't hear you!"

"Um, yes, I got it." Nicholi realized it was time to stop acting like a douchebag and focused on Nicholas.

"Just because you're sitting here in my home doesn't make you part of this family. You need to earn it, and that comes from respecting the ones above you, to the side of you, and me. I can't believe I'm saying this, but I'm going to give you another chance to prove yourself to me, and if you succeed, you will become part of the family as an associate."

Nicholi's eyes lit up as he waited to see what Rozzito had in store for him.

"I have a contract that I need you to carry out. I need you to find the man in this picture and ice him for me. Can you handle it?" Rozzito handed Nicholi a picture of Tomas Rainer, chief of the Vancouver Police Department.

"What did he do?"

"It doesn't matter what he did." He slapped Nicholi on his head. "But let's just say he was an old friend who betrayed me, and now it is my turn to return the favor. Put a bullet in his head. He'll get the message. And I want the both of you to end whatever this thing is between you now. It doesn't look good that my captain is always bickering with a newbie. You both are making me look bad, and I am getting pissed off. Keep it up, and I'll take you both out one by one. Now, Bobby, I want you to make sure Nicholi finishes the job the first time, and report back to me when he's done. You both got it?"

"Yes," Bobby and Nicholi responded in stereo.

"Good. Now, get outta here. I need to rest my eyes and this throbbing pain in my back. Look, you start acting like my captain, and you, Nicholi, show some fucking respect to him. Miguel is waiting to take you to the jet. Go, and shut the door behind you."

Chapter Sixteen
Perception

Ten to one, my BlackBerry displayed. No messages, no
e-mails, and no calls. Odd seeing how I depended on this dang
contraption to rule every minute of my day. I swore it was
broken, but the screen was bright and my scroll wheel was
moving amongst the icons on the front screen. I just figured
since it normally went off with e-mails constantly that
something must have happened to it.

It had just been less than fifteen minutes since Daniele
had stormed out of the cafe and two fewer slices of pie to carry
with me. I couldn't take the whole pizza with me, but I
managed to stuff four into a small carryout box and two on top
of each other folded up New York style. I figured I could treat
my taste buds a few minutes longer while I headed back to the
administration building. I was truly amazed that Daniele had
found that cafe. It was a less-than-desirable hole in the wall, but
it had to-die-for pizza. I had to hand it to her, she was right. I
would kill for this, and to top it off, not a spot of grease on me.

I managed to devour the slices like the opposite sex would've done.

No wonder they could fit so much into their mouths. Tuck, fold, and stuff—it was just that simple. My only gripe was, don't wear expensive shoes to a place like that, or you will soon realize you get more than you bargained for, like gum stuck to the bottom of your shoes. I could feel the ground playing tug-of-war with my feet as I walked across the slight incline to Cherry Street. I stopped in front of Seattle Mystery Bookshop. Lifting my leg, I could see the gum stretching out like one of the old toys I remember from the orphanage, Stretch Armstrong. Same color, too.

"Eew, this is disgusting!" I mumbled as I rubbed the bottom of my left shoe against the curb several times to remove the sticky gum.

At least I knew one thing was for sure; I could grab a free sample of Seattle's Best from inside the bookshop as long as I purchased something. That's what the sign said on the door. Perfect timing, as my blood-to-coffee ratio was dwindling, and I needed a pick-me-up if I was going to have to spend the next few hours digging through court files.

Walking through the glass doors leading to the bookshop, I could see what they meant by a free sample of coffee after walking down a couple of steps right outside and in front of the entrance to the store. There was a small table with a black sheet draped over it and a single pump-action coffee dispenser and white Styrofoam cups no bigger than a kitchen Dixie cup with a sign taped to it saying, "Please go to the counter first."

Looking to my left and then to my right, I could have just quickly grabbed a sample and been on my way, but I was quite sure I would be plagued with an illness or be cursed with warts by the coffee gods if I tried to sneak a sample without buying something.

Cute bookshop, as I could see looking in. I could see the mystery theme portrayed inside with painted streaks of blood on the ground and furniture near a dead-body tape outline on the floor. I had to go in. I was sure I could find a bookmark or something tiny to buy for a few bucks to get my much-needed sample. Opening the front entrance door, I made my way to the counter, where I was met by a young man with a name tag— Edward—behind the counter. He was wearing a blue sports coat and a green button-down shirt that seemed to work against his freckled face and red hair.

"Cute little bookstore. I really like it."

"Why, thank you. Are you just saying that to get a free sample of coffee?" Edward looked at me, grinning.

"Oh, no. I read the sign outside and thought to myself, 'A free sample of Seattle's Best, heck yeah, can't pass that up, so here I am."

"Welcome again. The only catch is you have to buy something. My manager's little secret to get folks to come in and perhaps buy some books. Business has been slow lately, so..." Edward looked around the store, lifting his head up and down and lowering his voice. "Your secret is safe with me."

I smiled back as I realized something about Edward. "I get it."

"Get what?"

"Well, this is a mystery bookstore. And by the way, I love the theme."

"Thanks. That's what we we're aiming for."

"It makes sense now. You're Archie from the comic book? What I mean is, you're in character, right?"

"Wow, how did you know? I just love Archie Andrews, all of his mystery adventures. I practically own all of his comic books and merchandise, but my mother, whom I still live with, hates the very fact that I don't want to leave home. I mean, it's not like I don't want to. Who I am kidding? Of course, I don't want to. It's just that I'm twenty-seven and still need my mother. Is that too much to ask? God, she can be a bitch sometimes. She just doesn't get me."

"OK, I think I'm going to pass on the free coffee sample."

I was weirded out by this young man who had mommy issues and slowly walked backwards the way I came in. It wasn't worth the free sample, which really wasn't free if you had to buy something from inside. It was more like bait and switch, and I was not about to be caught up in this scenario.

"No, wait. I'm sorry. Guess I kind of got carried away there for a second. My bad. Tell you what. Go ahead and grab a couple of samples, and don't worry about buying anything. Let this be our little secret." Edward held his left index finger up to his lips as he waved to me with his right hand to go on.

I couldn't wait to grab the free samples and get out of there. Wow, it takes all kinds, but it was very fitting for a man like that to be working in a mystery shop. The free samples were more like coffee shots as I slammed them all together as quickly as I got them. I could see Edward looking at me through the glass, smiling. Smiling back, I made my way out the entrance back on Cherry Street and headed to the corner of Third.

It didn't take long before I passed James Street and made it to the outside of the courthouse. Once I got past the numb feeling in my feet, it was all smooth sailing, but I was quite sure I would feel it tomorrow. This was a bad idea, wearing them on my first day, their being new and all.

I had to get to the administration building, and the only way I recalled being the quickest was taking the underground walkway. I remembered seeing the stairs and the golden sign on the wall with a big black arrow pointing downward at an angle, suggesting that was the way to it. Pulling on the main doors of the courthouse, I could see the stairs to my right. I made a quick dash towards them, hoping to avoid Officer Calloway once again.

Good lord, these stairs were fit for athletes. There must have been at least thirty steps before I made it to the walkway. So much for not sweating; the air inside the walkway was stifling with an overabundance of musty scent. It reminded of the times I spent hiding out down in the basement of the Alexandra House, trying to avoid the warden, Miss Simons. Identical feel and smell, if you ask me. The only difference now was the hideous cracked concrete floor that was painted a burnt orange color. I didn't see the connection there, but who was I to judge?

I made my way across the underground walkway and up the stairs to the first floor of the King County Administration Building. No need for me to stop over at the information wall, as I recalled I would find Judge Northrup's assistant, Sally, on the fourth floor. Checking my BlackBerry, I saw the time was now twenty-five past one. Still no new messages or e-mails, and Beauford must have forgotten to call me back, too. I was hoping I could catch up with him and perhaps find out when exactly he was coming to my home, maybe even catch a ride a day early and sleep on my couch.

Staring at my phone was not going to make it ring. Still, I thought by now he would have called, seeing how it had been a few hours. I could call him, but that might seem too forward. Besides, I didn't even have his number. *Focus, Alex.* I couldn't believe I was getting sidetracked thinking about him again. It was obvious he had me hook, line, and sinker, and I was a dangling fish at the end of the line.

I had no choice but to shove my BlackBerry into my purse to avoid staring at it. My uncle always told me when I was growing up that a watched pot never boils. I never did understand that until I was in college. The simple fact is, the more you watch, the longer it seems to take to boil. In my case, I was driving myself nuts waiting for something to happen with my phone standing there waiting for the elevator doors to open.

For once, I was getting on an empty elevator. So much different, I could actually hear music coming from the tiny speaker on the panel. How fitting…the words, "It's just the power of love," filled the six-by-six box. Impeccable coincidence, to say the least. Was this a sign and Huey Lewis was trying to tell me something, or was it more overactive brain messing with me? Thank goodness the elevator came to a halt on the fourth floor.

Something must have been wrong. The floor sign said, "Vehicle Tags and Renewal" to the right and "Job Applicants and HR" to the left. This couldn't be right. I knew the judge specifically stated the fourth floor. I was confused because this couldn't have been the floor I needed. It didn't even resemble anything like a place to store court files, but I decided to walk to the left away from the elevators in the center of the building floor and see if I could find someone who might be able to help me.

"Excuse me. Can you tell me where I might find someone named Sally, Judge Northrup's assistant?"

I had come across a robust man dressed in a tasteless off-blue-colored suit, half his shirt exposed and belly overlapping his waist. He was gulping what looked like a MacDonald's hamburger. He pointed in the direction I was walking, making Neanderthal grunt noises.

"Oh, OK, guess you mean this way." I hugged the wall, letting him squeeze by as he made his way towards the elevators. I watched him with a perplexed look on my face. Had man reversed gears and gone backwards in time? It takes all kinds, but this surely topped the chart for me today.

I made my way down the hall until I came across an open section with a few chairs against the wall to my left and a counter to the right. Not a person was sitting in the chairs or standing in front of the counter except an elderly woman.

"Hi, can someone tell me where I can find a Sally?"

"You have to take a number."

"I'm sorry, what did you say?"

"You have to take a number!"

The elderly woman pointed at a red number machine attached to the wall next to the counter. The red ticket dispenser was bolted to a white sign with a red arrow pointing down, "Please take a number" written on it. A digital panel attached just above the machine displayed the number three. I was baffled as to why I had to take a number. I was the only one there. The number I pulled was five. I looked over at her. All she did was blink her eyes at me for a minute before speaking again.

"Next, please."

I walked up to the elderly woman and handed her my ticket. She looked around as if there was someone else before me, calling out for number four. Maybe there was someone before me, but at that very moment, I was the only person standing there, and all I could hear was the ticking of the clock on the wall. My precious time was being sucked down the drain, in a manner of speaking, and I felt like I needed to say something.

"If I may, can you please just tell me where I can find a woman named Sally?"

Nothing but a stare. This old woman meant business until a stubby, fat, odd-looking woman dressed like a dwarf version of Marilyn Monroe came walking up behind the counter.

"Mom, I told you to tell me when someone was here."

"Wait, this is your mom?"

"Yes, sorry. I wanted to bring her to work with me to get her out of the assisted living place today, hoping it would make her happy."

"Oh, I thought she was serious with this ticket thing."

"Mom, I told you not to play around with that stupid ticket machine. Sorry, this used to be the place to submit job applications, but since our space across the way is being renovated, we're forced to be here in this cramped area. We barely have enough room for me let alone the boxes full of court files."

"Are you Sally?"

"Yes, I am. Hang on a second. Mother, please leave that alone and go in the back. I have your favorite cookies on my desk. OK, where were we?" Sally's mother slowly turned and smiled at me before leaving the counter.

"Sorry about that."

"It's all right. You're Sally, Judge Northrup's assistant, correct?"

"Yes, and you are?"

"Miss Henson. I was sent over here."

"By whom?"

"Your boss. He said I could see you about getting some files on the case I'm working on. Can you help me?"

"Sure, honey. Do you have a case number?"

"Case number? Um, let me check."

I started to fumble around inside my backpack. I pulled out my notepad, but all the pages were blank. I had not taken any notes earlier. This was not going to go well if I couldn't get any files to look at.

"Um, I seem to have misplaced the case number. Is there a way you can look it up by who is involved?"

"No, sorry. That case information is strictly confidential."

"OK, give me a minute." I turned around, went over to the chairs, set my bag down, and began to search frantically for any possibility of having the case number.

"You know, I get that stare all the time."

"What stare?" I looked back at Sally.

"Marilyn. I've been told I am a spitting image of her."

"Uh huh."

"What, you don't think so?"

"No, no, no."

"So, you're telling me I don't look like her, then?"

"No. Not what I meant."

"Yeah, well, you just said it again. Who are *you* supposed to be?"

"Wait, what? I'm not following you."

"You supposed to be a hooker or something dressed like that?"

"Hooker?" I looked down at my outfit and saw no resemblance to what Sally was referring to.

"Oh, relax. I'm just messing with you. You must be a newbie."

"That obvious?"

"Well, you are kind of saying so with your bra playing peekaboo."

"Sorry about that." I had forgotten that I had my top unbuttoned enough to give a hint of what I had to offer. I closed it up.

"No need. If you've got it, flaunt it. That's my motto."

"Well, not exactly mine. I was taking a friend's advice for my first day in court. She figured it might come in handy."

267

"Well, did it?"

"Not exactly. It was over before it started."

"Oh, you must be the lawyer Judge Northrup mentioned. You were supposed to stop by here an hour ago. Been waiting to take my lunch."

"I'm so sorry. I figured I would stop by after I met a friend for lunch."

"No worries. Mama's kept me busy. She thinks we're on a cruise ship. Dementia is starting to set in. I have what you want back here. Give me a sec."

Sally stepped away from the counter as I went back to my backpack and picked it up. A few seconds later, Sally returned and slapped a rectangular box on top of the counter, saying, "Here you go." I looked at her and then at the box. *Great. How am I supposed to carry that home?* She thought.

"Wow. Wasn't expecting a box."

"Yeah, I hear you, and I wasn't expecting to take my lunch late, either."

"Ouch. Guess I deserved that."

"You kind of did, but hey, think of it this way. I saved you hours of researching for it. It's all here. Enjoy."

Chapter Seventeen
Disclosure

What a perpetual first day this turned out to be, I thought as I stood outside the fourth-floor elevator. I was just ecstatic that all the files I needed were piled together by Sally. It was odd, to say the least, not having to dig deep and find files that would pertain to my case. Maybe Judge Northrup figured since I was new, he would make it easier on me by making sure everything I needed was there. That would mean he wasn't such a hard-ass after all, but I knew better than to assume that.

Finally, the slow elevator made it to the floor. All I knew was that I was happy to be leaving Seattle on my first day a few hours earlier than normal. Why hadn't Beauford called me back? I guess he had changed his mind and had run for cover. I would have after the encounter we had when we met on Pier 69. I needed to get ahold of Michael and see if he was available to take me to the airport, as well as one of my uncle's Learjet's.

I made it to the lobby of the administration building. When I stepped out of the elevator, I saw Timothy Beacon, my co-worker who had left me high and dry in court that morning chatting away on his cell. A few choice words came to mind, but I figured it wouldn't make a difference. He would just shake it off. I'd seen his type back in school and avoided them like the plague. Best I do the same and walk right past him, hoping he didn't notice me.

"Alexandria!" Too late. Timothy had spotted me from the corner of his eye. "Hang on a second, Peter. I see someone I need to chat with...OK, I'll ring you back afterwards...Bye."

"Miss Henson, wait. I need to talk to you." Timothy made a sudden stride to get in front of me, keeping me from walking forward.

"Alex, I want to apologize for earlier. I had to take the call. It was an emergency. Let me explain."

"Explain? What's there to explain? You left abruptly, leaving me standing there looking like a fool in front of the judge, jury, and courtroom. What more is there to explain other than that?"

"Look, I was called by one of our top partners from the firm and was asked to leave to address an important issue."

"More important than a trial case that you were lead prosecutor on? I had no idea this was at trial stage and thought I was observing, according to you."

"Weren't you supplied with the certified papers on the case?"

"Yes, but—" Timothy cut me off before I could finish what I was saying.

"Didn't you read them?"

"Well, I—"

"Well, what? If you had been prepared, you would have been able to take over where I left off. Doesn't matter. The case was declared a mistrial."

"Mistrial? Hmm, guess you didn't get the memo since you ran out on your case. No mistrial. I am lead now, and the case has been transferred to Vancouver SC."

"No, no, no. Our boss is not going to like that. This was supposed to be deemed a mistrial." Just then, Timothy turned around and quickly made a dash towards the underground walkway.

"Hey, wait. What did you mean, this was supposed to be a mistrial? Timothy?"

I stood there for a second, confused, before chasing after him. Timothy had made his way down the stairs very quickly and into the pathway as I struggled to get to the stairs carrying my backpack and box of court files on the case. If I was going to catch him, I was going to have to ditch the Gucci's and run barefoot. Somehow, this scenario seemed all too familiar. The only difference now was I wasn't chasing after a bad guy, or was I?

I knew I had to catch him and ask what the hell he meant by that comment. Looking down at my feet, I did the unthinkable. I took my Gucci shoes off and placed them on top of the box and hopped down the stairs barefoot. I figured I would be able to get in range to shout to him to stop. To my dismay, Timothy was halfway through the walkway on his cell, and I needed to get his attention, so I dropped the box and backpack, grabbed my shoes, and chased after him.

I wasn't sure why I took my shoes with me. I guess I figured in that split second that they were more valuable to me than my backpack and classified court files. I shouted out Timothy's name several times, but he never looked back. The only thing I could do was to throw a shoe at him, hoping it would hit him and get his attention. I had to get closer, so I made an effort, and as soon as I got close enough, I threw my shoe.

I watched it glide in the air towards him in slow motion, only to come down a few feet behind him, slide across the concrete floor, and stop against the wall. It wasn't even close enough to get his attention. I had to make sure the next shoe counted. I grabbed the heel and with all my might tossed the shoe tomahawk-style, hitting my target dead on the back of Timothy. It worked. He stopped and turned towards me as I ran towards him.

"Have you lost your mind?" Timothy shouted at me, picking up the shoe as I caught up to him.

"I tried to get you to stop and respond, but you kept walking. Didn't you hear me?"

"I heard you. I just chose to ignore you."

Timothy's comment instantly made my blood boil. I could feel my ears burning from the heat. Where did this guy get off? If I had had any sense, I would have grabbed my shoe out of his hand and whacked him across the head, but as I said, if I had any sense, I wouldn't have been there right then.

"Can I have my shoe back?" I chose to bite my tongue and ask for my shoe. Timothy looked at me, grinning, and tossed it to the ground. It landed in front of me as he walked away.

"What is your problem?"

"My problem? You seem to have it all wrong, missy. You're the problem."

"I'm the problem? How so?"

"Look, this case was supposed to go away. Somehow, you managed to get the case thrown to the Supreme Court, and Winslow and D'Entremont is not going to like this. Great job on your first day."

"Hang on a second."

"No, you hang on. Just because you have a fancy piece of paper for a law degree and money invested in this firm doesn't mean squat to me. You should know by now, coming from a wealthy family, when not to stick your nose where it doesn't belong. And honey, you think what happened today is the worst? You just wait and see because if the SC rules a guilty verdict, well, let's just say don't bother getting settled in at the office. In fact, if I were you, I might even strap on some Depends just in case you get scared and pee yourself in court." Timothy backed me up against a wall, as he got right up in my face.

"Such a shame. You had so much potential. We could have been a great team. Mmm, with a body like that, you could have slept your way to partner without even getting on your knees...of course, unless that's what you prefer. What a waste for a nice piece of ass like you. Your family isn't going to like this outcome." I impulsively slapped Timothy across the face after he made a sexual advance at me while sniffing my hair.

"Enjoy your newfound fame. It won't last long." Timothy pulled back with an evil smirk and walked away.

"Ha, nice knowing you!"

Timothy, with his back to me, lifted his left arm and waved to me as he walked up the stairs to the main lobby of the courthouse.

I was beside myself and had not expected that. He was lucky I slapped him with my right hand and not my left, which was tightly grasped around the heel of my shoe. That would have left a permanent mark. At least he got a sting out of it. What a total jerk this guy turned out to be. I felt like I needed a shower to wash his filth off me. I felt violated from his perverted gestures and comments. Something told me what had happened today was much more involved than just a trial case.

"What the hell have I gotten myself into?" I looked around. I was the only one there. I took a deep breath and slowly exhaled.

Looking directly across the walkway, I saw my other shoe lying against the wall in distress. I could only imagine what kind of damage I had bestowed upon it from throwing it and having it scrape against the concrete surface. I certainly wouldn't win Gucci spokeswoman of the year for my actions. At this point, I really didn't care as long as I could still walk in them. What's a few hundred dollars more down the drain? I already had sent my Prada's down to Davy Jones's locker, why not another?

I was just beside myself as I walked back barefoot to where I dropped my backpack and box at the other end of the walkway. I didn't know what to make of my encounter with Timothy. I felt more disturbed by his comments about my family not going to like the outcome if the trial got a guilty a verdict than his uncanny perverted male gestures.

Something didn't sit right. What did my family have to do with this, let alone the comment "money invested in the firm"? My uncle had made a few calls, as he was a well-known businessman, but money invested in the firm? I highly doubted that. My uncle tried to steer me away from law. There was no way he had money invested in the firm. Besides, if he did have money secretly invested, that would have made him a criminal, and my Uncle Nicholas was no criminal. I was quite sure of that.

Chapter Eighteen
Painting the Town Red

The Seattle skyline was cloaked in the essence of night as she so beautifully danced against the horizon. The hustle and bustle of the week was winding down as the weekend was ushered in with a cool breeze draped in a slight drizzle of rain from a storm off in the distance in Bainbridge. Tomas had decided to stay overnight in the city to celebrate their anniversary with his wife and two daughters. Earlier, Alex had given him a key with Nicholi's DNA on it in hopes of finding out who had attacked her.

Tomas used his favor card to get this to the forensics lab in Seattle, and results would probably be ready no later than Monday. Since he was coming back to town on Monday, he figured he would grab the results and share them with Alex then. The best part of being in Seattle was going to Guido's Italian Ristorante off Fifth, especially for dinner. Tomas and his family were walking distance from their hotel as they made their way towards the restaurant.

275

"Hey, girls, you ready for some great Italian food?"

"Daddy, I want ice cream."

"Maybe afterwards, girls, but not for dinner."

"Mommy, please, we don't like pasta." Tomas's girls tugged on both his and his wife's hands in a tantrum.

"Girls, stop it. You heard your father. After dinner, you might get ice cream, but you two have to behave. It's your father's and my anniversary."

Tomas bent down to talk to his girls. "Listen to me. Tonight is a special night for your mother and me, so please, let's not argue. Let's go in and have a quiet, relaxing family dinner, OK?"

"Yes, Daddy." Both girls nodded their heads yes as the family entered the restaurant.

"*Buona sera!* Welcome to Guido's Ristorante. How many in your party?"

"Just the four of us."

"*Si prega di seguire me.*" The host asked them to follow.

Tomas and his family followed the host to their table. The atmosphere was rather lively, as the chatting from all of the other tables seemed to topple at a high rate, making it hard for Tomas to hear the host, let alone his family. Just as they were seated, his cell phone vibrated loud enough to get his attention as well as his wife's.

"I know. Don't tell me. Work is calling you?

"I don't know. I'll just let it go to voice mail."

"You promised, my Tomas, that you would turn that dang thing off tonight."

"Look, honey, I am sorry, but being chief of police carries a heavy responsibility and my attention even when I am off duty." Tomas's cell vibrated again with an incoming text message.

"We need your attention, too. Please, just for one night, shut it off and spend time with us girls."

"Yeah, Daddy, please!" Both girls looked at their daddy, smiling.

"OK, just let me see what it's all about, and then I promise I will turn it off."

Tomas grabbed his cell and saw it was a text message. Reading over it made him feel uneasy, and from his body language and facial expressions, it was obvious to his wife that something was not right. Tomas began to scan the restaurant, looking around him, turning in his chair.

"What is it, Tomas?"

"Uh..." He cleared his throat. "Nothing."

"Nothing? Come on, Tomas, I know you better than that. Look at you. You're sweating. You get like this when something terrible is about to happen."

"No need to worry. Just some random text message," Tomas lied to his wife as he read the text again.

"Come out, come out, wherever you are. Ha-ha-ha. Sounds like I found my whistle-blower. Meet me out back, or your wife and two girls get iced. N.R."

"Tomas, you OK?" Tomas's wife knew something wasn't right.

"I'm fine. Hey, I'll be right back. I need to step outside and call someone."

"Call who? Tomas, where you going?"

Tomas had a bad feeling about the text he received. He knew damn well the initials for N.R. stood for his old acquaintance Nicholas Rozzito, and now the cat had been let out of the bag. Rozzito knew it was Tomas who blew the whistle on him. The only precautionary thing he could do in case his life was in danger was call 911 and report a crime before meeting Rozzito out back in the alley.

"Nine-one-one. Please state your emergency."

"Please come to Fifth and Cherry Street, back alley behind Guido's. A crime is being committed."

"What crime? Be more specific."

"Homicide."

"Sir, what is your name?"

"My name is Tomas Rainer, chief of police, Vancouver, BC."

"Mr. Rainer, you stated homicide. So has someone been killed?"

"Not yet, but if you don't hurry and dispatch a unit to this area, someone will be...me!"

"Who is threatening you?"

"Nicholas Rozzito."

"So, a man named Nicholas Rozzito is threatening your life?"

"What is with you people? I am reporting a possible homicide, mine, and I need someone to get over here quickly to make sure it doesn't happen."

"OK, sir, calm down. Please stay with me while I get a unit dispatched."

"Hurry."

Tomas lowered his cell from his ear, staying connected to the 911 dispatcher as he made his way around to the back alley. What he could see was a blurred figure standing in the dark as the rain pelted his face. Puddles of water began to build in the alley as he walked towards the figure.

"So, you figured it out, Rozzito. You're damn right it was me who blew the whistle on you, you scum-sucking lowlife. Come on, show me your face." Tomas's adrenaline kicked into high gear, as he demanded the cloaked figure reveal himself.

DEADLOCKED: A Trial Beginning

"All these years, I let you pay me off and control the police department. Hell, if it weren't for you and your organized crime, West Vancouver would be a ghost town. I have to hand it to you, Rozzito, your fishing company has brought the economy up, and for that, I looked away and accepted your dirty money. You conducted money laundering and drug trafficking, and for that, I am ashamed of myself for dishonoring my country, my city, my badge, and most of all my family. So, go ahead and kill me if you have the guts to do it. What, cat got your tongue?"

The cloaked figure removed his hood while keeping his face concealed in the alley darkness. He moved his arm from behind him, pointing a gun. Tomas didn't see that the unidentified person had drawn a weapon and had pointed it towards him until the figure walked closer into the light, illuminating the end of the barrel and part of his arm.

"Do it. Do it! Come on, pull the trigger and shoot me, you son of a bitch!"

The figure cloaked in the darkness walked further into the light, revealing his face. Tomas noticed vehicle lights come on down the alley, shining against the pouring rain. The lights turned off and on as if to signal something. Tomas thought about making a drastic move to grab the pistol strapped to his ankle in hopes of fending off Rozzito, but he stood there, cell phone in his right hand. He heard the faint sounds of someone trying to get his attention.

"Wait!"

All Tomas heard was two rapid loud bangs before being thrown backwards. His eyes closed, and he body hit the ground, his body becoming one with the puddles of water. Tomas still had not seen if it was Rozzito, but he was fading fast from his fatal wounds to the chest. Blood was exiting his chest and mouth as Nicholi pulled back his smoking gun and grinned with sheer evil. He walked over and stood directly above Tomas.

"Shh, don't try to speak. Save your breath. Wow, I have to say, you truly hate Mr. Rozzito." Nicholi walked around Tomas as Tomas tried to speak but couldn't as the blood spilling from his wounds began to fill inside his chest, choking the life out of him.

"You thought it was him. Funny, as it should be him lying where you are. No matter, that will come. You see, I am not who he thinks I am. N.R. doesn't stand for Nicholas Rozzito; it stands for New Russia, a new breed of organized crime. I have fooled him into letting me into his mob family, and let's just say he is going down. Shh, don't struggle. The more you do, the quicker your heart will stop pumping."

Lights flashed from where Bobby was seated in a car a few yards back to signal Nicholi to come on. Tomas tried desperately to reach for his pistol as Nicholi's ego raged on. Blood began to run down the alley from where Tomas was lying and into a drain. It didn't take long for the alley rats to smell it and emerge from the garbage Dumpsters.

"Well, it looks like you have a few more guests for dinner. Give my regards to the chef."

Nicholi figured Tomas was done for as he threw a dollar bill towards him, saying, "Here's your tip. Keep the change." He turned around smiling and walked back towards Bobby. The reaction on Bobby's face was a "whatever," since he had killed plenty of times, and it was nothing to him now. Nicholi had done exactly as Rozzito wanted, and this would secure him a place in the family.

"Get in the fucking car." Bobby impatiently waited for Nicholi while he gloated over his kill.

Tomas made a last-minute effort to reach for his pistol and tried frantically to hold it steady as his hand shook. He pulled the trigger. Nicholi suddenly dropped out of Bobby's sight, landing face first on the ground right next to the front bumper, legs twitching for a few seconds before his body shut down. Tomas had made a last-second effort to shoot his attacker as he drew in his last breath of life, hitting Nicholi in the back of the head, piercing his brain and killing him instantly. Bobby noticed that Nicholi was not in sight anymore and rushed out of the car, only to see his partner was lying down in his own pool of blood. Looking at where Tomas was and around him, he could hear the distant sounds of sirens coming closer. Bobby had no choice but to call Rozzito and give him the news.

"Is it done?" Rozzito responded to Bobby.

"Yeah, but the kid is dead, too. Guess Tomas must have shot him before he died."

"You know what to do. And Bobby, make sure no one links this to us, *capisce?*"

Bobby responded back to Rozzito, acknowledging his order, and went around to the trunk. He opened it before grabbing Nicholi's body and stuffing him in. He said a few words: "*Che peccato, Jamook!*" meaning "such a pity, you idiot," as he slammed the trunk lid and drove off recklessly just before the Seattle PD arrived.

****

Sitting in my seat next to the window, I could see the storm clouds intensifying as my cup of coffee danced and jiggled on top of the table. Something about flying always made me nervous. When I think it is going nice and smooth, that's when all hell breaks loose, and I get scared out of my wits. The clouds seemed to conceal the lightning energy going from gray to white. It reminded me of when I was thirteen, sitting in my uncle's living room with him as he watched old Hollywood war movies. The explosions from the bombs looked similar to the ones in the clouds.

281

"*Excusez-moi*, Miss Henson."

"Oh!" I was startled by Chantal, Rozzito's other female stewardess, as she touched my shoulder.

"I am sorry for scaring you. Please fasten your seat belt. Looks like we are in for a rough flight, and the captain said we will have to divert our course and head towards Sidney instead of Port Angeles."

"Why, is there something wrong?"

"No, no, just too many storms in the area."

"How will I get home?"

"No problem. The captain has contacted Sidney, and your ride will be waiting for you. So try to say relaxed as it might get a little bumpy."

"Thanks, Chantal."

"*Je t'en prie,* Miss Henson. Would you like me to take away your cup?"

"Oh, I'm still nursing it, *merci!*" I was not about to give up the coffee, even in the midst of a bumpy ride.

Chantal left my side as I watched the coffee cup rattle across the table, catching it before it almost tumbled over onto the ground. One good thing about having to land in Sidney, I would be home sooner in order to go and see Natalie, although I did like riding the ferry. It would be there next time. The right wing of the Learjet descended. I could see we were making a directional turn before leveling off as distant lightning battled the dawning of the horizon.

I felt so bad for not making a better effort to find out about Natalie, and as soon as we landed, I was going to have my driver take me to the hospital before going home. I had to know if she was all right. My thoughts were scattered as I felt suspended in the air when the plane dropped out of nowhere, sending what was left of my coffee onto the seat across the table. I was not expecting that and was glad I had buckled my seat belt.

The captain came on the radio to let us know what was going on. "Sorry about that. We're going to try and get below the storms. Hang tight."

The Learjet dropped another twenty feet or so within seconds, sending my stomach into a tizzy as I grabbed onto my seat for dear life. The turbulent pockets of air sounded like a snare drum as they pelted off the bottom of the plane. All I could do was close my eyes and hold on as the pounding noise faded. I could see the bright light shine against my closed eyelids and knew we had successfully dropped beneath the storm. Looking out the window, I could see the massive thunderclouds still very active with energy just above us. I was sure glad we made it through that and survived.

"As you can tell, we are below the storms, and it should be smooth sailing into Sidney. We should be touching down in twenty-five minutes, according to the captain." Chantal had unbuckled and walked over to my seat to tell me we had cleared the storm. I was just grateful for the captain's flying skills to get us out of that mess. My hands were frozen to my seat still as I slowly removed them, leaving indentations.

****

Quick chirps from an unmarked Crown Victoria pulled up next to the alley entrance near Guido's Italian Ristorante. The scene of Tomas's demise was crawling with Seattle PD officers trying to keep the public onlookers from moving in on the crime scene. Two other officers were stretching out the yellow tape, marking a square perimeter where Tomas's lifeless body lay. Flashes sparkled against the rain as forensics took photographs of the scene.

"Jesus Christ. Sean, get those people back so Seattle's finest can do their jobs. Before you know it, the media will be

283

swarming this area like flies on your wife's bad cooking."
Homicide Detective Skip Vasquez, assigned to the case from
Seattle's West Precinct, made his way up to alley entrance and
past the wall of officers.

"I'm on it. Hey, move those people back. We can
barely breathe." A random light flashed from the crowd of
people. "Sean!" Detective Vasquez yelled to Sean, another
detective from the same office.

"I got it. Who took that photo?" Detective Sean Jenner
yelled into the crowd of people to get that camera. Detective
Howard lifted the tape up and bent down to walk underneath it
into the area of the crime.

"Hey, Skip!"

"What?" Skip turned around and looked in Sean's
direction.

"Look who just showed up."

"Christ, there goes the neighborhood."

"I heard that, detective!" Veronica Barber, former
girlfriend and field reporter for KIRO-TV Channel 7 Eyewitness
News, yelled at Skip. "We have a right to report the news to the
public."

"Yeah, yeah. Can you hold off for a few minutes so we
can conduct our investigation of the scene?"

"So, what you are basically saying is to not do our jobs,
sort of like what you couldn't do when we used to sleep
together?" Laughter came from every direction as Skip drew a
disgusted look on his face.

"Are you still burnt about that?"

"Hey, we would still be a thing if you would just have
taken that magical pill, but no, you would rather have ED over
me."

"Can we please not talk about this right now? Christ,
everyone now knows I have problems with my plumbing. Sean,

please escort Miss Barber and her camera playmate behind the crowd so I can do my job."

"Relax, Detective Jenner. I can escort myself, but you can't keep us away too long, Skip. It's the people's right to news.

"Yeah, yeah, why don't you go play with your microphone and leave me the hell alone?" Detective Howard quietly mumbled beneath his breath as he gestured with his hands to move her back.

"Who's the vic?" Skip asked an officer standing near the body.

"One of us."

"One of us? A downed officer?"

"Yes. His name is Tomas Rainer, chief of police in Vancouver."

"What's he doing here?"

"Don't know yet. We can't get his wife and two kids to talk." The officer pointed over near the back of the ambulance to Tomas's widow and two girls crying and staring at Tomas.

"Come on, folks, cover the body up and pay some respect to his family, for crying out loud." Skip ordered the officer to get someone to cover the body. The officer pointed to his fellow officers as they grabbed a blanket out of one of the squad cars and covered Tomas.

"Any signs of a struggle?"

"Only two holes in the chest, a blood-soaked dollar bill stuck to him, a .22 ankle pistol in one hand and cell in the other. The guy had rats all over him, too, from all the blood. Here's the kicker—his cell phone was still on, and..."

"And what?"

"Nine-one-one operator was on the other line the whole time, and apparently, the chief was the one who called."

"You get the name of the operator?"

"Yeah, 911 is sending over the recording to your office. Oh, and one more piece of the puzzle—the 911 operator stated she heard the name Rozzito mentioned."

"Hmm, don't know anyone by that name."

"Funny, as we also found an alarming text on the phone saying he was a whistle-blower, and it was signed N.R."

"You got the cell?"

"No, but we can have forensics once they are done send it over to you."

Skip nodded his head in agreement.

"Thanks. Let's keep his identity quiet for now as it looks like we have a cop killer on the loose. We don't need this going viral."

Chapter Nineteen
Impromptu

The past seventy-two hours had been a sadistic roller-coaster ride from hell. I'd rather have been back in Paris enjoying my break from life than going through what I just did. I felt as if my mind and body were part of a reality show, and I was next in line to be kicked off the show. It just didn't make sense to me. Thoughts of my uncle being caught up in a scandal like my case were just not possible. He was just a simple businessman trying to make a living. It seemed to me society had it all wrong.

I get the fact that it is easy to construe things wrong and point the finger at someone. Just because someone happened to be in the line of work that my case was about didn't automatically link him. Still, what Timothy said back in Seattle was very alarming and hit a nerve. I couldn't have cared less at that moment that he had insulted me and tried to verbally rape me. That was just typical of men that have complex issues and hide behind them. I was beside myself thinking that in some

287

way or somehow, my uncle might have been part of this, and it was killing me to even think that, but what if he was? Then what would I do? I couldn't defend him because he might be on the opposing side in this trial. I couldn't defend him because he is family. What I really felt at this moment was deadlocked.

It wasn't long after Alexandria landed at Victoria International Airport that she was picked up by one of her uncle's drivers, only this time it wasn't a luxury limo or even a taxi. She was in the back seat of a Chevy Tahoe, the very same one Bobby had driven a few days ago. Little did she know that this vehicle was responsible for Natalie's ordeal, let alone other criminal activities? The Tahoe belonged to Rozzito; however, it was registered to the strip joint Tawny's that was near the airport. Rozzito used this mode of transportation to drive him around the island of Vancouver to conduct his organized crime plots. This would keep him under the radar and not draw attention to him.

"Can you take me to Jubilee Hospital?" I looked at the driver as he stared back at me through the rearview mirror.

"Of course. Are you sick?"

"No, just need to see a friend there."

"You know I have strict orders to drop you off at your home."

"Strict orders? From who?"

"Your uncle. Once he found out that you had to fly into Sidney due to the storm, he gave instructions to take you right home once you landed."

"It's not like I'm on a leash. Please, I won't tell my uncle. I really need to see my friend. Just drop me off there, and I'll get a taxi home."

"I don't know, Miss Henson. If he finds out, I might..."

"Might what?"

"Nothing. OK, just make sure you get home safe." The driver's eyes stared at me with sincerity.

"Relax. Wow, you act like my uncle is going to hurt you or something. This is just a courtesy ride because I missed my ferry ride due to the storms. Trust me, my uncle is gentle and the kindest man I have ever met. He would not hurt a hair on a fly."

The driver kept looking down at the road and back at me through the rearview mirror all the way to the hospital. It was a creepy twenty-minute ride seeing his beady brown eyes staring at me, and I was glad it was over as he pulled into the drive to the hospital main entrance. I didn't wait for him to stop as I opened the door, tossed my backpack out, and hopped out, reaching for the box of evidence.

"Thanks for the ride."

The driver nodded his head and drove off. I watched him round the turn as he exited the hospital drive before he punched the gas. I just wanted to see Natalie, make sure she was OK, and head home. I needed sleep or I was going to be like a zombie the next day at Pierre's event.

I was tired of lugging around the box. Where was my knight in shining armor now? I still couldn't believe he stood me up and hadn't bothered to call. I couldn't think about that right then. I picked up my backpack and strapped it on and carried the box. I made it through the automatic doors and towards the information desk.

"Hello. I was wondering if you could help me." I plopped the box on top of the counter as an elderly woman with a nametag saying "Estelle" stared at me.

"You do realize this is a hospital, don't you?" Estelle squinted her eyes with disgust at me for a second and then looked at the box.

"OK, I'm sorry. It's just this box is heavy."

"Well, kindly remove it!"

"Um, OK. Relax. I'm moving it. Didn't mean to offend you,"

I made a face, taking her off guard. This elderly woman was quite put off at the box touching the countertop. She sat there and snarled at me and motioned me with her hand to hurry up and remove the box. As soon as the box was barely off the countertop, she quickly pulled out a sanitized wet napkin and wiped down the countertop, mumbling, "Kids. The only thing they're good for is germs."

"I'm sorry." I leaned in to read Estelle's name tag. "But can you please tell me where I can find a patient?"

"Well, for starters, you came to the right place."

"Yes, I know that. That is why I am here. Are you going to help me, or do I have to find someone not working at the information desk to help me?" I was getting a little bitchy because this was adding stress to my already stressed-out day.

"Fine. All you had to do was ask me nicely."

"I did...uh...whatever, OK. Can you please help me?"

"Now, that wasn't so hard."

I wanted to pull this woman's false teeth out and give her a piece of my mind, but I didn't want to waste what little dignity I had left on her and decided to just smile at her. Besides, the more I thought about it, the less I felt like a civilized woman. My first day as a lawyer was nothing as I had imagined; it was more like a jail sentence now. It seemed everywhere I turned, there was confrontation. I was not quite sure I was up to the task.

"You have a name?" Estelle said to me as she pulled up the patient screen on the computer. "Name? Do you have a name for the person you are looking for?" Estelle snapped her fingers because I had faded off.

"Ah...yes, sorry. Must have blanked out for a second. Natalie."

"Last name?"

"I'm sorry, I don't have that." I looked at Estelle, who was frowning.

"Now, how am I supposed to help you if you don't know whom you are looking for?"

"I'm really sorry. This female isn't really anyone I know."

"Excuse me?"

"No, what I mean is, she was involved in a car wreck outside my place a few days back and was brought here. I just wanted to see how she was doing."

"Listen, darling, that is so sweet of you, but if you don't have a last name, I can't help you, unless you can remember roughly when she might have arrived."

"Uh, I think it might have been around eleven at night, or was it later?"

"I don't know. I wasn't there."

I shook my head in response to Estelle's remark. "Can you search between midnight and four in the morning?"

"The only Natalie in the system I see was admitted last Thursday."

"That's got to be her."

"Unless the person you are referring to is in grammar school; then she would be the one, but I am going to take a wild guess and say no."

"No, she had to be my age. Mid-twenties."

"Well, if you are in your mid-twenties, then that must make me in my mid-forties." Estelle cracked a joke as she tried to make light of my comment.

"No, really, I am only twenty-five."

"Relax, it was just a joke, but the way you look now makes you look older. Oh, I think I found her. Female, mid-twenties, five-foot-four-inches, dark brown hair, arrived last Wednesday. Admitted for possible head trauma, released from ER, and looks like she is still registered here in PC."

"What's PC?"

"Patient Care. Take the elevators to your left, go to the fourth floor, and your person of interest is in room 412."

I grabbed the box and darted across the lobby floor towards the elevators. That was all I wanted to know, not the extra bullshit I got from Estelle that delayed me from getting to Natalie. It seemed as if lately, everyone either had an attitude against me or was just being an all-out asshole. I was not sure why because I was not trying to come across that way. It was just a simple question asking if I could find someone.

"You're welcome!" Estelle shouted across the lobby at me before sitting back down.

"Thank you." I turning my head towards Estelle, softly saying, "You crotchety old shrew."

Ding! The doors to the elevator opened and I entered, giving Estelle one last glance before hopping aboard. I knew she would be watching me, and what better way to express my gratitude than looking at her with a fake smile and grinning sarcastically. The look on her face was priceless as the doors shut.

The elevator stopped at the fourth floor. I exited and walked around the corner. Something about hospital smells made me feel nauseous, almost as if it was too sanitized and smelled like a bagful of rubber bands I once sniffed as child. It just had that same odor. To my surprise, there was not a staff member in sight. The floor seemed awfully quiet as I looked on the wall for room number 412.

Rooms 400 to 420 were to my left, and 421 to 430 were to my right. It was just very shocking to not see someone up here tending to the patients if something were to happen. A few cough noises came out of a room as I glanced in walking by. It looked like a shriveled up old man trapped in his decrepit so-called body. He turned his head, covering his mouth with a white handkerchief. His eyes told a story, yet I saw him only for a second or two. Sad, if you ask me. I bet most of the folks up here were left alone to recover or yet, the worst, to die.

This made me feel bad inside for not calling or coming sooner to see about Natalie. Walking down the hall and looking into each room made me think how precious life was and how much we take for granted. I hoped if I ever ended up in a patient care facility, someone would come and see me.

"Nurse?" A shallow request came out from room 405 as I quietly walked past.

I stood there in between room 405 and 406 and looked around for a hospital staff person, but I didn't answer back. What was I going to be able to do? It wasn't like I had credentials to be a nurse, yet this person was crying out for help, and no one was around besides me.

"Nurse, please, I need your help." Another request came from room 405, but this time it sounded a little bit more in distress.

I was only a few rooms away from Natalie. I didn't know what to say as I stood there quietly. I could keep on going towards Natalie and ignore the cry for help, or I could do the right thing and turn around and respond to the cry.

"Someone, please, I just need to keep up and use the lavatory. Hello? I just need to get up." The old man started to softly cry underneath his breath.

I knew what I had to do. I placed the box of evidence down once again and took off my backpack, setting it on top.

"Just a minute. Be right there." I figured, what the hell? No one else was there to help, so I decided to walk into room 405. What I wasn't prepared for was my emotions to kick in. He was a frail old man, skin so thin I could see his skeleton, a few gray hairs on top of his freckled bald head, with dried tears on his cheeks.

How could anyone not give a shit about this man? It broke my heart to see him, and I hadn't the foggiest idea who he was other than the fact he was here with no one to help him.

"Please, I need to use the bathroom. Can you help me up?"

"Here, let me come closer. You can wrap your arms around my neck, and I'll slowly help you up."

"Thank you. I have been calling for someone to help me for some time now."

"I am sorry. I don't work here. I'm actually here to see someone."

"I knew it. The moment my eyes caught yours, I knew you were an angel. I thought for a second I was going to be going to heaven and was excited."

I helped him sit up and stand, holding his arm as he slowly put one foot in front of the other while pulling his metal stand on wheels that was connected to tubes from a bag hanging from it. He couldn't stand straight anymore. The years that had passed looked like they had gotten the better of him as his back was permanently arched downward.

He glanced up at me to let me know he could take it from there. I watched him slowly turn around and smile. The door made a creaking noise as he slowly shut it. I stood outside the lavatory door for what seemed like an eternity, but it was only a few minutes. The door opened, and the old man blinked his eyes and said, "Thank you, child."

"You are quite welcome. Here, let me help you back to your bed."

"You sure you're not an angel?"

"No...Well, sometimes." I cracked a smile and giggled.

"What's your name?"

"Alexandria."

"What an angelic name. Thank goodness you are not mean like the others."

"Others? What do you mean? Here, wrap your arms around my neck again...There you go...Now, lower yourself slow and easy…. Let me help you with your legs."

"What are you doing? Don't touch that patient!" I was startled as a hospital staff member walked in on me.

"I'm sorry. He was crying for help, and no one was around."

"Look out. Here is Nurse Ratchet," the old man mumbled to me.

"If anyone saw you doing this, you would be subject to HIPA rules and would be tossed out of the hospital. Now, step away from him."

"Sorry, I was just—" I was rudely interrupted.

"Just what? Helping out a patient who happens to have strict doctors' orders to stay in bed due to his severe case of dementia?"

"Um, I meant no harm...He called out for someone... Perhaps I'll just leave you to tend to him."

"Perhaps so. Who are you looking for, anyway?"

"A woman in room 412 named Natalie."

"Ah, yes, the woman who was admitted with head trauma."

"That's her. Is she all right?"

"Honey, the only one with head trauma around here is me putting up with patients."

"So, what you are saying is she's OK?"

"If she isn't, then I'm the one with dementia and not Herman right here."

"Oh, thank God. That's good news."

"The only thing she has is a bump on the forehead and has been kept here for observation just in case she developed a concussion."

"Thanks. Sorry about earlier."

"Well, just don't do it again."

"Bye, Herman. Nice to meet you." I waved to the old man as I turned and walked out of his room.

"Look at me, Herman, not at my boobs," said the nurse.

"She was an angel sent to take me home."

"Yeah, and I'm Sheena, Queen of the Jungle."

"Oh, wow, queen of the jungle. You're an angel."

"OK, Herman if you say so. Now lie back and close your eyes and rest."

I could hear the nurse and Herman fading a little as I approached room 412, where Natalie was supposedly recovering. I felt a little nervous and stopped. I almost turned around and walked away, but I didn't. I could see from the round black and white clock on the wall that the time was approaching 6:30 p.m., and visiting hours were over at 7:00. The door to room 412 was open a hair. I knocked ever so gently, saying, "Hello?"

"Come in."

I pushed the door slowly as it hardly budged from being so heavy. Natalie was sitting up and watching TV. I didn't know what I was going to say as I tiptoed into her room. What I needed to say was, "How are you doing?" but I just smiled as she looked at me and said, "It's you. You're the one who I saw right after the crash. It was as if you were an angel."

"That's twice in one day I've been referred to as an angel. You sure you don't have dementia from that bump to the head?"

"Not that I'm aware of."

"It was just a joke. Hi, my name is Alexandria. We haven't been formerly introduced since, you know."

"It's OK. You can say 'the crash.' Come in and sit down."

"Oh, OK." I felt kind of awkward being there, but I went over and sat down, placing the box on my lap and backpack near my feet. "I wanted to come sooner, but unfortunately, I couldn't due to my job."

"Oh, no worries. I haven't felt like having people visit since all the last visitors were from the police department."

"Well, since it was a hit and run, I'm sure they were just doing their jobs."

"Yeah, I know, but the last two didn't seem like police officers."

"What do you mean?" I leaned forward, gently took Natalie's left hand, and placed it between both my hands.

"Well, they both seemed a little odd."

"Odd? Odd how?"

"It doesn't matter. It's not like you need to know that."

"No, please go ahead. I want to hear."

"I don't know, honestly, but I felt from what they were asking me that they didn't seem like police officers, but more like someone higher up."

"Higher up? What, like a sergeant or detective?" I was kind of lost as to where Natalie was going.

"Yes...no. Not a detective, much higher like a—"

"A chief?" I interrupted Natalie by blurting out.

"No, um, let me think for a second. More like a government level."

"Government? You sure?"

"Not totally. Guess I'm a little foggy still from the accident."

"It's OK. The main thing is you're OK."

"I know what it was now. Both of them took turns asking me about the car that ran me off the road and kept drilling me if I had seen the driver's face, but I kept telling them no. It happened so fast, so I couldn't remember." Natalie started to form tears in her eyes as she spoke.

"Hey, it's all right. No need to cry. You're going to be OK." I reached over to the side table, pulled a Kleenex out of the box, and handed it to Natalie.

"Thanks."

"You are welcome."

"It just seemed really odd to me because it didn't feel right. One of the men didn't have a local accent."

"What do you mean?"

"One had a deep French kind of accent, and the other sounded like a bad attempt to sound Southern."

"Hmm, that is odd. Maybe it was just the way you perceived it being in the state you were at the time."

"Maybe so, but after they left, I got to thinking about their question if I had seen the face of the driver, and all I can remember is..." Natalie paused as she looked around the bed and table for something.

"What is it?"

"You happen to have a pen and paper handy?"

All I could think of was maybe she was going to give me a sketch of the driver's face, and if so, that would come in handy because she still needed to call the police department and file a report from the previous Wednesday. I could hand over the sketch for Natalie's case. I managed to find a pen inside the table drawer and a hospital patient care pamphlet.

"Here, not sure if this will do, but it's all I could find."

"Oh, thanks." Natalie began to write out what looked to Alex like a bunch of letters.

"Here, this is what I remember right before I was run off the road, but it wasn't a car like the police thought. It was a truck or a van." Natalie had written out the letters "1NAMTIH" on the pamphlet and handed them to me.

"Strange, what does this mean?"

"I don't know, it was just the last thing I remember before seeing you."

"Visiting hours are over now." The nurse came around and interrupted my and Natalie's train of thought.

"Oh, OK. Wow, seven already?"

"Visiting hours open tomorrow at nine. You can come back then if you like, but I think she is being released then. You going to be the one we release her to tomorrow?"

"Oh no, I'm just visiting." I looked away from the nurse and over at Natalie.

"Unless you don't have anyone to take you home. I could come back. I don't have a car, but I would take you home in a taxi."

"No, I have my brother coming in from Seattle tomorrow. He'll take me home."

Looking back at the nurse, I could see her tapping her watch as a signal for me to wrap things up and leave. I wanted to ask Natalie more about the two last visitors but figured it really didn't matter. It was probably just two men doing their jobs, and Natalie was just still dazed from the hit to the head. I folded the hospital pamphlet in two and tucked it into a side pouch of my backpack. I strapped it on and reached for the box.

"I am so relieved that you're all right. I was worried you were in a worse condition."

"Hey, thanks for coming by. Sorry for the other night."

"Pff...No need to apologize. Wasn't your fault. Well, I'm going to go now. Take care, and get yourself well."

My emotions almost got the better of me as I started to get teary-eyed before smiling back at Natalie.

Chapter Twenty
Retribution

Gray, puffy storm clouds were forming, and light rain started to freckle the concrete walk area. The northern sky was succumbing to the fall of night as the sun slowly tucked itself underneath the horizon. It looked as if the weekend was off to a bad start. One thing I didn't have on me was an umbrella. It was almost deja vu, as this was all too familiar. Thank goodness the hospital had a front outside covering that would provide shelter from the oncoming rain.

I guess it was time to call a taxi again. I was so wrapped up in seeing Natalie, I hadn't even thought about how I was going to get home. I promised my uncle's so-called driver I would get home safe. I was tired of lugging the box and backpack around like some traveling gypsy, and I could have died for a hot, steamy, relaxing shower right about then.

If I had had my way, I would have just dumped the box into my backpack, but I was certain that would have turned out bad, too. At least my arms would be free from the dulling

sensation that had started to overcome them. Once again, my
BlackBerry vibrated out of control inside my backpack. I hadn't
answered it from before because my hands were tied up, and I
had totally forgotten about it even though it had been a mere
few minutes go.

*All right, all right! My life would be so much easier if I
would invest in one of those wireless ear doohickey things to
connect with my BlackBerry.*

I couldn't have cared less as I dropped the box right
where I was standing, almost right on top of my foot, and swung
my backpack around. The sheer thought of silencing the damn
phone would be music to my ears.

"Hello?"

"Hey, it's me."

"Me who?"

"Beauford."

"Oh, now you decide to call. What happened to calling
me back in a couple of hours?"

"I'm sorry. Something came up."

"Something came up? That's the best you've got?"

"Uh…" He cleared his throat. "You see, it—"

"Listen, I have had a really, really bad day, and when
you called, it was not a good time, but I was looking forward to
hearing from you, and I didn't."

"Alex, I am sorry."

"I thought we could have had a great weekend and
maybe get to know each other better, but I'm not sure that is a
good idea."

"Alex, give me a chance to explain."

"Hey, let's just face it. We're two different people
whose ships crossed in the night, and let's call it that."

"Let me explain."

"My life is complicated right now, and even though I like you, I don't have time for a serious relationship. I have this new case that is stressing me out. I'm standing outside, inches away from being soaked again by this blasted rain."

"Alex... Alex."

"What?" I blurted out loud as I was caught up in thoughts flooding my head.

"I was just going to say, I would like to see you now."

"Now? Um, I would find that kind hard since you're there and I'm here in Victoria."

"And where is it that you think I am?"

"I'm not in the mood for a guessing game, Beau."

"Wait, you just called me Beau?"

"Yes, and too bad if you don't like it. It just sounds so much sexier. You've got a problem with that?"

"No."

"Good, because I like you more with that name."

"Well, in that case, let me pick you up and take you to dinner or for a cup of coffee."

"Did you not just hear me? I'm in no mood for games. I can't take much more bullshit or many more false promises, so please stop toying with my mind. I've got to go."

"Alex, I'm here in Victoria. In fact, I'm looking at you right now."

"What? How? Where?... Why?" My eyes glazed over in excitement while I wiped the tears that had formed in my eyes from the sheer stress of the day.

"I'll explain over dinner. Look straight ahead, and I'll flash my lights." Beauford twisted the rental car light switch back and forth, rapidly revealing to me that he was truly there.

"How'd you know where I was?"

"It's complicated, but first let me get you out of this rain."

Beauford put the car in drive and pulled up beside where I was standing. The passenger-side rain-soaked window opened. I leaned down a bit and looked inside. It was truly him. My knight in shining armor had come to my rescue again.

"Hi."

"Hey," I responded with a slight smile. Beauford just sat there.

"Oh, shoot! Where are my manners? Let me help you."

Beauford unbuckled his seat belt and exited the car. I watched him as he walked towards me. The rain began to soak his shirt and revealed the outline of his sculpted abs. His hair quickly became soaked while his glasses covered in raindrops made my insides tingle. He rounded the front bumper of the rented Jaguar XJ series. Nice car, but he was my main focus as he approached me. Before he could say another word, I did the unthinkable. I leaned in and planted my lips on his, kissing him.

I knew he was caught off guard, but as my eyes were closed and our lips locked, I felt his warm hands embrace both sides of my head. What seemed like an eternity was merely a half a minute, but as I pulled my lips away from his, opening my eyes, I could see his were still closed. If his heart pounded any faster and louder, I could have seen it against his shirt. I had no idea why he was already here but didn't care. If he played his cards right, this weekend, he might just get lucky.

I watched him stand there in the rain for a few seconds more before snapping my fingers to get his attention. Guess my kiss was like a spell for him to stand there with eyes closed and speechless. "Hey!"

"Um, wow, that was a nice surprise." Beauford pushed his glasses back towards the top of his nose.

"Sorry."

"No, don't be."

I looked at him and could tell he was mystified and excited at the same time. However, I really wanted to get out the rain. I smiled at him and kept glancing down at the door until he finally got my drift.

"Here, let me grab your stuff."

"Oh, OK...umm...hmm."

Beauford was walking circles around me, bumping into me and looking like a lost puppy as he picked up my box and almost spilled the contents out onto the wet concrete. I watched him scramble about for a few seconds. I guess my kiss did put a spell on him. He almost took my arm off pulling at my backpack.

"Whoa there, cowboy. I've got this. Can you get the door for me?"

I smiled at Beauford as he realized he was acting goofy all because I had kissed him. It wasn't like he had never been kissed by a girl before, or was it, I thought? I watched him walk around the front of the car. He had a little extra pep in his step. It was kind of cute and sexy at the same time.

"So, you're probably wondering why I'm here."

"Sort of, but I get it. You wanted to surprise me. That's why you're here, right?"

"Uh, yes, ahem, yep...You caught me...Guilty!"

"What I don't get is how you knew exactly where I would be since we haven't spoken to each other all day."

"Well, you see—" I interrupted Beauford as he was about to tell me some kind of a lie.

"Are you some sort of...?" I paused for a second as Beauford focused on my eyes.

"Sort of what?"

"Oh, nothing. Just for a second there...I don't know, I guess I was going to refer to you as a stalker or a spy...something like that."

"Who, me? You kidding me?" Beauford responded in a higher tone of voice before clearing his throat.

"I know, right? Silly me, thinking you of all people being a spy." I giggled, cracking a smile.

"Wait. So you don't think I have what it takes to be a spy?"

"I didn't mean it like that."

"If you didn't mean it like that, then how did you mean it?"

"What I meant to say is—"

"Is what? That just because I look geeky, you think I can't do that sort of work?"

"That's not what I meant." I went from being in a happy place to all of sudden feeling rather uncomfortable.

"OK, get in the care and we discuss it on our way."

Beauford opened the door as Alex got in. She watched him walk around the front of car and get in smiling at her before driving off.

"Then what?" Beauford inadvertently pushed down harder on the accelerator, causing the Jaguar to speed up.

"You're going a little too fast. You might want to slow down."

"Why, you feel I can't be a race car driver either?"

"You're starting to scare me. Please."

"I swear, just because you look a certain way, people misjudge you."

"Oh my God, you are insane. Slow down before you hit something or someone." I grabbed ahold of the "oh shit" handle as Beauford swerved in and around other cars and the distant sounds of horns quickly came and went.

"Oh, I see, now I'm insane."

"More like a jerk. Please stop the car."

"Why?"

"Stop the fucking car now!"

Beauford pulled the car over to the side of the road and put it in park. I couldn't believe what had just happened to me. What the hell had happened? Something didn't feel right. My right hand was still glued to the safety bar above my head as my heart raced uncontrollably. I wasn't sure what to do, as he looked straightforward out the windshield.

"Alex, I'm sorry. Please forgive me."

"Just take me home."

"I didn't mean to snap there."

"I don't need any explanation. I just want to go home."

"All right, at least let me make it up to you over dinner."

"I don't feel hungry right now."

"How about a drink? I really am sorry for whatever just happened. I kind of got carried away there for a moment. It wasn't really who I am."

"And exactly who are you? I barely know you, yet I feel drawn to you. I can't explain it, but I...don't know."

"OK, I get it. Last time we met was during a rainstorm, and I didn't exactly impress you. Still mad at me for snapping the heel of your knock-off boot?"

"Wait, did you just say knock-off boot?" My face suddenly became distorted in disbelief at what I had just heard.

"I didn't mean it like that."

"Just stop, please. Take me to dinner, and maybe I will forget this ever happened."

It didn't take Beauford long to realize I wanted to go. He put the car into drive and pulled away from the side of the road. Knock-off boot...typical male, not understanding the meaning of Prada, let alone I would never be caught dead wearing a fake. I paid good money for those boots, even though they were on sale. What does he know? He's a geek who plays with shit all day, literarily.

****

Ring...ring...ring.

"Hello?"

"You trying to double-cross me, Rozzito?"

"Who is this?" Rozzito was sitting in his cigar-smoke-filled office. He didn't recognize the voice on the other side of the line.

"Oleg...Oleg Nikita."

"Who the fuck is Oleg Nikita? I don't know any Oleg Nikitas."

"You even think about double-crossing me, and I ..."

"You'll do what?" The phone went dead, and a dial tone was all he could hear.

"Hello...hello? *E Figlio di puttana!*" Rozzito hated being threatened and yelled out, "You son of a bitch!" grinding his teeth together while slamming the handset repeatedly down on his desk, breaking the top part off.

"Mr. Rozzito, is there something wrong?" Frankie, one of his young foot soldiers, was standing outside his office and heard the commotion.

"Yeah, this phone is a piece of shit. I don't know what happened. It just broke."

"Ha-ha-ha, Looks like you had a fight and the phone lost." Frankie cracked a huge smile on his face.

"Is this funny to you?" Rozzito walked up to Little Frankie and grabbed his shirt right under his chin, making Frankie choke a bit

"No, Mr. Rozzito."

"You scared of me, Frankie?"

"No..." He was gasping for air. "Mr. Rozzito."

"Are those tears in your eyes, boy?" Rozzito paused for a few seconds as he stared at Frankie. "Answer me!"

DEADLOCKED: A Trial Beginning

"No, Mr. Rozzito." Frankie barely was able to get those words out as the wind was being choked out of him.

"You sure? Seems to me you just peed yourself out of fear all over my nicely polished hardwood floors" Rozzito stepped back as Frankie accidentally relieved himself out of sheer fear of Rozzito and what he might do to him.

"Make sure you clean this up. Have Rosemary order me a new phone, one that won't break under pressure."

Rozzito let go of his grip and patted down Frankie's shoulders, locking eye contact with no smile upon his face. Frankie held his neck, trying to suck in some air. Rozzito looked up and down at Frankie, giving him a disgusted look before walking away.

"Oh, once you're done cleaning up here, go and tell Donnie to meet me out back, and call Philippe and have him prep the yacht for departure. I have some business we need to tend to. Frankie, don't be ashamed. It's OK. Sometimes even grown men cry and accidentally, well, you know what I mean." Rozzito turned around and laughed as he walked down the hall towards the grand stairway.

****

Bubbles filled the top of a frozen beer mug as Beauford stood and watched, wedged between two other males packed at the bar. I could see him standing almost sideways, leaning in, as the noise inside Lucky's Bar seemed to deafen my ability to think, sitting at a tiny table in the middle of the place. I'd heard of Lucky's only from the TV commercials I would catch at home in between my channel surfing. I hadn't lived in Victoria long enough to venture out by myself other than to the harbor each workday.

I was still mad at Beauford for the shit he had just pulled in the car. I wasn't too sure what that was all about, let alone why it had happened. Beauford glanced back at me from the bar with a look signaling to me to be patient as I sat there, thirsty. Little did he know I would have rather gone to a little place to eat than here because I was starving, but I was sticking to my act to be mad. I wasn't really mad any longer. Heck, I don't think I was ever mad. I was just stunned the he was actually here with me. I pinched my cheek to make sure this was real as he walked up, spilling the top of the beer mugs, revealing they were beyond capacity.

"Whoa, sorry about that. Did I get any on you?"

"No, I'm good. Hey, you don't mind if we go outside on the patio, do you? Kind of loud in here."

"Oh, sure. It is loud in here."

I pushed the chair out away from the table and headed with Beauford towards the patio that faced the harbor across the street. Seeing if he would be a gentleman, I figured he would stop and open the door. My thoughts were correct; he opened the door and smiled at me. That alone brought him back into good graces with me. *A simple act of chivalry will go a long way*, I thought as I looked up at the "Lucky Bar" sign. I wondered how they came up with that name as I cracked a smile.

****

Water danced across the bow of an M2 catamaran, leaving mini-whitecaps in its wake. An image was coming and going out of focus. Engine sound from the boat made a gurgling, muffled sound before coming to a stop, rocking up and down as the waves combed the bottom of the vessel. A faint, high-pitched noise in less than half a second switched from the fall of night to ambient green light.

"*Voyez-vous quelque chose?*"

"*Rien encore.*"

"*Continuez à chercher. Bonne ont dit qu'ils seraient dans cette zone du détroit.*"

DEADLOCKED: A Trial Beginning

Two men aboard a subdued marine vessel concealed by the blanket of the night searched the waters close to the international boundary line that separated the United States and Canada. Intel reported possible drug-related activity in this area in the past and got a tip from in inside source that a deal would be going down at some point tonight. The men exchanged comments as to whether or not there had been anyone spotted in the area who looked suspicious, but there hadn't.

The hard part was, this stretched a good distance of ninety-five miles and was protected by the Constitution of International Maritime Act of 1791, grandfathered into the Principle of Equidistance set between Canada and the United States. This only meant that while vessels were inside the boundary, they would be protected from local and foreign acts of engagement, better known as a safe zone for many who partook in criminal activities.

A sudden horn blast out of nowhere startled the two men. An oil tanker heading for the Salish Sea spillway had snuck up on the little vessel undetected. The captain of the tanker sounded the horn to avoid running over the little M2 craft. Waves rocked the M2 violently, causing the Frenchman standing in the bow to lose his footing and be tossed to the floorboard of the vessel.

The driver of the vessel made a drastic attempt to move away from the oncoming surge of waves from the tanker, as it passed by just yards from colliding. It was so close, if any closer, the men could have touched the hull of the tanker. She slowly yet firmly pushed forward past them, revealing her name. The name *Nautilus* stood out between the encrusted rusted hull and white lettering that the sea had tried to erase. It was massive in size, stretching a whole 1,159 feet, just shy of being a supertanker.

She had thrown the M2 off course. The driver made a dashing 180-degree turn and pulled away, making its way to the stern of the tanker. It was clear now that the name of the vessel was indeed the *Nautilus*, based out of Anchorage, Alaska, said the words displayed on the back hull like a car license plate. A sounding gesture came from the mouth of the horn that proudly screamed out her presence, signaling a farewell as the *Nautilus* slowly faded into the night. The erratic waters subsided, giving back the stability that was momentarily robbed from the M2. Looking out into the night to the north, the Frenchman wearing the night vision goggles spotted something. He dialed in the focus, speaking to his counterpart.

"Luc, je crois que j'ai repéré quelque chose," meaning he might have spotted something such as a possible vessel in the safe zone. A few distance lights shined through the lens. Maybe it was the vessel they were looking for, and perhaps the one that Rozzito was aboard.

"Allez, allez, allez. Permet de le découvrir!"

"Go, go, go!" shouted Edgar, the Frenchman who just happened to be Alex's abrupt, rude neighbor, as the M2 engines churned and lifted the bow out of the water. She darted off in the direction of the possible spotted vessel. Edgar in fact had been working undercover for the past two years as a foreign operative agent with the Canadian Security Intelligence Service (CSIS) on a joint mission with the United States government to combat illegal money laundering and drug trafficking over international waters.

His mission was to track down the alleged notorious Canadian Mafia ring lord, Nicholas Rozzito, who had graduated from being a mobster to being public enemy number one. Edgar was to help bring him and his criminal organization down in a joint mission with the National Security Agency, as well as work with the United States Central Intelligence Agency,

Coastal Defenses, and local and foreign law enforcement, under the direct supervision of ECHELON, the world's most in-depth spy network, better known as the Communication Security Establishment, an extended arm of the North Atlantic Treaty Organization (NATO).

****

"I just love this place." I closed my eyes and took in a deep breath of the harbor air, talking softly to Beauford.

The night sky had drifted in, and the once-revealing sun had changed hands with the rising moon, giving a glow that tickled the harbor water. Sweat formed on the outside of my frosted beer mug. This was fitting for the day I had had and not what I had thought of when I had awoken that morning. The rain had long stopped, and the air just seemed cleansed. Looking over at him, I could see a gleam in his eyes as he studied my face.

"Anything new going on with your crappy job?" I could have said a thousand different things, but this one seemed to be the only one to surface off the tip of my tongue.

"Oh, same old stuff. You know how it is when you work with crap all day."

"I don't, actually. You can tell me, but only if you get me another round of beer."

"Um, sure."

It was in that instant that Beauford turned from being geeky to sure of himself. I watched him snap his fingers, and with that snap, he attracted the attention of one of the waiters who had walked outside the door. He came over to the table, as if he been demanded to do so. I was actually rather turned on by Beau's mere composure, and if I could I, would have forced myself over the table and onto him. But I planted my butt, which was slightly elevated out of the chair, back down on the seat.

313

"Yes, can I help you?" the Lucky Bar waiter asked the two of them.

"Two more rounds of the house beer for me and this lovely lady."

"Actually, I think I changed my mind," I quickly blurted because beer didn't seem too fitting anymore.

"Oh, OK. Um, whatever she likes, then." Beauford sat back with a slight hint of a smile and pushed his glasses back to the top of his nose.

"And for you, ma'am?"

"Do you have any pineapple that you could mix with some rum and a splash of vodka...oh, and crushed ice?"

"No, ma'am, we do not have any pineapple at the moment. All the pineapples available have been sold out for a special event this weekend."

"Well, rats. I guess I'll take some peach schnapps, orange juice, and a splash of whatever your vodka is over ice, then."

"OK, so one beer refill and one Fuzzy Navel with a splash of vodka. Will that be all?"

"Yes." Beauford smiled at the waiter, and me but I wasn't quite done yet.

"Actually, you got anything to munch on? I'm a little hungry."

"Right now, we have a special on a dozen huge deep-fried scallops served with lemon herb dipping sauce and a side of pork crisps, enough for two to enjoy for under ten loonies."

I looked over at Beauford, and he nodded his head in agreement. I looked at the waiter and told him that would be fine. The waiter turned, stopped, and turned back around towards me.

"Gustave Crush, right?"

"What?" I asked, looking at him.

"The drink you wanted, Gustave Crush, right?"

"Yes, but how did you know that?"

"It's no secret. The owner of the *Victoria Cove*, Mr. Gustave, has spread the word about one of his employees who created it. Oh, it is to die for."

"Yes...yes. I had one last Wednesday when I was aboard the ship and met Pierre. Oh my God, it was like drinking a piece of heaven."

"Indeed. You met Mr. Gustave?"

"Yes, briefly, but he has invited me to his event this weekend in Sooke Harbor."

"Yes, that's why we have no pineapple. No one does. He has purchased all that could be found at the last minute for his event."

"Well, I guess I'll be getting my fill of them tomorrow. Why don't you make me a bigger-than-normal glass for my drink?"

"Yes, ma'am."

"Don't you think you should slow down? I mean, mixing drinks can mess with your head."

"Relax there, cowboy, I can hold my own. Besides, with the snacks, I will be just fine. Why don't you tell me about your fancy job?"

"It's OK, nothing that important. Like you said, it's just a shitty job."

"I didn't mean it like that."

Little did Alexandria know, but inside her purse, her BlackBerry was vibrating from an incoming call, yet she could not hear it because she had silenced the ring at the hospital. Daniele, her friend, was trying to reach her.

"Yes, you did. Lots of people make fun of people who work with, you know, the stuff I do."

"Oh, come on Beau. I was just messing around. Must be the beer talking." I looked down at my almost empty mug and quickly threw back the last swallow of the Lucky Bar's finest.

The waiter arrived just as I finished, placing down a huge glass of Fuzzy Navel, and it looked ravishing. It was so big, I am not sure I was going to be able to finish it, but I would give it one hell of a try.

"OK, one huge Fuzzy Navel for the lady and one beer for the gentleman. Your food order will be up in just a few minutes."

Thank goodness for the timing of the drinks. Beauford didn't seem too pleased with my sarcastic tone. There was something strange about him. I couldn't quite put my finger on it, but I was still not quite sure how this had all come about tonight, with him being there already and all. Seemed a little odd. I certainly wasn't going to think about it much more. Besides, my drink was calling my name.

Ha, he might have been a gentleman, but the more I looked at him, the less I wanted him to be. I couldn't help my urges because I wanted him to take me and have his way with me, but I knew that would portray me as being easy. My insides started to tingle, and my skin became hot. I had to focus on something else. I stared at my yummy drink.

I took a huge sip of my drink through the straw as I looked at Beauford. I could tell he was watching my every move in disbelief that I was downing the drink so fast. A true newbie cardinal rule mistake—chugging a frozen drink would ultimately lead to frozen head syndrome.

"Easy, now. You know what happens next if you're not careful."

Chapter Twenty-One

Turning Over stones

Pitch black painted the surrounding canvas of nightfall as Edgar and Luc charted towards the possible spotted vessel; however, they were soon not alone. A joint venture from both sides of the international boundary line had commenced towards the target undetected and with stealth like reflexes, like a pack of sharks smelling a drop of blood from miles away, homing in on its prey.

Deep inside the safety net of the boundary, somewhere between the Haro Strait and the Strait of Juan de Fuca, Rozzito's yacht, the *Bella*, had come to a stop. Armed foot soldiers aboard her secured the vessel's perimeter as Rozzito awaited his arrivals. History recorded it that this area was known back in the heydays of the late sixties and early seventies as the center of the smugglers war, hence giving the name Smugglers Cove to a nearby stretch of water near the western side of San Juan Island.

A war between Mafia families and justice organizations that lasted several weeks and was recorded in Canadian history books as one of the bloodiest maritime wars since the early days of British Naval battles lined the bottom of the straits with her memories of a once-powerful Naval fleet. In fact, in undocumented acknowledgments and eyewitnesses, some even said that the late American labor union leader, Jimmy Hoffa, had been spotted in this area near the time of his going missing and his death.

According to local history records, it was wrong, and the late labor union leader was taken out towards the area by opposing gangsters, shot in the head, and tossed overboard in Smugglers Cove. Of course, this was just speculation, as the body of Jimmy Hoffa, like many other stories, had never been found, yet why would it if he had become a meal for a pack of hungry sharks?

"Alpha three two, this is Bravo three two, we are Oscar Mike to possible target zone, over."

Ten miles further up north near the Turn Point Light Station, an American Coast Guard vessel was en route to the possible location of the drug activity, heading down the outskirts of the safe zone. Her radar signature disguised her as a frigate.

"Bravo three two, this is Alpha three two, Charlie Mike, out."

"Alpha three two, Bravo three two, change of tact. Stand by, Alpha three six, over."

The United States Coast Guard and Canadian Coast Guard ships along with several small M2 vessels on both sides of the line suddenly were told to stop and hold their positions by command of operations. Intel reports might have been wrong, and verification of target and tip might not have been so valid after all. ECHLON had ordered all units to standby until further notice as precious minutes burned away, closing the window of opportunity to seize Rozzito under the cloak of night.

****

Beauford and I were still outside Lucky's Bar on the front patio, enjoying the night breeze. I could tell Beauford was getting a little uneasy with me drinking and all.

"So, tell me why you're really here." I looked at Beauford while sipping on my second frozen drink.

"What do you mean?" Beauford responded, cautiously looking me straight in the eyes.

"Oh, cut the crap. I'm onto you."

"I honestly don't know what you are referring to, Alex."

"You know, you're cute and sexy when you defend yourself. Your cheeks get red, and your face glistens. Isn't that my job, to defend?"

"OK, I can see this is the alcohol talking."

"Oh, relax, you party pooper." I broke out laughing.

I was starting to feel woozy from the drinks and could tell Beauford was not laughing back at me. I think the waiter had the bartender add just a tad too much vodka, but it was so good. I couldn't help myself as I started to talk louder and laugh. I'm sure I could be heard by passersby on the street, but I couldn't help it.

"You know, I have your watch."

"My watch?"

"The one you were looking for when we first met." I had started to slur my words as Beauford sat there poker faced. "Oh, don't look at me like I'm drunk."

"Well, you kind of are, Alex."

"No, remember, you were under the table, and you hit your head...Coffee went flying all over the table, splashing onto my chest...Course, I think you were trying to sneak another peek at my tattoo between my legs underneath the table like most boys did in high school. I know you want me. You were just being you. Don't lie."

"OK, clearly you are not making sense. I think it's time I get you home." Beauford looked around and noticed people on the patio staring at us. He saw the waiter inside the bar through the window and got his attention.

"Yes, now we're talking," I said. "Take me home and have your way with me. I'm ripe and ready for you."

I was surely was under the influence of the drinks, making me react as if it truth serum were spilling out my emotions. The waiter had stopped by the table, smiling at seeing me unwind outwardly as Beauford paid the man. An old couple who just so happened to walk by the patio stopped and watched me make a fool out of myself before making a comment towards us.

"You should be ashamed of yourself, talking and acting like a hussy."

That did it! I don't know what I was thinking, but I pushed the chair away from the table and staggered towards the old couple.

"Alex, don't do it. Come on, let's get you home."

"Relax, I'm just going over to say hello."

I motioned Beauford to stay put as I staggered towards the iron black fence near the sidewalk, almost tumbling over a chair, but I managed to catch myself. Beauford almost made a dash towards me as I looked back at him, but he stayed put next to the waiter, who had a big fat grin on his face. It was almost as if he knew I would be drunk off my ass from the drinks. God, I was such a lightweight from two drinks, or was it more? Oh yeah, I had had a beer, too.

"Hello there, old wrinkly people." I had no idea my alcohol blood count was far beyond the norm as I rudely commented to the old couple.

"Young lady, you need to watch what you are saying. If you were my child, I would throw you on my knee and spank you."

"Bet you'd like that. Spank me, Daddy." I had no idea what I was saying, but I almost threw up as I turned around and lifted my dress, showing my butt and smiling at the old man, who now stared at me with eyes wide open.

"Heavens to mercy! Come on, Morty, this is the work of the devil."

"Hang on, Ethel."

"Morty McDonald, I don't believe you. Getting all hot under the collar over a drunk young woman." The old lady looked at me and then her husband in shame, giving him an evil look.

"Oh, come on, Ethel. She meant nothing. Look, at least I don't need any pills tonight." Morty smiled at me, opening his eyes up wide before turning towards his wife.

"Oh my word, get that thing away from me." Ethel started to walk away fast as Morty smiled and chased after her.

"OK, time to go, Alex. I think you've embarrassed yourself quite enough for one night."

Beauford grabbed my arm and pulled me towards the exit as the waiter lunged over, laughing out of control. Somehow I think he had a hand in my drunken condition.

"Yeah, if you still want me, you'd better take me home and have your way with me."

****

Darkness surrounded the *Bella* as she sat there motionless. Rozzito, on the other hand, was enjoying a cigar while he toyed with his lighter, flipping the top open and closed. He knew he was being watched from afar. Word from his communications specialist aboard the yacht had alerted him.

"Mr. Rozzito, your guests are en route and should be here in a few minutes."

"Good...good. *Grazie!*"

The radar signatures had indeed fooled his personnel, broadcasting as mere harmless vessels as the strike team waited impatiently to proceed and move in on him, hoping to catch him in illegal activities.

"Any activity on the screen?"

"Just a few frigates and some small vessels miles away from us in either direction."

"Very good. This new paint job with radar cloaking from our friends to the north is working. To be safe, why don't you send out our precaution? It will broadcast our signature and fake out anyone who might be looking for us. Oh, and make sure the welcome package is set. We don't want whoever finds the vessel to feel their efforts were in vain." Rozzito started to laugh and shake his belly in his comfy chair before coughing on the smoke from his cigar.

"Right away, Mr. Rozzito."

"Leo?"

"Yes, Mr. Rozzito?"

"What is the status of our deal?"

"On its way to Alaska. The weapons are safe and sound aboard the *Nautilus*. The captain of the ship said they hadn't seen any suspicious traffic other than a small boat that happened to be in her path, but it was scared off when they were surprised by her presence. Not a threat by any means, just a couple of drunken fishermen. Seems the new whisper motors are indeed working. Got to hand it to the Russians for their advanced technology."

"Ha, it seems so."

"The helicopter is on approach."

"Good. That is all, Leo."

Cocky and way out his normal league of being an organized crime boss, Rozzito had struck a deal with a new northern ally called New Russia, otherwise known as N.R, a new Russian Mafia organized crime outfit. He had made an arms deal to supply them with US-made weapons, a deal worth over ten million, and his take would be at least 250 large. Rozzito had raised his stakes in organized crime and was no longer just considered a Mafia boss but had more of a global stature, with a little help from inside sources.

"Alpha three six, this is Foxtrot Alpha Romeo, over." Foxtrot Alpha Romeo, FAR for short, was the joint strike mission's aerial recon and communications plane.

"Go ahead, Foxtrot."

"SAT has an inbound bogey on approach to target, over."

"Roger."

"Bravo three two, it's a go for capture. Proceed with stealth. Do not engage target, over."

"Alpha three two, Bravo three two, hold short of four left."

"Roger. M2's, proceed to target. Do not engage. I repeat, do not engage inbound aircraft to target. Cover and conceal and report back, over."

"Affirmative."

****

The unidentified helicopter had made its way to Rozzito's yacht and had landed at the stern of the vessel. Engines only were tuned down to a steady idle as two men exited the craft heavily armed. Rozzito stood there as a man exited the helicopter wearing a suit. Rozzito waved him forward to where he was standing before walking inside the vessel.

"You realize the danger of meeting here? For Christ's sake, Rozzito, these waters could be crawling with government agents."

"Relax. You afraid of your own people?"

"It's not my people I'm afraid of. If we were ever caught, this would break treaties between countries, not to mention treason for violating the national security of both sides of the fence."

"The ship is radar invisible. Besides, if they knew we were here, don't you think we would know about it? As a precautionary move, I've already handled it, just in case."

"Handled it? In what way?"

"Don't worry about it. Sit, relax. Here, smoke a cigar. They're Habaneros from Castro's personal stock, not one of those fake Cubans your papa probably smoked when you were a boy."

"Whatever. How'd you get those? Never mind. I don't need to know. I'll pass, thank you."

"You seem nervous, Mr. Pasquale. For a man of your position and stature, you seem uneasy. Do I make you nervous?"

"What kind of question is that?"

At that very moment, Rozzito made eye contact with Donnie, signaling him to quietly come over.

"It's a simple question. Either I do or I don't."

"I deal with thugs like you every day. Nothing different this time."

"Watch your tone. No need for name-calling."

Just then, Rozzito stood up as if to stretch and gave Donnie the OK to move in. Donnie quickly took his wire that he had wrapped around both hands and moved in slowly. Rozzito motioned his head and chin to his men as they snuffed out the life of the two men who had stepped aboard the vessel, shooting them both in the head with silencers.

Both bodies fell into the water as the pilot of the helicopter made a desperate attempt to prepare to take off but was stopped by a gun to his head. Mr. Pasquale had seen from the corner of his eye one of his men fall into the water and leaped out of his seat.

"Hey...hey! What the hell is going on here? You just kill one of my men?"

"Sit down."

"You realize what you just did? You just killed a United States government agent and signed your own death warrant."

Mr. Pasquale, none other than the United States Comptroller General for weapon sales, selected by the United States Congressional party, suddenly realized he was not in a good position. Donnie came up from behind him and pulled him back down in his chair with the force of his wire, firmly cutting off precious oxygen to his head. Rozzito's anger had surfaced, and he pulled out his weapon of choice, an Italian dagger.

"You know what your problem is? You Americans get too greedy, and all of a sudden you think it is OK to throw your weight around like you have some sort of fucking power." Rozzito raised his voice while waving around the dagger in front of Mr. Pasquale as Donnie firmly held the wire against him. Gasps of air gurgled out of the mouth of the comptroller.

"You think you would fly in here on your fancy bird, step into my world, and walk away, smiling like nothing ever happened?" Rozzito paused for a few seconds and stared at the helpless man gasping for air.

"*RISPONDIMI!*"

Rozzito lunged towards Pasquale, screaming the words "answer me" while placing the dagger's shaped side up against the skin between his top lip and nose. The only way the comptroller was going to be able to answer him was if Donnie backed off and removed the wire. Rozzito snapped his fingers and motioned Donnie to move away as Pasquale leaned forward, head down, coughing.

"The deal has changed."

Pasquale raised his head up slowly, looking Rozzito straight in the eyes and covering his mouth. Blood oozed between his fingers. The dagger was sharp enough to cut the skin between his lip and nose. However, Rozzito made sure he left a mark for Pasquale to remember.

"Deal change? There are no deal changes. Who the fuck do you think you are, anyway? The only reason why you and I are here this very second is because I allow it."

"No...No...No, you see, you have it all wrong. I admit, I am a thug, as you put it. Hey, bada Bing... bada boom. It's in my blood, and yes, I do things that, well, some would say are unethical, but meh, I say they aren't. You say 'po-tay-toe.' I say 'po-tah-toe.'" Rozzito, while dangling the dagger around in a figure-eight motion, spurted out some humor.

"What does that have to do with it?"

"It has everything to do with it, Mr. Pasquale. We are both carved from the same fabric."

"No...No...No, that is where you are wrong." Pasquale stood up as if to defend his comment.

"Am I? *Si metta a sedere!*"

"I'm sorry; I don't understand your stupid Italian."

Rozzito glanced over at Donnie. Pasquale followed his look and saw Donnie getting ready to come at him again with his wire-wrapped hands.

"Sit the fuck down and listen to me."

"You are way out of your league, Rozzito. You have no idea what you're getting yourself into."

As soon as Pasquale made his comment, Rozzito suddenly smacked him across the face. His left cheek was grazed by Nicholas's boss ring, which happened to scrape the skin deep enough to draw blood.

"You can beat me, shoot me, hell, even dismember me, but if you kill me, there will never be a deal, let alone a deal change. So I advise you to take your cut and be on your miserable, pathetic way, as this meeting never happened."

"You listen here, you little maggot. I took this deal because I don't give a rat's ass about you, your government, the Canadians, the Russians, or any other *Figlio de puttana* who is a part of this little operation of yours. I took it because of the money. Nothing better than the smell of dirty money."

"You don't get it, do you? You can go around calling everyone a motherfucker, but the reality of it is, you are just a lowlife piece of shit, just a pawn in this chess game."

"Oh, so you do understand my stupid language. Well, you go back and tell your boss I said, *Ciao*. Oh, and tell him the deal has changed. Now my take is five hundred large, and I want safe passage for my shipping vessels to and from the United States, never to be stopped or questioned. Have the authorities from both sides just look away as I conduct my business."

"You have got to be joking. What you're asking cannot be done."

"Not only will it be done, I want to never be linked to this deal and never see your face again on my water because if I do, you won't just get away with a few scratches, if you know what I mean."

"My boss just happens to consist of 535 members who report to the president of the United States. What you are asking cannot be done simply by saying it. This takes a vote in order to get approved."

"So, what's the matter? You'd better see to it that it does get passed, or let's just say, one by one, starting with the closest person to you, they will end up dead. Your only child, Marisa, is it?" Rozzito pulled out a photo of Pasquale's eighteen-year-old daughter and placed it inches away from his face.

"Don't you ever threaten to harm my daughter? She is just starting out in life."

"Then I guess we are done here, yes? Do as I ask, and not a hair on her pretty little head will be harmed. Don't do as I ask, and well, let's just say I will make sure she gets treated like a whore before she is torn alive into pieces and tossed overboard for fish food."

"You as much as lay a finger on my daughter, and I will—"

"Will what? Come and kill me?" Rozzito and Donnie started to laugh uncontrollably. "Get the hell out of my face, and get that piece of shit ride you call a helicopter off my boat."

"Oh, just so you know, this water we happen to be on isn't yours. It belongs to the United States and Canada, and you, sir, are on borrowed time. You can't hide between the boundaries forever. This is extortion!"

Rozzito waved Pasquale away as he ran towards the helicopter. Two black duffel bags full of American bills were tossed into the backseat area as Pasquale boarded. He kept eye contact as the pilot brought the bird up to speed and lifted off into the dark.

****

Lights reflected off a twenty-inch chrome wheel as the passenger-side front wheel of the Jaguar rolled to a stop, nudging the curb right outside my apartment. Beauford looked over at me as my head was plastered against the window with my eyes closed.

"Hey, sleepyhead, you're home." Beauford put the car in park and exited.

My head was spinning, and I felt like I could puke at any second, but I didn't want to ruin my chance of finally scoring with a man. I swallowed hard to push back down the urge to throw up. I could see him from the side mirror as he made his way to my door. He opened it, leaning in to unbuckle me. Smelling his cologne at that very second tingled my insides, and in my drunken state, I grabbed him, locked lips, and started to French kiss him. His eyes opened, and he pulled his tongue out of my throat and backed out of the car doorway.

"What's wrong? Wasn't that OK?"

"Um, no, I liked that part of you, it's just..."

"Just what?"

"Did you by any chance almost puke?"

"Why do you say that?"

"Well, because I could taste what seemed like the food we had a while ago."

"I am so sorry. Get me inside and let me freshen up, and we can continue."

"Oh, OK, but if you're not feeling so well, don't you think that kind of action is going to make you seasick and throw up?"

"Hey, let's slow it down. I may be in a drunken state, but who said anything about getting laid?"

"You did, at Lucky's Bar. You told me to get you home because you wanted me."

"I did?"

"In fact, you told a few people that. So...we're here now."

"Wow, is that all I am to you, a piece of ass?"

"No, um, not at all."

"Relax, cowboy, I was just kidding. Just get me inside and let me freshen up, and we'll go from there. Oh, grab my stuff, willya?"

"OK...um, sure." Beauford looked at me for a second or two before grabbing my backpack and box. He followed me up the stone walkway to my door.

****

"*Cette attente est stupide. Bientôt, les fenêtre d'opportunité va fermer.*"

Edgar, standing on the edge of the bow of the M2, was getting angry about why ECHELON orders had been halted. Looking over at Luc, his counterpart and M2 driver, he blurted out how it was stupid to be waiting around because the window to capture Rozzito was closing. Looking through his night vision goggles, Edgar scanned the water's horizon and dialed in the lens, but he could not find the once-flashing lights that could possibly have been the target. Nothing but water, darkness, and the sound of the waves lapping the side of the hull.

"*Oubliez les ordonnances, allons-y!*" Edgar looked over his shoulder, telling Luc to ditch the order to stay put and move towards the possible target.

"*Ne soyez pas stupide,*" Luc responded to Edgar, telling him to not be stupid.

"*Pour tout ce que nous savons que navire aurait pu être un détournement de nous jeter hors,*" Edgar said sarcastically, referring to the ship heading towards Anchorage, Alaska, as a possible diversion to throw them off.

"*Ha, ce serait drôle à bord d'un navire à patiner droit adopté nous.*" Luc laughed as if to say that would have been funny to use a ship to sneak past them.

"*Appelez-le et vérifiez.*" Edgar told Luc to call it in and check just in case. To him, that would have been too easy but a perfect way to avoid the joint strike mission to capture and seize whatever deal was going down. Little did both of them know, the ship in fact had been used in a deal, a weapons deal, to be exact, a ten-million-dollar cargo consisting of American-made weapons on its way to outfit Russia's new organized pockets of crime.

****

After Beauford followed me into my home, I stumbled my way upstairs as he walked into my living room and placed the box on top of the dining table.

"Give me a few minutes, cowboy. Make yourself at home."

"OK. I'll just be waiting in the living room."

Beauford sat down in the La-Z-Boy chair and quickly realized how comfortable it was, pulling back on the lifter and extending the foot area, smiling. "I could get used to this."

"What did you say?" I yelled down from upstairs.

"Um, nothing. Just saying how nice your place is."

"Thanks. My uncle pretty much helped me pick this place out."

"I noticed you don't have any pictures on the wall."

"Well, that's because I haven't had time to put any up."

I realized just then I had snuck up on Beauford because he seemed startled to hear my voice, but the reaction on his face was even better.

"Um...wow...you look ravishing."

"Thanks. Not too forward?"

"No...No." He cleared his throat. "You look fine." Beauford could not help that his vocal cords suddenly shot up a few decibels.

My head was still spinning from the drinks, but I had managed to put on a button-down dress shirt. I had just never buttoned it up, revealing my stomach area, partial cleavage, and a pair of bright red-laced panties peeking out from behind both sides of the shirt dangling freely. I figured, what the hell, if this was going to happen, I might as well go for it. Besides, I could see he didn't mind. I just hoped I could keep from puking.

"You are so beautiful, Alex. I had no idea."

"Oh, you're just saying that because you're about to score."

"No, really, you are...wow."

"I have to be honest with you, I have never, you know, done the whooptie-whoop."

"I'm sorry. What's whooptie-whoop? Is that some sort of dance or game?"

"Dance...game, no. I mean, I have never, you know." I kept nudging my head to the side, pointing my eyes down at his midsection in hopes he would get the idea.

"Oh!" Beauford glanced down towards his waist, opening his eyes wide.

"Oh, God, no. What is with you men? Ewe."

"What? What did I do?"

"I meant I have never had sex with a man before."

"Oh, so you are still a virgin?"

"Well, when you say it in that tone, it sounds like I have leper syndrome."

"I'm sorry, not what I meant."

"Well, are you going to just stand there? Better make a move before I change my mind about this." I knew I was not going to change my mind, but by saying that, perhaps he would get over being shy and approach me.

I could still tell he was nervous, yet so was I, not to mention my stomach was still feeling like a boxing match was going on. So I decided to invite him over to me with my index finger, and that did the trick. He moved towards me and softly touched my shoulders. No fireworks there as I stared at him.

Was I going to be the first one to make a move? What was it going to take to get him to embrace me?

Then it happened. He leaned in and kissed me. Well, it was more like a peck, but that's all it took for him to break the ice as I closed my eyes and felt him kiss my neck softly and gently. My heart must have gotten the message because my body felt hotter than it was a few seconds ago. I could hear my pulse pump through my ears as my heart began to race. I had no idea what was about to happen, but it did. Beauford had without my knowledge reached under my shirt and cupped my left breast, and the unthinkable happened.

Instead of being excited to have him touch my skin, my reflexes did the opposite, and my left knee just so happened to contact him in the groin area unannounced. It happened so fast, I had no idea I had done it. I could see the look on his face was pure disbelief.

"I am so sorry. I didn't mean that."

"It's OK. Guess I had it coming for touching you without asking."

"No, I mean, I want you to touch me. It was just a reflex. I wasn't expecting it, and your hands are cold."

I felt like the moment had changed in a blink of an eye. I suddenly didn't feel the urge to continue, but I wanted to. I had no idea how he would react to me, so I had no choice but to remove my shirt in hopes of grabbing his attention again. It worked.

"Tell you what," I said. "Why don't you grab one of the kitchen table chairs and bring it in here?" At that very moment, I burped quietly and almost felt like I was going to puke, but I played it off. "Place the chair right here and sit down."

"What do you have in mind?"

"Sit. You'll see."

Beauford placed the chair right in front of me and sat down. My head felt so heavy, like it was barely sitting on my shoulders, but I wanted to impress him by giving him a lap dance. I never had done one before, but from all the chats with my friend Daniele, I figured I could do it since she always went into more detail than I ever cared to hear. Besides, I figured this way, I could keep the room from spinning out of control and slowly connect with him, first by touching one another, rubbing my body over his. Perhaps this would enhance the moment and lead to more.

"What are you doing?"

"Shh, just sit there and hush." I placed a finger over his lips before straddling my legs on both sides of his.

I felt awkward and shook a little, purely out of nervousness, but I managed to gain his undivided attention grazing my chest over his face. I could tell from sitting on him, rubbing up against his pants, that he was beyond excited. I had to admit, so was I as I tried desperately to keep from making a gasping sound every time I moved my hips, but I started to move and grind as I got deep into my crazy idea. The only thing that went wrong next was I made a foolish newbie mistake. I started to swing my head backwards and to the side just out of excitement as my heart pumped blood through my veins uncontrollably.

When I looked up at the ceiling that did it. I couldn't hold it down, and the unthinkable happened. I looked at him. He was opening and closing his eyes in pure enjoyment before I projectile vomited all over his face and shirt. The boxing match was over and the bell rang is what happened. All that motion and swinging my head to please him was over the top. I sat there for a few seconds, not knowing what to do. My head was spinning out of control, but I just pushed myself off him and fell down on the floor flat on my butt.

I couldn't move and started to bawl out loud. Tears flooded my eyes and rolled down my face. I was so embarrassed for what had just happened. Even I couldn't understand my own words as I tried to tell him I was so sorry for what just took place.

Chapter Twenty-Two
Wrenching Dismay

Tick tock was the sound echoing in Edgar's mind, as seconds turned to minutes with precious time fading to seize the element of surprise. Sitting and waiting for orders that might never come, Edgar grew anxious and knew if something didn't happen soon, this would all be in vain. Rozzito would slip through, and they would have to try again another time, leading to more corruption to happen.

"*C'est bull. Venir sur Luc, permet de passer.*" Edgar looked at Luc, shouting how this was bull and to go.

"*Non, commande n'a pas gibing nous le commande.*" Luc responded by telling Edgar that he wasn't going to go since command had not given the approval.

Frustrated and about to throw his gear down on the floorboard of the M2, Edgar stopped and paused as the radio made a beeping noise, followed by a few seconds of silence. Luc and Edgar waited, eyes glued to the radio in hopes of getting the order to go.

"Alpha three two, Bravo three two, order is go for capture. Target confirmed. Capture, do not kill. Expect hostile situation...Proceed with caution. On the move. Over."

"Three six, this is Bravo team, affirmative."

"Three six, this Alpha team. Roger that."

"*Commande positive.*"

Luc responded to command, then dropped the microphone attached to the radio, leaving it to dangle. He slammed the M2 into full throttle, lifting the front like a whale cresting. Edgar braced himself as the twin diesels churned out all 960 horses against the peaceful water. Perhaps Rozzito had not left the area yet, and the go for capture would still be immanent for a successful mission despite ECHELON stalling.

****

Rozzito's yacht had left the Smugglers Cove area and had already started to head northwest towards the peak of the Salish Sea. So far, his vessel had avoided radar, and he had been able to conduct his meeting under the cloak of darkness. The arms deal was done and on its way, his bank account was now plus-500 large, and he couldn't have been happier. Now it was time to make one more stop before heading back towards English Bay.

Strapped to the bottom of the vessel, tightly sealed from water, Rozzito was making a personal delivery to one of his clients. The deal was to meet in an undisclosed area around Boundary Pass where there was an uninhabited island not prone to attention. One hundred kilos of pure cocaine that was sealed, spread out, and attached would be removed and handed off for the lump sum of eight million, leaving him with a nice profit of two million to add to his half-million payday.

Little did he know that from all four angles of his nautical position, a joint mission was being conducted for his whereabouts to arrest him for illegal activities, not to mention

337

the order already in place to capture him so that he would appear by order of the Supreme Court for such allegations Monday morning, the same court hearing that Alexandria, Rozzito's niece, would be leading as prosecutor in the trial of the International Maritime Crime Division against the English Bay Fisheries Local 509, Fishing Workers of Canada. The key to Rozzito's being undetected was the little boat deployed carrying his former signal as a decoy, giving him the ability to travel right through any possible warning nets and out of the boundary.

Chatter on the com went back and forth between teams on a channel frequency only they could communicate on, but there was no spotting of Rozzito's so-called yacht, the *Bella*, just normal frigates, oil tankers, and cargo ships passing through the night and maybe one or two small vessels, none with the radar signature that would unzip the whereabouts of the Mafia boss.

Rozzito's yacht made its turn towards the bottom of Boundary Pass near Turn Point Light Station where Alpha three two was scouring the waters outside of the boundary line.

"Mr. Rozzito, it seems we have a United States Coast Guard ship a mile to our starboard side. Looks like they're actively searching the water at high speed, as well as a Canadian Coast Guard frigate to our port side about two miles out."

"Thank you, Leo, but are they coming our way?"

"They don't appear to be."

"Good. They can't see us. Flip the remote control switch to turn on the signature broadcasting just in case. Perhaps it's just an exercise. Don't worry about it."

"Yes, Mr. Rozzito."

"Leo, I will be retiring to my cabin. Do not disturb me until we arrive at our next destination. I need a few minutes of shut-eye."

"Yes, Mr. Rozzito."

Rozzito walked up to Donnie and whispered in his ear. "Donnie, make sure nothing goes wrong. The kid is nervous about some Coast Guard activity."

"Yes, boss. Probably some exercise. They tend to do that sort of stuff."

"That's what I told the kid, but you know what to do if something..."

"Go rest. It's all under control."

Rozzito looked at Donnie and stuck out his lip and chin as if to agree, and then he walked inside towards his cabin.

****

The M2 boat with Edgar and Luc traveled up the Haro Strait at full throttle until Edgar waved with his hand to signal Luc to slow down. With his night vision goggles dialed and focused, Luc's radar picked up a faint signal as well. The M2 came to a slow trot as the SAT radio began to chatter.

"*Qu'est-ce que c'est?*" Luc shouted to Edgar, asking him what it was.

"*Je pense que j'ai vu une lumière clignotante dans la distance,*" replied Edgar, stating he thought he spotted a flashing light in the distance, perhaps a vessel.

Luc pushed the throttle forward, giving a gentle nudge against the hull in an effort to move closer to the potential vessel.

"*Alpha trois six, c'est le M2 Bravo, plus?*" Luc called into command Alpha six with the M2 call sign to report the possible sighting.

"Roger, go ahead, M2 Bravo, and for God's sake, speak English."

Luc stared at the microphone for a second or two before responding. "Alpha three six, radar signature strong...possible target...location...latitude 48.60399...longitude -123.18825 north, northeast, over?"

"Roger M2, proceed and report. All units proceed towards grid coordinates latitude 48.60399, longitude -123.18825, just southwest of Henry Island, and rally up with M2 bravo, out."

Luc pushed the throttle forward some more, again almost knocking Edgar off balance while cracking a smirk. He was getting some slight enjoyment out of watching Edgar in the bow of the boat. Edgar, on the other hand, did not care for Luc's sudden gesture to leap the boat out of the water. Even though it was dark, looking through the night vision goggles back at Luc inside the driver's seat of the boat, he could see the grin on his face. Without Luc being able to fully see Edgar, Edgar fired a pistol just above the top of the boat near Luc. This was his way of getting Luc's undivided attention.

"*Sacrebleu. Quelqu'un a tiré sur nous.*" Luc, without realizing it was Edgar who had fired the shot, stuck his head out the side window and yelled out that someone was firing on them.

Edgar, smirking, happened to look towards the front of the M2 and saw what looked to be a small boat as the radar signal heightened rapidly. Luc pulled back on the throttle and maneuvered the M2 to the side of the small boat drifting aimlessly in the water. The radar was pinging a flat line, mimicking the *Bella*'s signature, but it certainly was not Rozzito's yacht as they had hoped it would be. To keep the small boat from drifting past them, Edgar scrambled to obtain the reach pole system and pulled the boat close to the side. Inside the unmanned boat was a wooden box with a dark image on the side. Edgar couldn't make it out from where he stood and yelled out to Luc to keep the M2 steady because he was going to board the small craft and check out the box.

The small boat rocked too much against the waves that bounced off the M2, so Edgar reached for a tie rope and managed to secure the small boat up against the side of the M2 and leaped into the boat.

"*Qu'est-ce que cest?*" Luc yelled out to Edgar, asking him what it was.

"*Je ne sais pas m'accorder une minute,*" Edgar immediately responded to Luc, stating he didn't know yet and to give him a minute to find out.

"*Je vais appeler les sat dans. Il y a quelque chose qui cloche avec cette signature,*" responded Luc, stating something wasn't right about the radar signature, and he was going to radio command.

It was hard for Edgar to make out the symbol on the box looking through the ambient green light from the goggles. He took them off. Reaching for his black issued Army-style flashlight clipped to his utility belt, Edgar looked out into the water before shining the light directly at the side of the box, revealing a skull with crossed bones and the word "Explosives."

Immediately, Edgar knew something was wrong, yet instead of warning Luc, he attempted to open the wooden box from the top and discovered his worst fears.

"Get the fuck out of here! It's a trap!" Edgar shouted out to Luc in English.

"What?"

"Quick, loosen the rope from the boat. It's a bomb, and it's counting down, with only twenty seconds left. I must have armed it when I opened the top." Edgar turned to Luc frantically while trying to loosen the rope from the small boat.

"*Fils de pute!*" Luc shouted, meaning "son of a bitch," and stumbled towards the control center of the M2, throwing the gear in reverse.

The M2 backed away in a violent motion as Luc watched Edgar stand there as he turned on the spotlight. All he could see was Edgar gesturing "in the name of the Father, the Son, and the Holy Spirit" across his chest while jumping overboard feet first. The small boat erupted in an explosion, lighting up the water's horizon.

The blast could be seen for miles. The Canadian Coast Guard and the second M2 homed in on the grid coordinates of Luc and Edgar's whereabouts. Luc had moved the M2 just far enough back before the explosion, yet pieces of the boat still pinged the side and windshield, cracking it. Out of sheer reflex, Luc had ducked down, and the last thing he remembered seeing before the explosion was Edgar about to jump off the boat.

Pieces of the once-small vessel lay scattered across the water in flames. Luc desperately shined the spotlight back and forth over the carnage, calling out to Edgar, but there was no response.

Right about that time, the second M2 boat rounded the backside of Luc's M2, circling around the outside perimeter of the wreckage. The Canadian Coast Guard frigate stopped fifty yards away from Luc while communicating over the SAT radio to him, but he ignored it and continued his search for Edgar.

"M2 Lima Foxtrot, what the hell happened, over?" the captain of the Canadian Coast Guard frigate tried to communicate with Luc.

Luc scanned the water standing on the bow of his vessel, shining his flashlight into what looked like a war zone of burning debris, calling out for Edgar. The other M2 kept moving in a 360-degree turn, shining its floodlight over the debris area as well. Luc started to turn away from the water when he felt a hand grab his foot, which startled the hell out of him. It was Edgar. He had miraculously survived the explosion.

DEADLOCKED: A Trial Beginning

****

A loud screeching noise, followed by a grasping jolt, came from the engine room of the *Bella* as dark pillows of smoke rose from within the room and out from the back of the yacht. Her diesel had engines overheated and seized, causing the propulsion to stop and leaving the vessel helpless in the water, adrift four miles out from Rozzito's next rendezvous.

"What in God's name was that?" Leo shouted towards the captain of the yacht.

"Damn it," the captain replied while looking at the computerized instruments.

"What's wrong?"

"Both engine alarms are showing malfunctions on the screen."

"How can that be? These engines are indestructible. I had them inspected before we left harbor."

"Well, it appears they are not."

"Can you just push a button and restart them?"

"What, are you fucking kidding me? You can't just push a button and all is good. We're dead in the water right now."

"Oh my God. I'm a dead man. I promised Rozzito we were good to go. He's going to kill me." Leo panicked and tweaked around in place, fearing the worst.

"Well, you'd better go and let him know."

"Let who know?" Donnie had caught Leo and the captain by surprise as he entered the control room of the *Bella*.

"Um, we seem to have some sort of trouble at the moment. No need to worry," said the captain.

"What kind of trouble?" Donnie replied with a disgruntled tone.

"Just some minor issue with the engines...We should be on our way momentarily."

"Don't lie to me. Engine trouble means we won't make our next stop, and Mr. Rozzito isn't going to be happy about that."

"It's being worked on as we speak."

"Well, you'd better make sure we're up and running fast. Damn it. I'd better go and let Rozzito know."

"That's Mr. Rozzito. Have you forgotten all respect for who I am?"

"No, Mr. Rozzito," Donnie quietly responded but keeping eye contact.

"You may have worked your way up the chain of command, but I am still the don, and when you mention my name or greet me, you will show some fucking respect, you got that?" Within a blink of an eye, Rozzito whacked Donnie across the face with his backhand. The look of sheer fear was on Leo's and the captain's faces, but not Donnie's. Donnie slowly brought his face back to the front with a scowl. He knew if he said what he wanted to, something terrible would happen. Blood would be spilled and this was not the time.

"Now, someone do me the honors and tell me what the fuck is going on?" said Rozzito. "Why are we stopped, and what was the awful noise?"

"We experienced engine failure.".

 Leo responded.

"Engine failure? Impossible. I was told these engines were indestructible."

"Apparently not. I have the engine room crew assessing them now and working on bringing them back to operational status."

"I'm sorry, Mr. Rozzito." Just then, Leo panicked for his life and darted past Rozzito, almost knocking him over as he left the control center and ran out the side door to the outside of the yacht.

"Che cosa l'inferno?" Rozzito yelled, "What the hell?" as Leo had pushed him with enough force to almost knock him off his feet.

"Shoot that lying son of bitch!" Rozzito stared at Donnie, but Donnie didn't move.

Leo had stumbled down the stairs, losing his footing, and he fell flat on his face. Lifting his head and looking up towards the control center before getting back up, he tried to make his way to the front of the yacht in hopes of jumping overboard to safety to avoid being killed.

"Shoot him now!" Rozzito, beet red in the face, ordered Donnie to kill Leo.

"Let him go," said Donnie. "He's just a kid. Forget about him. Come on, let me help you up."

Rozzito went from grinding his teeth to letting Donnie pick him up with both hands. Donnie gave Rozzito a hug out of respect in hopes of derailing his thoughts of killing the young man fleeing for his life. Donnie wrapped his arms around Rozzito, kissed both his cheeks, and made a sudden gasping sound. His eyes and mouth went wide open as he staggered back away from Rozzito, looking down at his stomach as blood saturated his shirt.

Rozzito had a hidden sleeve knife that had pierced the right side of Donnie's torso. Donnie squinted his eyes in horror as he staggered outside the side door and tumbled overboard while Rozzito wiped his blood from the knife and retracted it.

Rozzito demanded the captain hand over his sidearm. "Give me your pistol, and shine that floodlight at the bow of the ship. You want to end up like him, too?" Rozzito looked at the captain.

The captain unclipped the safety strap, pulled out his gun, and slapped it into Rozzito's hand. He toggled the floodlight switches. Nicholas made his way out the side door and to the top of the steps. He saw Leo about to make it the front of the boat. He aimed the pistol with his right hand and pulled the trigger several times, hitting Leo in the back once and another round fatally in the back of the neck. Leo stopped in his tracks for a second before stumbling to the edge of the bow. Blood spewed out of his mouth as he slowly took his last breath, leaned over the bow, and plunged into the water.

At that very moment, horns blasted. Lights from an oncoming vessel had illuminated what just happened. It was the United States Coast Guard frigate Bravo three two, which happened to be in the general area when the automatic distress signal was triggered, carrying the radar signature of the vessel when the computers reported an engine failure, an important new feature Rozzito had no idea existed when he had bought the *Bella* and had her engines overhauled.

"This is the United States Coast Guard. We know who you are, and we will board your vessel, Mr. Nicholas Rozzito. Do not try to anything foolish or we will fire upon you and sink you."

Across the water about twenty yards, the captain of the Coast Guard frigate called out towards the *Bella*. The ship was equipped with a front 57mm gun that was pointing directly at the mid-hull of the vessel.

"Lieutenant, if he as much as flinches an inch, blast that son of a bitch out of the water and send him straight to Davy Jones's locker."

"Aye aye, Captain."

"Master Chief, take your men and prepare to board the vessel and apprehend Nicholas Rozzito."

"Yes, sir."

"Master Chief, remember, he is wanted alive because he is due in court Monday for his trial as well as the murder of whomever it was that fell overboard."

"Petty Officer Wilco, have they fished the person out of the water yet?"

"The men are on their way, sir."

"Very well. Let's go get them, boys. ECHELON is counting on us."

****

"I think they plan on boarding us, Mr. Rozzito."

"Relax. They've got nothing on us. Just play it off as if we were having some engine trouble after coming back from a nice outing."

"But the shooting..."

"What shooting? I didn't shoot anyone."

Rozzito looked down at the gun and then back at the captain. Rozzito was wearing his gloves, so there was no trace of his fingerprints, only the captain's.

"The way I see it, you did it. You got a problem with that?"

"No, sir, um, I mean Mr. Rozzito."

Rozzito leaned his head from side to side to lessen the tension before straightening out his suit coat and walking towards the bow of the yacht where the US Coast Guard cutter *Savannah*, code named Bravo three four, had pulled her 230-foot hull up against the *Bella*, dwarfing her tiny 120-foot length. There was no sense in Rozzito and his men defending the *Bella*, as they were outnumbered and outgunned. The only logical thing to do was to act calm and smile, as if they were just a bunch of people who were in need of some help with a crippled yacht.

Rozzito stood there on the deck and waited patiently for the Coast Guard crew to secure against his vessel before being greeted by the master chief and his armed crew.

"Nicholas Rozzito?"

"Yes, that is I."

"By the power invested in me, you are hereby under arrest for drug trafficking, money laundering, extortion, illegal business activities, violation of the Constitution of International Maritime Act, and murder."

"Whoa, whoa, whoa. Murder? I think you have the wrong person, officer. That's quite a list of accusations, don't you think?"

"It's master chief."

"What?"

"I am not an officer. I am a United States Coast Guard Master Chief, and you, sir, are hereby under..."

"You have the wrong person. I am just a simple man. Take it easy...watch it...this suit happens to be a Brooks Brothers worth more than your salary." The master chief's crew quickly took Rozzito into their arms.

"You can't do this. You don't have any proof of all that you said. Besides, until you slap the jewelry on my wrists, you are violating my rights." Rozzito stuck out both his arms and hands, gesturing a plea.

"Sir, you gave that up when you decided to be who you are." At that very moment, Master Chief O'Connell cuffed his hands.

Rozzito was in shock as he looked at his hands. He turned to his crew and blurted out a few words. "They have nothing on us, boys."

Master Chief O'Connell shook his head to the side as his armed crew took that as a signaling order to remove Rozzito, place him under arrest, and detain him in the holding cell aboard the *Savannah*.

Chapter Twenty-Three
Coup de Grâce

The sun began its daily routine over the horizon as men from the United States Coast Guard wrapped up their apprehension of Rozzito and his men. To no surprise, they had discovered what Rozzito had carefully concealed under the hull of the *Bella*. An underwater diver surfaced, reporting to his fellow team the discovery of the cocaine. This was not the time or place to remove the drugs, but they reported the find to command. It would be only a matter of time before the *Savannah* and the *Bella* set sail for English Bay, where Rozzito and his men would be handed over to local authorities before being processed and booked. There was no way he was going to get out of standing trial for his criminal actions Monday in Supreme Court, let alone any chance for escape. There was enough evidence to keep him from seeing the light of day again, and the tough part was, Alex had no idea what had transpired over the night since her passing out and leaving Beauford running to clean up the aftermath of her drinking, not to mention

349

the fact she was about to prosecute a trial against her own flesh and blood come Monday morning.

Lying in my bed, I could feel the pain in my temple pounding like a dull drumbeat. I had no idea how I had gotten there. I wanted to open my eyes, but I knew if I did, my head would explode from the raging headache that had taken over the circumference of my forehead like a cerebral assassin. My eyes ached at the very touch, but the slight circular pressure on them and my face amazingly brought me some relief.

It didn't take long before I noticed a distinct, familiar smell. The only thing was, I had never smelled it so strong before. It was almost too strong, yet my senses knew the smell of Arabica beans being brewed. I didn't even recall setting the pot on last night. Strange, but perhaps I had. I just couldn't remember.

I truly felt like a train had run me over. What day was it, anyway? Clanking noises came from downstairs, and it hit me. I pulled the bedspread up and noticed I was not wearing any clothes. In fact, I was stripped down to my birthday suit. As I pulled myself up and sat on the side of the bed, the pounding in my head seemed to lessen as I took in a deep sigh and yawned.

It all started to come back to me, and I realized the clanking noise must have been Beauford, but how? The last thing I recalled was leaving the bar. Had he taken advantage of me? Not that I would have minded, but I would have liked to have been coherent, at least. No, he was too much of a gentleman to do that to me. What the hell had been in the drinks?

It didn't help the fact my room was bright from the sun shining in through my window. The blinds were open, and I knew if I was going to be able to move, I would have to close them to give my eyeballs a rest. Lucky for the kid across the street, I forgot I was naked and walked towards the window. I reached for the blinds, but while raising my arms up, I could see the little pervert looking into my window.

I pulled the sheers closed, covering the window up, but then I thought, what the hell. If he was looking for a quick show, why not open the sheers back up and give him what he wanted? That would teach his father a lesson for making those remarks against me the previous morning. My head hurt if I moved too fast, but I turned around and closed the sheers, leaving only my breasts exposed. I figured a minute or two and the kid would probably go into convulsions and drop to the ground.

Figuring by now he had had a good long, hard look, I opened the sheers, only to see my neighbor from a few houses down, old Ms. Marzetti, a 92-year-old widow looking up at me in utter disgust. I felt so embarrassed and felt the need to open my window and explain.

"Hi, Mrs. Marzetti. It isn't what you think it is." I was numb to the fact I had stuck my head out the window, still exposing myself for anyone to see as I tried to explain my actions to the old woman.

"Well, it *is* what you think it is, but I can explain."

Old Mrs. Marzetti just squinted her eyes and gave me the tar-and-feather look of disgrace, pointing her cane up at me and calling me a hussy. Can't say that I blamed her. What was I thinking, exposing myself out the window? That was not who I am. It had to be my head not being right. "Ugh" was the only noise I could muster as I closed the window and my sheers before throwing on some undergarments and a long T-shirt.

As I came down the steps slowly, the overwhelming coffee smell seemed as if it instantly made my head feel better. My eyes were amazed to see Beauford standing there with his back to me in the kitchen area that was exposed from the stairs. He was actually using the coffee contraption my uncle had given me. The horrible noise coming from it reminded me of an old-time steam locomotive from all the push, posh, bubbling, and gurgling sounds.

"So, making cow pies, are we?" I felt that making a joking comment would break the ice and get his attention.

Beauford turned around while sipping his fresh cup of cappuccino. "Mmm, that is some good coffee. Good morning, Bella."

"Ugh, not sure about that. My head is pounding like that movie *Jumanji*." I gestured is if to animate the pounding of drums against my head, yet Beauford gave me a look of emptiness.

"I'm sorry. Jewmunchie? What is that? Some sort of Jewish zombie?"

"Oh, never mind. I don't want to push it by thinking too much."

"Oh, *Jumanji*. That's that movie where Robin Williams's character as a kid got sucked into a magical board game and was released by two kids decades later, only to find out that the world he lived in would soon follow him because the game was still in play."

"Yeah, that's the one. You really need to get a hobby. I was just making a…oh, never mind. So, how is it?"

"How is what?"

"The coffee, silly."

"Oh, delicious. You want a cup? I could whip you one up."

"Thanks, but did you happen to possibly make my regular coffee?"

"You are in luck. I took the leisure of brewing a full pot for both of us, but I was intrigued by this wonderful coffee goddess, so I naturally had to examine it. Hope you don't mind?"

"No, not at all. I wouldn't know how to use it, anyway. It was just a housewarming gift from my uncle. Can I have a cup of coffee, please?"

"Oh yes, sorry."

I waited patiently for him to pour me a cup of coffee. A few cups of that, and I would be back to normal. Well, if normal meant caffeine plus Advil, then, yeah, I would be as good to go as a spring chicken.

"Here you go. A little cream and sugar already added, just the way I recall you liking it."

"Thank you."

"Don't mention it."

I stood there sipping on my coffee for a minute, looking up at him. He had a big fat grin on his face. I couldn't imagine why, but I had to know. I was trying to muster enough courage to ask him what had happened last night while sipping my coffee some more. Luckily for me, he beat me to it.

"So, what a crazy night last night."

"I guess so, but I don't remember much other than being at the bar."

"Yeah, you were thinking the waiter at the bar must have put something in your drink because you were out of your mind last night."

"That bad, huh?"

"Well, I wouldn't give you an A+, but I'd sure give you a B for best effort, considering the conditions."

"And what might those be?"

"You don't recall last night…here in your condo, do you?"

"Sorry. I'm thinking since I woke up this morning in my birthday suit that perhaps…well…we kind of did something."

"To say the least, I would have to agree."

"Was it at least everything you hoped it would be?"

"It was OK but not exactly."

"Oh, so what you're saying is it sucked?"

"Not entirely."

"Did I at least satisfy you?"

"Hmm, not exactly."

"Oh for God's sake, was I really that bad in bed?"

"I can't say."

"What do you mean you can't say? It's either a yes or a no." I was starting to get a little irritated at Beauford's short two-to-three-word responses.

"Well, no, then, is my answer."

"Wow. You sure know how to make a girl feel bad."

"No, it's not that. I...I mean, we didn't do anything. Well, you did, but that isn't the point."

"Well, something certainly happened in order for me to wake up naked."

"Yes, I agree. Something did happen."

"Then what?" I asked, standing there inside the entryway to the kitchen.

"You sure you want to know? Maybe it's best if we just forget about tit...I mean it." Beauford pushed his glasses back up his nose and turned to face the coffee machine. "You really want to know?"

"YES!" I raised my voice in response.

"Here, let me pour you some more coffee, and you might want to sit down."

What on earth could have been so bad that he was avoid telling me? I know I had never slept with a man, but could it have been so awful that he was ashamed to tell me, and that is why he was dancing around the subject? Perhaps he was the one that was ashamed. Maybe he couldn't contribute to the cause. Look at me, silently cross-examining this ordeal, yet I couldn't stop picturing him undressed. My head didn't hurt anymore, and even though I had no freaking idea what had happened here last night, it didn't matter if it was bad or good. My body shivered in pure attraction to him, sitting there staring at him.

"You ready for this?"

"Will you please just tell me so we can move on?"

"Where do you want me to start? At the bar or here?"

"So, you're telling me this started at the bar? I don't recall that as well."

"How about I just start from your place, and let's just skip the bar scene?"

"Why is there a kitchen table chair in the middle of the room?" Alex walked past the chair where she had Beauford sit last night during her drunken stupor and sat on the couch.

"You insisted I grab the chair and place it in the middle of the room."

"Why?"

"You really don't remember?"

"No, I don't, but I'm starting to wonder if I should know about it, either."

"OK, let's just forget about it, then."

"No, continue on." I knew I wanted to know what the heck went on last night since I was truly not aware of my actions.

"You had me sit down, and you become very erotic towards me and were doing things I had never imagined in you."

"Like what?"

"Well, my granddaddy back on the farm used to call it when a female cow and male bull..."

"Beau, please don't refer to us as cows or some scientific explanation of what happened."

"Um, well, let's just say you sat on me while facing me and began to move around on my lap."

"Oh no."

"Oh yes. Quite exhilarating watching you. I have to say, I was slightly aroused up until you…"

"What?"

"You don't want to know."

"You can't go all the way and not finish."

"Ha, you didn't, but you did manage to ruin the moment. Profoundly disturbing, but under the circumstances, I can't hold a grudge."

"Oh my God. What did I do that was so bad? You make it sound like I was horrible." I started to get teary-eyed.

"No…no…no. Don't cry. It isn't that."

"What was so bad, then?"

"Hey, it's OK. It wasn't that bad. It's just that you puked all over me."

"What?"

"I said, you puked all over me. I mean, really puked all over me."

"OK…OK. I get it. Wow, I am so sorry."

"Then you slid off my lap, or maybe you pushed yourself. I'm not sure exactly. My eyes were closed. You fell to the floor, landing on your butt and I presume passing out."

"You must hate me," I said, crying yet laughing slightly at the same time.

"No, I barely know you enough to hate you yet," Beauford said softly with a joking tone and smirking.

"Well, that doesn't sound comforting. You have got to stop that."

"Sorry, just trying to lighten the mood."

"So, nothing happened last night after that?"

"After I carried you up to bed, I had to remove your shirt since it had quite a bit of puke on it, but I did not take advantage of you, and I certainly did not remove any other clothing that you had on. I won't say I didn't stand there for a few minutes looking at you, though."

"I'm so sorry for last night. I wish I hadn't been drunk. I promise to make it up to you."

"It's all right. You don't have to unless you really want to."

"I want to. Come here and give me a kiss."

I was really happy Beauford was there with me, considering what all had gone down since last Wednesday. I wanted to at least show my affection by giving him a kiss good morning. Leaning forward towards his lips, I figured I would get him back for staring at me instead of covering me up right away. As he was about to touch my lips, I pulled back and acted like I was about to puke. The look on his face was priceless.

"I'm kidding! That's for staring at me topless and not covering me up."

"Good one." Beauford smiled and then kissed me.

"You are such a great kisser. You sure you don't want to…you know?"

"I think for now I am going to take a rain check. I've kind of lost my desire at the moment."

"Oh, OK. Well, I'm going to go take a shower. If you want, you can use the shower around the corner in the bathroom downstairs. You did bring stuff for that, right, and a set of clothes?"

"Yeah, I just need to get my overnight bag out of the car."

"OK. I should be ready to go in less than an hour. What time is it?"

"I don't have a watch on, but your clock says 11:37 a.m. What time is the event today?"

"I think he said around two, but I'm sure if we get there a few minutes early, it won't hurt."

"OK. I'm just going to step outside for some fresh air and make a phone call."

"Sorry about last night again. I'm happy you're here." I smiled while holding the stair railing before going upstairs.

****

The sound of pounding on a closed steel door rang through the tight walkway below the deck of the Coast Guard cutter *Savannah*. Rozzito was locked behind a steel door. He was being detained and was causing a ruckus yelling out, "This is a joke, and I'm being set up." He was demanding to speak to his lawyer. The joint mission to capture Nicholas Rozzito, the don of Canada's worst Mafia crime family, had been successful despite the few who had lost their lives, good or bad.

Inside sources tipping off his whereabouts had led the authorities from both sides of the boundary line to apprehend him along with any of his accomplices. ECHELON leaders were thrilled about the news of the capture and began to work towards bringing down Rozzito's empire, starting with an admission of guilt.

The Canadian Coast Guard cutter *Tesla*, aka Bravo three three, joined the *Savannah* along with the remaining M2 catamaran. The *Bella* dangled tightly behind the *Savannah*, attached by marine-grade rope. Her bow was cuffed just like her owner as all four vessels set sail for English Bay in Vancouver.

An individual wearing a DEA jacket approached the door where Rozzito was being detained. It was guarded by two men, both of whom came to attention. The individual hesitated for a moment and took a deep breath of air before nodding his head to have them unlock the door. The door opened and then closed behind the individual, as Rozzito stared in utter disbelief at whom he saw.

"Surprised to see me, Nick?"

"It can't be. I saw you fall overboard."

"I'm still in shock that you had the audacity to stab me, your right-hand man. For what? Letting an innocent man save his own life, or at least try to until you popped one into the back of his head?"

DEA Officer Shane Olsen, aka Donnie "The Wire" Bonnachi, stood across the table where Nicholas stood. Rozzito shrugged it off as if taking a life were no big deal. The stab wound Shane received hadn't been deep enough to kill him. In fact, diving overboard and hitting the cold water had slowed the blood flow, ultimately saving his life before being rescued by the Coast Guard. Rozzito instantly knew he wasn't there for a family reunion and saw the letters on his jacket.

"You little shit, I outta…" Rozzito darted towards Shane, quickly stopping in his tracks with his arms pointed upward as Shane revealed the 9mm strapped to his waist.

"Easy, Nick. Quite ballsy, under the circumstances."

"Go fuck yourself, you lowlife scum."

"Now, is that any way to talk to your right-hand man?"

"I want you outta my face, you little prick. Don't I get a free phone call? I think I need to phone my attorney."

"This isn't jail."

"Then you're holding me against my will, and I will have your badge, you little fucking weasel. Think you can burrow your way into my circle of trust, my life, and my family? I trusted you like a brother!" Rozzito shouted at Shane, foaming at the mouth.

"Sit down," Shane ordered Rozzito as he held the side that was cut, but Rozzito, perturbed, frantically walked back and forth in the room.

"Now!" Shane sat in his chair with his index finger pointing down and against the top of the table.

Rozzito's face was blood red, boiling from anger, as he approached the table. Not before he showed his disrespect by spitting in Shane's face, he pulled the chair out from the table harshly and sat down, snarling towards Shane.

"I guess I had that coming." Shane took a handkerchief out of his jacket and wiped the spit off his face.

"I trusted you, and this is how you repay me, by being an informant. Nothing more than a pig. You ate at my table, broke bread with me, drank my wine, and now this...betrayal."

"That's how the game is played. You're just lucky I survived, or you would be charged with my murder, too."

"You ain't got nothing on me. As far as I'm concerned, you may have won today, but tomorrow..." Rozzito sat back in his chair, snarling and laughing.

"We'll see about that. One way or another, we will get a confession, but that doesn't really matter because I know all your dirty little secrets and operations. That's right; get beet red in the face. Not so tough now, are you?"

"I should have cut you deeper so you would have bled out. Then you'd be fit to be with me because your stinking body would be cleansed of this shit."

"Oh, just so you know, your niece has been appointed lead prosecutor for your trial on Monday. I wonder what she would think about you now once she finds out you stole her family rights, killed her parents, and stole everything she was entitled to."

Shane scooted the chair back, stood up, and walked to the door, making one last comment to fuel the situation before locking the door behind him. Rozzito, in a moment of rage, shouted, "You piece of shit! I am going to rip your head off and shit down your neck, you son of a bitch." He stood up, glanced down at the chair, picked it up, and tossed it against the locked steel door. Shane waited outside the door with his back to it, waiting for the cue he had succeeded in pissing Nicholas off even further. Raising his right hand with index finger pointed, he made a gesture swooping the finger down saying, *One for the good guys, zero for the bad guys.*

"Make sure he doesn't get too comfortable. We don't want to send the wrong message, now, do we?" Shane turned his head towards the two men guarding the door before walking away.

****

Time had passed as Beauford drove up behind a line of cars waiting to be directed to park near the Sooke Harbor House. Pierre Gustave's yacht the *Wanderer* was down at the marina.

"This friend of yours must be pretty important." Beauford turned and looked at me, inching the car forward.

"I barely know the man. I just figured since he was kind enough to extend the invitation, I might as well come, but I guess so. Wasn't that Simon McNeil who just got out of that limo?"

"Who?"

"Seattle tycoon." I tried to describe the man, but Beauford responded by shaking his head as if he had no idea.

"You know, Simon McNeil, the guy who sold his Internet Company back in the late 90s for 250 million and later that year won the state lotto for 400 million."

"Sounds to me like the rich get richer and poorer get, well, shafted."

"What's that supposed to mean?"

361

"Nothing, just saying."

"Just because you have money doesn't make you a bad person."

"I didn't say that."

"I mean, my uncle, for instance, worked hard all his life as an honest man to have what he had, and he gave me everything I ever wanted and always told me what was his was mine. Does that make me a bad person, too?"

"No Alex, relax, that's not what I meant."

"Anyway, I just thought I saw someone important since you mentioned Mr. Gustave must be important."

Just then, Beauford pulled up to a man directing the parking and rolled down his window.

"You here for the Miller wedding?"

"Um, no, we're here for the Pierre Gustave event." I leaned over towards the driver's window, practically in Beauford's face as he leaned back and caught a scent of my perfume.

"What's your name?"

"Alex, Alexandria Henson, plus guest."

"Ah, yes, Miss Henson. Says here you are part of the VIP guest list."

"Oh, OK."

"Pull right over there and park. I will have Tommy, my helper, drive you down over to the harbor where Mr. Gustave's party is."

"Thank you. For a minute, I thought we might have been in the wrong place since you mentioned a wedding."

"No problem, ma'am. It gets like this around this time of year. Everyone wants to book the Harbor House for weddings, and the hotel gets overrun. Please pull over there and park, and we'll get you to your destination."

"Thank you, officer." Beauford rolled up the electric window as he pulled over to the side parking lot, put the car in park, and turned it off.

"VIP. Seems to me you made quite an impression on the old man."

"Oh, stop. Why, are you jealous?" I smiled at Beauford.

"Should I be?"

"Maybe if he was younger, but chances are you're in luck because I am only interested in a hot young stud."

"Oh, shouldn't he have come with you instead of me?"

"I meant you, stud." I leaned in and kissed him on the cheek.

"Oh, nice." Beauford smiled. His phone, lying in the drink holder, vibrated.

"Aren't you going to answer that?"

"Probably nobody."

"Well, it has to be someone since it's still ringing." I thought it was odd for him not to answer the phone and started to question his motives.

"Yeah, maybe you're right. I'm going to go..." Beauford pointed outside and smiled at Alex before exiting the driver's seat.

Something was weird about that man. Who doesn't answer their phone? I was puzzled since he seemed a little edgy quite suddenly. His face went from normal to beet red. Maybe this guy was playing me, and it was his wife or girlfriend calling him, wondering where the hell he was, since he was with me last night. Oh no, my involvement with him could lead to breaking up a marriage or relationship. I felt a sudden cramp in my stomach, almost as bad as my monthly visitor, but I decided to get out of the car and take a deep breath of air and not think about what it could be. I was quite sure I was overreacting, and it was nothing. Besides, if Beauford was being taken care of at home, he wouldn't be out looking for it.

"Everything all right?" I asked Beauford as he walked back towards me leaning against the back of the car.

"Yeah, just a wrong number."

"A wrong number?"

I was confused since I had watched him talk to the so-called wrong number as if the other person on the end was a friend. Maybe he was just being overly friendly with a stranger. It was nothing. I was just excited and nervous to see Pierre again and introduce him to Beauford.

"What time is it?" I asked Beauford.

"Not sure. I haven't been able to locate my watch since last week."

"Um, about that. Somehow, your watch ended up in my backpack. Don't ask me how, but I actually have it here in my purse. I meant to give it you Friday, but we all know how that turned out." I reached into my purse and handed Beauford his watch.

"Oh, how awesome. I thought I had lost it."

Chapter Twenty-Four
Ascendancy

Within minutes, I could see the harbor as we approached riding on the golf cart. What a beautiful place. I remembered coming up here with my uncle to spend the day relaxing out on the water. My uncle would take his yacht up the coastline to the harbor at least twice a summer to treat me to a day of relaxation and sightseeing. I never got tired of looking at the wonderful scenery and gazing upon the horizon, wondering what lottery I had won to be so lucky to have such a wonderful uncle to care for me all those years. Little did I know the sinister side of my uncle was about to come out and be revealed to all.

I never imagined just how huge Pierre's yacht, the *Wanderer*, would be. This vessel had to be at least 200 feet as it made the pier look tiny up against her.

"Alexandria, Alexandria, is that you?"

I turned around to see whose voice it was and realized it was Gino, my uncle's childhood friend from the old neighborhood.

"Gino, is that you?"

"Yes, my child, it is me, Gino. *Grazie…grazie Mon ami.*"

I couldn't help myself and ran over to Gino and gave him a great big hug.

"Alexandria, you are all grown up! What a beautiful angel you are!"

"Oh, Gino, stop it. You're going to make me blush!"

I was so caught up with seeing my uncle's old friend, I forgot where Beauford had gone off to. I turned around to look for him, but he was nowhere in sight. *That's odd. I wonder where he went in such a hurry,* I thought. By now, several key guests were arriving, and I knew by the way they looked that they were either royalty or someone important. Looking back around to Gino, I excused myself to go look for Beauford. Walking down the walkway in the direction of the Harbor House entrance, I took a good look to see if I could spot Beauford, but he had just up and disappeared. Maybe he was back at the yacht and looking for me, so I decided to switch directions and head back from where I came.

I could see the deckhands were preparing for the arrival of guests on and outside of the Yacht. Out in front of the entrance to the pier on the grassy knoll, the workers were setting up tables and chairs for guests. Lavish decorations outlined the grounds.

"Miss, would you like a glass of champagne?"

"Oh, I would love one, thank you." Turing around, I saw it was Beauford. "Where did you go?"

"I had to go use the little boys' room, but by the time I had returned, you were gone."

"You just up and left. I had no idea you were gone. You could have told me."

"Sorry, you're right, but I almost didn't make it, so…"

Looking at him, I couldn't be upset. I smiled as I took the glass from him and took a sip. What a refreshing taste of delicate grapes ripened to perfection!

"Compliments of Mr. Gustave!" said Beauford.

"Really? Is he here? Did you meet him? I was hoping to introduce you to him." Alex replied with a frown.

"No, that is what the sign said on the table when I took the glasses of champagne."

Just as I took another sip, I could hear a low whirling noise overhead. I looked up, shielding my eyes from the bright sunlight, to see a sleek black Sikorsky 76B helicopter approaching the helipad off to the right of the grounds next to the docks. That had to be Pierre Gustave. Talk about a grand entrance, this man sure knew how to arrive in style. I watched the helicopter descend with such precision. Seconds before touching down, the gear appeared from the underside of the helicopter. It touched the grass, barely making an indentation.

The side door opened up, and the stairs extended downward to the ground. I saw Gustave peer through the doorway and make his way down to the ground. I wondered if he even remembered me. I grabbed Beauford's hand and dragged him with me to greet Pierre.

"Alexandria, so glad you could come."

"Hello, Pierre. I wouldn't have missed it for the world." I leaned in and kissed Pierre on the cheek.

"Who's this young, handsome man with you?"

"This is my friend boy...I mean boyfriend...Beauford." I stumbled over my words. Pierre was as surprised as I was at my saying the word "boyfriend."

"Well, Alex's friend boy...I mean boyfriend"—Pierre winked at me—"feel free to wander about the event and mingle as well as step aboard my latest and magnificent state-of-the-art yacht, the *Wanderer*."

"I am honored to be here. Thank you for having us."

"The pleasure is all mine, but I must excuse myself and be a good host. Please, for goodness' sake, feed her something. She looks like she is starving. Your favorite drink is being served, Alex, and everything is on the house, so drink up." Pierre smiled at both of us before kissing me on the cheek again and giving a strong handshake to Beauford. "Oh, and make sure you stick around and see my latest sponsorship. You won't be disappointed, and Alex, come find me before you leave. I actually am glad you came because I have something for you."

As soon as I agreed to find him before we would leave the event, Pierre was off, and I was left standing there, feeling awkward for blurting out that Beauford was my boyfriend.

"So, I'm your boyfriend? I hadn't realized we had graduated to that stage yet."

"Sorry. I was just caught up in the moment, and it sort of came out unexpectedly. Don't worry if it made you feel awkward. I panicked and didn't want him to think I was just with a stranger."

"Stranger? You are batting zero for two…wow."

"No, I didn't mean it like that." I stopped and turned into Beauford and kissed him passionately for what seemed like an eternity, and not in a bad way. "Doesn't that show you I am very interested in you?"

"No complaints here," Beauford replied with an excited grin.

It wasn't easy for me to say what I wanted to say, but I felt he would get the big picture if I just kissed him passionately, and his reaction was spot on.

"Come on, I'm thirsty. You have got to try this drink I had last week on the ferry."

"Are you sure that is a good…whoa…idea?" Alex had tugged on Beauford, leading the way towards the open bar, catching him slightly off guard.

I was no stranger to the elaborate setup Pierre had going on here for his event. Fine dining and linens with crystal centerpieces full of fresh-cut white roses gave off a touch of class. White roses, I presumed, were a sign of friendship. My uncle threw events like this most of my life, so it was not a life-changing moment for me, but Beauford, on the other hand, seemed in awe.

"This Pierre guy seems to know quite a few people."

"I would imagine so. He does own the *Victoria Cove*."

"The same one that you boarded at Pier 69 the day we met?"

"That's the one."

"Makes sense now. Hey, you want to take a tour of his yacht?"

"Sure, just let me get a drink first at the bar over here. Oh, look, it's Bernard the bartender from the other night. Hey, Bernard!" I shouted to Bernard, who was standing behind the outdoor bar.

"Well, if it isn't the lovely Miss Alexandria. How are you?"

"I'm fine, Bernard, but I would be so happy if you could whip me up one of your special drinks again."

"Coming right up. For you?" Bernard looked at Beauford, asking for his drink of choice.

"A can of Coke."

"Just a can of Coke? You sure you don't want to spice it up a bit? This is an open bar, no charge." Bernard looked at Beauford, smiling as he made my drink.

At that moment, I heard my BlackBerry buzz inside my purse and looked at Beauford as if to let him know I was going to step away for a second and see who it was. He just knotted his forehead. I think he understood me, but I think he was distracted from the blender noise Bernard was making.

It was Daniele's number. Before I could answer it, she must have hung up. My phone displayed that I had missed seven calls from her. How could that be? I knew when we parted yesterday she wasn't exactly herself, but I didn't think twice about it. I figured when she was ready to tell me about it, she would, like old times. Damn it, I felt so foolish for not realizing she had been trying to reach me. I had been so distracted the last twenty-four hours, hell, I didn't even know how I was managing.

Looking over at Beauford, I could see him looking back at me as I raised my hand, displaying all five fingers, as if to say, "Give me five minutes."

"So, Alex's guest, you have a name?" Bernard said from behind the bar.

"Beauford."

"Hmm, never heard of that name before. Sounds like royalty."

"Ha, more like a lady repellant, if you ask me. Not sure what my parents were thinking." Beauford shrugged his shoulders while cracking a smirk.

"Well, can't be too much of a lady-killer seeing how you're with her. Mmm, she is so hot!"

"Easy there. Guess you're right, just something about her."

"Say, that is a fine looking watch. Where did you get it?"

"It was a gift I received when I graduated training for the NSA," Beauford replied with a serious look towards Bernard.

"Say what?" Bernard quickly responded as Beauford started to smile.

"Ah, that was a good one. You almost had me convinced there for a second…NSA," Bernard replied, giggling.

"What's not to believe?" Beauford looked at Bernard, smiling.

"You serious? Come on. Look at you. Now, if you'd said something along the lines of a teacher or scientist, then yeah, but an NSA agent?" Bernard gave Beauford a look of disbelief. "No way, but no offense."

"None taken. The watch accessorizes my look."

"Hey, what are you talking about?" I had snuck up from behind Beauford.

"Just making small talk here with Bernard, waiting for you to return."

"I was admiring his watch. Here you go, Miss Alex, one very yummy frozen drink as you like it."

"Thanks, Bernard. Mmm, that is so good."

"Ever since last week, it has been a hit."

"So, tell me, Beau, what does the inscription, "Never Say Anything," on the backside of the watch mean, anyway?"

"Oh, just an old motto." Beauford quickly nudged me to turn and walk away as he winked at Bernard. I watched his facial expression elaborate some truth in his reference to NSA connection.

"What was that all about?" I looked at Beauford as they walked towards the yacht.

"What do you mean?"

"Oh, don't go playing stupid on me. The turning around and looking back at Bernard. Did I miss something?"

"Just two guys having a little fun."

I didn't know if Beauford was telling the truth or not, but something was quite odd after Bernard asked him about the inscription on the inside of his watch. Nevertheless, it was a great feeling having my arm wrapped around his as we walked down the pier. Beauford actually surprised me as he leaned in and kissed the top of my head. I knew I was happy that he had come after all, despite his little temper tantrum he had had in the car Friday.

"Say, wouldn't it be nice to own one of these boats?" Beauford said.

"I guess so, if you don't already have one."

"That's right, I forgot. Your uncle owns a big yacht called the *Bella*."

"How did you know that? Have you been looking into my past?" I said with a slight tone of hesitation.

"You must have told me."

"I don't recall mentioning anything personal about my uncle."

"Hmm, you know what? I think I saw a picture of your uncle's yacht lying on your kitchen counter near the coffee machine."

"From the pile of pictures I had stacked one on top of another?"

"Yes, I do believe that is where I saw it. I admit, I did browse through them before you woke up this morning."

"Strange, I don't recall having a picture of my uncle's yacht, but hmm, interesting."

Beauford was indeed lying to Alex, as he never saw the stack of pictures near the coffee machine. In fact, his undercover intelligence had slipped out and had almost given him away, but for now, he would play along and agree with her to avoid being exposed.

"Hey, I have a good idea. Let's go to the top deck and watch all the festivities from there for a bit. Then if you like, we can tour the boat."

"Sounds romantic."

Beauford smiled at me. He was a gentleman, letting me

board the *Wanderer* first. This was nothing like my uncle's and was way sleeker. My uncle's yacht was nice and fancy, but it reminded me too much of a yacht straight out of a Mafia movie. Pierre's, on the other hand, was sleek, elegant, and luxurious. Everything about the yacht seemed to be carefully considered and added. I could see how one would want one.

As we reached the top deck and came out the glass sliding doors near the stern, it was just magnificent. The view, the breeze blowing through my hair, and Beauford's cologne tapping my nose were breathtaking. Watching him lean over the railing and seeing the sun cast its warm spell on his face drew me in further. I couldn't resist, so I moved closer and wrapped my arms around his, laying my head against his tight, firm arm.

"Wow, what do you think that circular object is down there in the water?"

"Not sure, but I would love to kiss you right now."

"Oh, OK." My eyes lit up.

If only God had a camera and could have taken this picture of him and me kissing with the sun shining on us, it would have been heaven sent. I couldn't wait to kiss him and made my move, locking my lips with his, and then it happened. Sounds of streamers filled the air with a demanding pitch. Was I dreaming? It was almost like fireworks going off as we kissed. I felt frozen in time, my lips locked to his, and for that very moment, I felt like a princess from a fairy tale. That soon ended when we were caught off guard.

"Well, perhaps you two would like a room." Pierre startled Beauford and me as he approached us, smirking. "You're just in time for my demonstration."

What I thought was fireworks were indeed fireworks, just not from kissing Beauford. The circular object that was in the water had lit up with sparks coming out all around it. Men stood at the edge of the water with what seemed to be bow and arrows. With his hands, Pierre motioned us to watch.

"Is that what I think it is?" I said, looking over at Pierre.

"Watch, child, watch." Pierre was beside himself, overjoyed as he motioned Alex to watch for what was about to happen.

This was surely straight out of a King Arthur storybook as the men were dressed in battle armor. There had to be at least ten men with bows and arrows, and now all the arrows were being lit on fire. I felt kind of nervous, scared, and excited all at the same time waiting for them to lean back and launch the arrows. I assumed they were for the circular object just a few yards off the side of the *Wanderer*. Praying they all hit the target and not having a stray one hit us, I squeezed Beauford's arm, and for some reason I grabbed Pierre's left hand at the same time. He looked at me and smiled. It was comforting, to say the least.

In a precision-like matter, all ten arrows left the bows and came straight down on their target, the circular object burning even after it hit the water. All of a sudden, people started clapping as if to celebrate what had just happened.

"I don't get it. Why are they clapping? It's not like the flames went out."

"Exactly, Alexandria, that's the point. This is my proof of concept for fireproof water," Pierre explained with a gleam in his eye like a giddy little schoolboy. "You see, Alex, there is a clear Plexiglas round cylinder out there with water in it, separate from the strait water and mixed with a precise chemical that I have been working on that forms a barrier around the water, keeping it from extinguishing the flames from the arrows."

"I still don't understand. Isn't water supposed to put out fires?" I was still a bit confused.

"Wait a minute. I recognize this now." Beauford's eyes lit up like bulbs.

"Go ahead, young man," Pierre said.

"The Jaden Effect. Reverse combustion energy where fuel, oxygen, and energy exist as one, yet instead of producing heat, it is reversed and is cool by reversing the chemical reaction to bounce backwards at the point of ignition, acting as a barrier; therefore, fire stays lit and does not go out."

"Exactomundo, my boy!" Pierre leaped in excitement, patting Beauford on his back several times.

"You're telling me this is real?"

"As real as the feelings this young lady has for you."

Beauford looked at me and smirked as he looked back at Pierre, joining him in nodding his head as if to say "well done."

"I can't believe what I just witnessed. There have been many countries with top scientists, especially Russia and America that have tried this theory in efforts to provide a better rocket fuel protective liner for space travel. They've failed, and some people have lost their lives trying to perfect this theory, yet here I stand witnessing the very proof of concept that the Jaden Effect does work. Thank you, Mr. Gustave. I am honored to have seen this."

"You are quite welcome, my boy. That was quite a mouthful, but indeed you are right." Pierre leaned in towards me. "I like this young man. He's a keeper." I blushed. "Well, I'd better get down to my fans."

"Oh, please do," said Beauford. "Sorry to have kept you."

"Nonsense. The pleasure was all mine. Alex, I took the pleasure of giving a package to my security advisor standing at the end of the pier. Please take the package and look at it when you get home. I think you might want to see what it contains." Pierre leaned in and kissed me on both cheeks, then shook Beauford's hand firmly before saying goodbye and departing.

I knew it was time to leave the party and head home. I

had no clue what the package would contain, but I would look at it later on. I just wanted to go home, be with Beauford, and spend some quality time with him, if you know what I mean. It was the least I could do to make up for last night.

****

It wasn't long before Beauford and I left Pierre's party and headed home. As soon as we arrived back at my place, I grabbed Beauford and pulled him inside and shut the door behind me. I threw myself on him. What seemed like hours for both of us turned out to be all night and all Sunday of making up for lost time before the sound of my alarm went off at five o'clock Monday morning. Startled by the sound of the alarm, Beauford actually rolled over and fell out of bed.

I couldn't help myself from giggling as I crawled over to his side of the bed and looked over towards the floor. He was lying there facedown, butt naked. I thought about sliding down and climbing on top of him, but I was rudely interrupted by my smartphone going off.

"Ha, saved by the bell," I said. I rolled over towards my nightstand, reached for my phone, and realized I was exposed from my chest up. I quickly looked towards the window and said, "Oh, thank God," when I saw that my blinds were shut.

I missed the call, and the screen revealed it as a restricted number.

"Oh. I hate when that happens."

"What's the matter?" Beauford asked with a muffled voice, his mouth still against the floor.

"I keep getting missed calls and restricted numbers."

"Maybe the person trying to call is just dialing wrong."

"Perhaps you're right. Guess it's time to get up and get ready."

"That's right. Today's the big day, huh? You should be excited."

"More like scared and nervous. What if I screw up?"

"Well, don't screw up. Problem solved," Beauford responded as I just gave him a look.

"Ha-ha. Easier said than done. Hey, don't you have to work?" I said, changing the subject.

"Yes, I guess I'd better get ready and go. I have to drop the car back off in Sidney, but I thought at least we could ride there together and then go our separate ways."

"That would be nice. Can you at least make me a cup of regular coffee?"

"Certainly."

I didn't even think about it as I threw the covers off me and stood up, but when I started to walk to the bathroom, I realized I was naked as well. It didn't take Beauford long before I heard a whistle coming from behind me.

"Oh, stop it. Haven't you had enough to last you awhile?"

"Yeah, you're right, but that butt of yours is driving me nuts."

"Well, I can take care of that for you if you'd like."

"No, no offense, but I don't think I could...well..."

"Well, what? Get it up?"

"Exactly. Too many hours of nonstop action has retired me for a spell."

"Better rest up for this weekend."

"What's this weekend?"

"You have to ask?"

"Oh."

"I was thinking I could come and stay the weekend at your place."

"Oh, is that what you thought?" Beauford smirked at Alex with a playful reply.

Chapter Twenty-Five
Zero Hour

It was 10:05 a.m., and sun blanketed the city sidewalks. News camera crews started to line up outside the Vancouver courthouse with anticipation of the morning that was to come. KATN Channel 4 out of Alaska had the exclusive interview with the district attorney upon the conclusion of the morning's proceedings. Arriving early on the scene, the news crew had already staked a claim at the front entrance of the courthouse. It was a surreal scene. As far as the eye could see, news vehicles and camera equipment were trained on the entranceway. Today marked the first time in the city of Vancouver's history that such a high-profile case had been tried here.

"Check…check." Andrea Newman, eyewitness reporter for KATN, checked her Mic operation as all eyes turned towards the approaching caravan of police squad cars.

One by one, the squad cars passed the main entrance and headed towards the rear of the building. Quickly, Andrea motioned for Ted, her cameraman, to move to the front of the plaza to be ready for the morning news update. Ted set up the camera and pointed it towards the street where Andrea was standing, quickly adjusting the camera lens to get a clean focus on her.

"We are live in 5, 4, 3, 2, 1," Ted whispered to Andrea.

"Good morning, Vancouver. This is Andrea Newman reporting live from Provincial Court of British Columbia, New Westminster Courthouse, where in just a short while, notorious mob Don Nicholas Rozzito is set to stand trial for international drug trafficking, money laundering, and numerous allegations of murder. It has been reported that his organization is responsible for the deaths of over thirty people, including an officer of the law, the late Tomas Rainer, Seattle's former chief of police, who was gunned down last Friday evening where nearby his family was having dinner."

"Oh boy. Looks like you're going to have your hands full, Miss Henson." My limo pulled up to the courthouse in between the parked media vehicles and passersby. "Would you like me to escort you into the courthouse?" my driver asked.

"It's OK. I think I can manage. Besides, I'd rather deal with the crowd out here than in the courtroom." I looked at the driver staring back at me through the rearview mirror, visible through the blacked-out window that was half rolled down.

"Guess that makes sense. Allow me to get your door."

"Thanks, Sebastian."

"My pleasure."

Sebastian exited the driver's seat, walked around to my side of the car, and opened the door for me. The noise coming from the crowd was intimidating. Not only were there news media and law enforcement present, but there were protestors as well with signs that read, "Fry in hell" and "Death to the Don." One in particular stood out amongst them all and read, "We forgive, just not you." Who were these people?

I hadn't met the person on trial yet, only his not-so-with-it lawyer, but I felt sorry for this man, and I didn't even know him. I shouldn't have, really. If the things the public was saying he did based on their chants and signs were true, may God have mercy on his soul. I was just glad it wasn't my family on trial. That would be too much for me to bear. Somehow, I had this knot in my stomach. I wasn't sure if it was because of my nerves or the ill feeling that it was somehow my uncle. I hadn't heard from him in days, and something was very strange. All this was too close to home for comfort. It didn't add up, is all I am saying, but my mind was now in overdrive from watching the crowd from inside the limo.

Nonetheless, I had been abruptly placed here today, no thanks to that creep Timothy from my firm pulling that disappearing stunt Friday. I intended to make myself and my employer proud by being lead counsel and bringing this man to justice.

My car door swung open, and the sound decibel increased a hundred times over. It suddenly came to a halt as I stepped out of the car and was almost punched in the face by several microphones from news reporters. I wasn't prepared for their questions and felt this overwhelming sensation.

"Miss Henson, how do you think this is going to go?"

"Don't you think it's wrong for someone like you to be lead counsel for not ever having a case under you?

"Isn't it true you slept your way here?"

"I beg your pardon. How dare you make accusations like that?" I fired back, defending herself.

"What's it like to be part of an organized crime family?"

"What? I have no idea what you're referring to."

"How can you sleep at night knowing you have bloodstains on the back of your hands?"

"Bloodstains? I...I...have no idea what you are

referring to."

Frantic shouts came from behind the intrusive reporters in the crowd. "Might as well cover the mallet in blood as your so-called justice is just like being guilty of murder!" I squinted my eyes and tried to see who had said that, but all I could see was a couple of tall bald guys dressed in black coats with shades on. However, they seemed to be not looking back at me and pushed forward towards the stairs outside the courthouse.

"Miss Henson, isn't it true your uncle basically paid for your scholarship and you aren't a real lawyer?"

That was the straw that broke the camel's back. I stopped as I placed my right foot onto the first step leading up towards the courthouse and turned around. It felt as if I was the one on trial and I was innocent, yet I felt I had to defend myself.

"Has it ever occurred to you that all the questions you are asking are pure bullshit?" I knew it before it ever came out of my mouth that those words would be the words that would haunt me going forward.

The microphones descended away from my personal space, and the crowd became deathly quiet. I turned around and walked up the stairs one by one, which seemed to take an eternity, only to make it to the door and hear the words, "What a bitch!" before the crowd started chanting again.

I was rather relieved to have the courthouse doors close, muting the outdoor inquisition. If this was a sign of what to expect now, I couldn't even begin to imagine what was to come next. All I knew was I needed to find some coffee. I didn't even care if it was instant coffee from a vending machine; I just needed some to calm my nerves.

I stood there as tears started to form in my eyes, and I knew I had to stay strong and fight them back. That would be all I needed on top of everything else, to have my mascara running down my face. Of course, it could be to my advantage to look scary. I started to laugh as I blotted my eyes with a tissue from my purse. Taking a deep breath to slow my heart rate down, I proceeded towards the main desk and asked for directions to my courtroom.

"Hi, excuse me. Can you tell me the room for the trial of the International Maritime Division against the English Bay Fisheries?"

"Well, that all depends. Are you a juror or spectator?"

"No, ma'am, my name is Alex Henson, attorney for Winslow and D'Entremont, lead counselor for the trial."

"Oh, why didn't you come in the back entrance?"

"I, uh, wasn't exactly informed on that."

"Yeah, we get that a lot. Well, you managed to survive the hounds."

"Excuse me?" I shook my head, confused, as the lady pointed behind her.

"Oh yes. They are quite brutal, and I'm afraid I made a comment right before entering the courthouse that might haunt me."

"Nah, relax, honey. Turn around and go up the stairs to the next level right there in the middle of the floor and head east. You can't miss the room. It's the one that's wired for sound."

"Um, OK. Thank you."

"If you want coffee or water before you go in, ask for Adrian, the guard. He will guide you to the private break room for something to drink, and the private lavatory as well."

"Thank you again."

I could not have been more nervous and wished Beauford was here, but I knew he had to get back to Seattle for work. After getting to the airport, I could tell he was sad to part, but I promised to come see him this weekend and kissed him goodbye for several minutes before boarding my uncle's Learjet that was waiting for me. To go from being with him to this was a total 360-degree turn, and it was up to me to get my nerves in order and be an adult.

I wasn't sure which way was east, but I took a logical guess it was to the left, and I was right. Walking into the lobby I noticed news teams bringing in cameras and running feeds and power cables inside the courtroom. I noticed the guard and darted across the floor as quickly as I could in my Gucci high heels towards him.

"Excuse me, are you Adrian?" I asked the guard.

"Yes, ma'am. How can I help you?"

"I'm lead counsel for this trial for Winslow and D'entremont, and the female guard down at the front desk said to ask you where I could get a cup of coffee."

"Ah yes, follow me." Adrian waved me to follow him.

I followed behind him for a minute or two, walking down a narrow hallway before turning right into a little break room that had two tables and chairs, a Coke machine, a candy machine, and a coffee machine.

"Just brewed her. Help yourself, and if you like, we have several kinds of flavored creams in those little cup packages or regular cream."

"Thank you. I just prefer coffee with cream and sugar."

"Ah, just the way I like it, too…simple."

Adrian was an old-timer for a guard and very polite and helpful. I didn't feel nervous anymore and felt very relaxed as I took a sip of the coffee.

"Mmm…that is good coffee. This tastes just like my friend's diner coffee back in Seattle."

"Well, funny you should mention that. An old friend of mine runs a diner on the pier."

"Are you kidding me? Are talking about Old Merl's?"

"Why, yes I am. I love his coffee so much, I convinced

the company that supplies his coffee to import some here."

"Wow, what a small world. Old Merl is like a grandpa to me."

"Well, you just go ahead and drink a cup, and don't be shy; grab another before heading into court, and good luck."

I still couldn't believe he knew Old Merl and that I had a cup of Devil's Blood just now. How ironic before entering the room I felt was going to be like hell today. But I knew it was time to face the music, and from the clock on the break room wall, I had a little less than five minutes, and I needed to skedaddle over there.

Walking across the lobby and entering the courtroom gave me an ill feeling. There was so much media presence, and the room was packed to the gills with spectators. I really didn't look around as I walked towards where I would be today. It sure felt like a walk of shame as I could feel their eyes looking at me every step of the way. As soon as I sat down, the bailiff yelled out, "All rise!" Everyone jumped up.

"Supreme Court of Vancouver, British Columbia, Department of Criminal Affairs, the Honorable Lucas Oliver presiding, is now in session. Please be seated and come to order."

Looking around, I saw Andrew, the lawyer, and he was accompanied by what looked like some hotshot with his hair slicked back and wearing an expensive suit. He noticed me looking and gave me an unwelcome creepy wink of the eye. He made me glance the other way, and I saw a familiar face. It was Judge Northrup. What was he doing here? Checking up on me to make sure I showed up? It wasn't like I wouldn't since I was under oath to appear. I watched the bailiff at the front signal to the other bailiff standing in front of a closed door. This must be the moment they bring in the accused person responsible for this trial.

DEADLOCKED: A Trial Beginning

I closed my eyes and prayed it wasn't my uncle, but as I opened my eyes, my heart sank and my throat swelled. My eyes were wide open as I shook from head to toe. It was my Uncle Nicholas dressed in a prisoner's orange jumpsuit, with both hands and feet in shiny bracelets. He spotted me and tilted his head, making a gesture that he was innocent. That was the meaning I could make out from the tears that flooded my eyes. How could this be? How could he be caught up in this horrible, horrible trial? I had to keep my composure and keep the judge from seeing my emotions, but my heart skipped every other beat. I felt betrayed.

The courtroom busted out of control with chants of filthy words and name calling. Judge Oliver slammed his gavel to bring order to the court. Every whack of the gavel made me jerk. I was in a fragile state and knew I was not ready for this. I had failed to review the files given to me by Judge Northrup's assistant, and I had walked in here today unprepared, and I had no idea why.

"Order in the court! Order in the court! I said, order in the court!" Judge Oliver yelled out to the crowd of spectators. The look on Judge Northrup's face was intimidating as he sat there with a huge grin upon his face. The man had no feelings, as it was my uncle who was standing trial as well as I. The media was eating it up as live feeds were being broadcast publicly over many channels, local and distant. I bowed my head in shame and rubbed my eyes.

I hadn't noticed the commotion coming from behind me as several cans of smoke were tossed into the courtroom, making a popping noise and fogging up the room. Someone had broken through the closed doors to the courtroom. I looked back over my shoulder, coughing, and all I could see through the white smoke while holding the center of my arm over my face was a middle-aged brunette female making her way down towards where I was.

Her eyes were locked on me as if we knew each other. She had pistols in both hands, pointing forward. I desperately tried to watch her every step as she passed me. Her eyes were glued on mine as I was bending over with my head cocked to the side. She turned to the right and pulled the triggers. She managed to get off several rounds that pierced my ears like a loud popcorn machine while yelling out, "You son of a bitch!" before vanishing into the smoke-filled room.

It wasn't until several minutes had passed before the smoke dissipated from the lower levels of the courtroom, revealing the aftermath. Throughout the ordeal that seemed like an eternity, I hadn't realized I had crawled under the prosecutor's table and was curled up in the fetal position. The entire courtroom echoed with horrific cries of panic, as people frantically moved about in every direction, fleeing the scene.

Raising my head and looking out from under the table, I couldn't see the woman who had turned my life upside down and placed me in this predicament. Where could she have gone? It wasn't like she could have vanished into thin air, but when I glanced around the room, it appeared she had. Standing to my feet and brushing my dress, I turned around in place, making a full circle, looking for my uncle, but I could not see him and feared the worst. Was he the intended target? My mind raced with anticipating fear. I wondered if he was wounded and lying hopelessly dead on the ground somewhere. I had to know and started to push my way through the crowd of people that stood between me and the last place I had seen my uncle.

"Excuse me...Please, I have to get over there." I made a desperate attempt to push myself through the frantic crowd, asking folks politely to move out of my way.

DEADLOCKED: A Trial Beginning

Looking through the crowd, I noticed Judge Northrup leaning over his chair as if he was holding his head down between his legs, perhaps to avoid any stray bullets that had come from the strange woman's gun. Maybe he would be able to tell me where my uncle was so I could go to him or at least know that he was OK.

"Judge Northrup," I said, waving my hand to get his attention.

What was wrong with the judge? I was trying to get his attention, but he still had his head down between his knees. Maybe he was scared and didn't want to lift his head up and see what the hell that was going on. I walked up to him and tapped him on the shoulder, but he didn't respond.

"Judge Northrup, it's OK. You can lift your head up now. Judge, are you OK?"

I leaned down in hopes of getting his attention once again, and when I didn't get a response, I decided to gently lift his head up. To my dismay, I knew now why he hadn't replied—because he couldn't. Judge Northrup had a hole in his head and was dead. My eyes and mouth were wide open as I staggered backward and slipped slightly in the pool of blood that now smeared the floor. I screamed at the top of my lungs as his lifeless body drooped forward towards me and slid off the chair and onto the floor. The next thing I knew, I was on my butt, being dragged backwards away from the judge.

The room felt like it was slowing down motion-wise as I watched the bailiffs surround the dead judge like a pack of wolves. The judge had been dealt a guilty verdict, yet the jury had had no chance to deliberate. His sentence was death, and this time, it wasn't the gavel that acknowledged order in the court.

www.ingramcontent.com/pod-product-compliance
Lightning Source LLC
LaVergne TN
LVHW051448080426
835509LV00017B/1702